BABY
NAMES
2019

Ella Joynes

white

This tenth edition published in Great Britain 2018 by White Ladder, an imprint of Crimson Publishing Ltd, 21d Charles Street, Bath BA1 1HX.

First, second, third, fourth, fifth, sixth, seventh, eighth and ninth editions published by Crimson Publishing in 2009, 2010, 2011, 2012, 2013, 2014, 2015, 2016 and 2017.

© Crimson Publishing 2018

The right of Ella Joynes to be identified as the author of this work has been asserted by her in accordance with the Copyright, Designs and Patents Act, 1988.

A catalogue record for this book is available from the British Library.

ISBN 978 1 91033 6 526

Printed and bound in Denmark by Nørhaven, Viborg.

Contents

Author's note

Baby names vary widely in spelling and pronunciation. To simplify things, this book usually lists each name only once: under the most common initial and spelling. If a name has an alternative spelling with a different initial, it may be listed under that letter also.

Information relating to statistics and trends in baby names is based on the most recent data at the time of writing.

Acknowledgements

I would like to extend my utmost gratitude to Beth Bishop and Kate Michell at Crimson Publishing for their patience and guidance throughout this project. To the many individuals and families I've had the fortune to doula for over the years, and who have graciously allowed me to share their baby names with the world, thank you. Love and appreciation also goes to Michael Turner, who has stuck around and offered endless helpful suggestions while I've worked on these wonderful books for the last nine years. And finally, the greatest thanks go to my own children, Owen Henri, Jasper Hugh, and Josie May. I fall more in love with them, and their names, every day.

Introduction

I'd say there's a fair chance that you and I have something in commmon right now: we're both expecting a new bundle of joy to join our families, and we're both a a loss on what name to pick! (Yes, yes, I know – but even authors of baby names books get stuck sometimes.) Well, after much taking of my own advice (and digging through every single name listed in this book), I'm happy to say we're finally close to a winner.

But what if you don't have a winner yet? What if you only have a list of names you absolutely *don't* want because you have that one second-cousin-twice-removed from your aunt's fourth marriage who you absolutely can't stand and there's no way on earth you'd saddle your baby with *that* name?

Well, take a deep breath and let us help. We *know* names here at *Baby Names 2019*. We know the names popular in the UK and around the globe, and we know the trends parents are setting: like choosing names that end in -a for baby girls, and that start with a J for baby boys. There's also a recent study that says we look like our names, and another that says you can tell which kids will be naughty at school based on just their first name. Yeah … we know about it all.

Inside you'll find out:

- how politics can shape baby name trends

- how to pick a name without any vowels

- why celebrities pick such unique names

- where to register your baby's name

- … and what to do if you change your mind!

Remember, this can be fun! Grab a pencil and a cuppa, dip in, and find some names you like. Use the tons of suggestions and lists we've given you, and work out whether one of them is your baby's future name.

Good luck! We're in this together!

Ella Joynes

Part one

Naming
your baby

1 Current baby-naming trends

It's no secret that humans are creatures of habit. We eat familiar foods, travel the same way to work each day … and apparently like to stick together when it comes to naming our babies. In fact, the biggest trend in naming babies right now is to … well … not be trendy. Just like pushing back against the craze for weird coffees and man-buns, we've decided as a nation that, actually, being traditional is classy again.

In 2018, we went one step further: we agreed, en masse, that our favourite names should match each other, and be as comfy and familiar as a pair of maternity yoga pants. Oliver stayed as the country's top baby boy name, and his twin sister Olivia has finally joined him on the podium after Amelia hung out there for six long years. In fact, the Top 10 names for both boys and girls stayed almost the same as the year before, with only two new entries across both lists: Lily and Muhammad, who shoved Poppy and William out of contention.

The Top 10

Boys	Girls
1. Oliver	1. Olivia
2. Harry	2. Amelia
3. George	3. Emily
4. Jack	4. Isla
5. Jacob	5. Ava
6. Noah	6. Isabella
7. Charlie	7. Lily
8. Muhammad	8. Jessica
9. Thomas	9. Ella
10. Oscar	10. Mia

Notice a theme here in the list for girls? Think they all sound a little similar? Look: there are eight names that sound strikingly alike: Olivia, Amelia, Isla, Ava, Isabella, Jessica, Ella and Mia. Even the two remaining names sound the same as each other: Emily and Lily. Clearly we enjoy familiarity. (And names that end in -a.)

Muhammad gets a raise

This spelling of Muhammad was the eighth most popular name for baby boys in 2018, moving up four spots from the year before. However, there are many ways to spell this popular and symbolic Islamic name, such as Mohammed, Mohammad, and Mohamed, and if all the various spellings were combined it would have been in first place! Experts have suggested a few reasons for the push up the charts, including an increase in the UK's overall Muslim population, an increase in the number of Muslim families choosing Muhammad over other religious names, and the recent successes of celebrities such as Mohamed 'Mo' Farah.

The theory behind the names

There are a couple of theories as to why we're all giving our kids the same names year after year. Personally, I think there's something to be said for the 'minimalism' movement. Lately we've taken to simplifying our lives and streamlining our possessions and choices like never before. Call it generational, call it recessional – whatever the reason, we are embracing simplicity and no-fuss living. The same could be said for names: why pick a long and complicated one when a nickname will do? Why search among thousands when you have a perfectly wonderful one right in front of you? Your baby will have enough mess and 'stuff' already, so let's at least make their name nice and simple.

The other theory is that parents are choosing names that they've heard for so long that they feel safe and familiar. This means that ANY name ending in -a or -ie/-y, or starting with O or A/E, is immensely popular right now, and we can all place winning bets on what our friends are going to pick for their newborns.

There's a comfortable pattern to the way we name our children that has prevailed for well over a decade now. Comfortable, you say? Tell me more! (Sitting, I hope, with your feet up.)

Here comes the science bit

Okay, I'm going to get a wee bit statistical for a bit, and break down some numbers for you. There are fewer names chosen for boys than for girls every year, which means that parents of little boys are even more likely to stick with what they know. For example, there are 1,600 more boys called Oliver than there are girls called Olivia, but they're both in first place on the charts. There are also close to 7,000 more recorded names for baby girls than boys overall.

Baby Names 2018 Key Statistics

	Boys	Girls
Individual names registered	28,200	36,600
Total registrations	357,046	339,225
Top names	Oliver (6,623 babies)	Amelia (5,017 babies)
Babies in Top 10	46,601	33,624
Top 10 names as percentage	13.1% of all names	9.9% of all names
Highest climbers (Top 100)	Arlo (up 53 places)	Luna (up 52 places)
Biggest fallers (Top 100)	Bobby (down 23 places)	Gracie (down 13 places)

Australia's Top 10

Boys		**Girls**	
1. Oliver	6. Thomas	1. Charlotte	6. Isla
2. William	7. Ethan	2. Olivia	7. Sophia/Sofia
3. Jack	8. Lucas	3. Mia	8. Chloe
4. Noah	9. Jackson/Jaxon/Jaxson	4. Ava	9. Grace
5. James	10. Lachlan	5. Amelia	10. Emily

For each name listed in the Top 10, there are greater numbers of boys with those names than there are girls in their respective list. Ultimately, this means that, while it might seem that parents aren't being that creative with girls' names, ending everything in -a or -y, the parents of little boys are branching out even less. You now need far more boys to be given the same name to reach a spot in the Top 10 than you do for girls.

This repeats itself throughout the 2018 data. There are now fewer babies being given the same name and a greater number of baby names being registered; last year there were 28,200 different names registered for baby boys and 36,600 for baby girls. The Office for National Statistics (ONS) counts each spelling as a separate entry, even if it's essentially the same name; for example, Lily is counted separately from Lilly, Lillie and Lili, and the spelling with the most registrations reaches a higher place on the charts. Hyphenated names are also separated; Lily-Mae, Lily-May and Lily-Mai are all counted as individual names in the UK's official statistics (see page 18 for more on hyphenated names).

This is not how all countries create their baby name statistics. Australia, for example, tallies names by sound, not spelling, which means that in ninth place for boys is Jackson/Jaxon/Jaxson, and Sophia/Sofia sits in seventh place for girls (see page 9). In fact, this affects the overall position for names quite profoundly. By combining spellings, certain names appear to be more popular than they would be if counted separately: although Jackson/Jaxon/Jaxson appeared in the Australian Top 10 for boys for the first time five years ago, neither of them would have been anywhere near there if they had been tallied separately.

Enough about our Aussie cousins; back to the UK. Elsewhere in our boys' list are names with a clear nod to royalty (royalty in the UK, anyway): George, 'Bonnie Prince' Charlie … and, of course, Harry (although Prince Harry's given name is actually Henry). They've all stuck around in the Top 10 for years – but with Harry it's probably as much a result of the Harry Potter phenomenon as our favourite red-headed prince.

The recent wedding of Prince Harry and Meghan Markle may see a boost in popularity for that Welsh girl's name. Meanwhile, the names Victoria, Matilda, Elizabeth and Charlotte have been big climbers for baby girls, being directly affected not only by England's Queens Victoria, Matilda and Elizabeth, but also our nation's smallest princess, Charlotte. Apparently, even tiny royalty has the capacity to rule over us all.

> Megan and Meghan are both Welsh names meaning 'pearl', which is rather delightful given how many jewels the newest duchess will be wearing over the forthcoming years!

Eleanor has been climbing the charts for the last two years, too. It's royal, it's traditional … and it just so happens to be this author's favourite name ever. My name. And I thank you for your consideration once again in 2019.

In 2018 there were 81 baby boys in the UK named Prince, which is more than the year before. This could be because of Our Will, but is more likely to be a result of the death of legendary singer Prince.

In Ghana in 2018, there was an outcry when officials started refusing to register babies with popular names they considered to be titles, such as

Prince, Nana (meaning Your Royal Highness), Owula (meaning Esquire), and Junior. Unfortunately this would have meant embarrassment for Ghanaian President Nana Addo Dankwa Akufo-Addo, and the scheme was promptly dropped after the public protested.

Biggest winners and losers

In an interesting development, several of the biggest climbers up the Top 100 chart for boys have been names ending in -ie/-y sounds. This is significant because the boys' chart is starting to sound an awful lot like the Top 100 chart for girls. Examples of this trend include Reggie, Albie, Jesse, Louie and Ronnie; and it might be an indication of the types of names we'll see appearing in the Top 10 over the next few years.

In the girls' list there are yet more names ending in an -ah sound, which all sounds very familiar. Take a look back at page 5 for a staggering display of conformity in the Top 10, and then check out the list below. I expect that Luna, Aria, Harper and Thea will all be around for many years to come. Harper is one of the most popular names for baby girls across the pond right now, so we'll have to see if we love it as much as

Biggest winners

Boys	Girls
1. Arlo	1. Luna
2. Reggie/Ezra	2. Aria
4. Jaxon	3. Harper
5. Finn	4. Iris
6. Albie	5. Felicity
7. Jesse/Louie	6. Charlotte/Beatrice
9. Ronnie/Caleb	8. Willow/Ivy/Thea

our American counterparts next year too. I'm firmly attributing the rise of Harper to the Beckhams and their daughter Harper Seven, and even though Robbie Williams calls his daughter Theodora by the nickname Teddy, I'm attributing the rise of Thea to him too. Long may the influence of '90s popsters continue!

So, it looks as though we're still very keen on using names that have traditional roots – but more and more of us are simplifying and shortening them. There's a reason Reggie is gaining traction ahead of Reginald, and Thea is swinging high ahead of Theodora and Dorothea. It's good news for both the traditionalists and modernists among us – everyone wins!

Other trends for high-climbers include old-fashioned names that were popular around 100 years ago, such as Beatrice, Iris and Ivy in the girls' names list. Biblical names also seem to be inching their way back into the mainstream, with Ezra and Caleb both climbing the charts in 2018.

Regardless of the reason, we are definitely seeing a return to traditional names, and a move away from names popular in the 1990s and 2000s,

Biggest losers

Boys	Girls
1. Bobby	1. Gracie
2. Lewis	2. Lucy/Jasmine
3. Liam	4. Molly/Lilly
4. Nathan	6. Ruby/Darcy
5. Jayden/Ryan	8. Holly/Summer/Martha
6. Jake/Blake	
8. Jenson	
9. Alex	
10. Tyler	

such as Jasmine, Liam, Ryan and Summer. In fact, this very book reported last year on Summer falling from a great height, and it seems the tidal wave away from popularity is just continuing. Poor Summer. This may be due in part to the '100-year rule' (where names that were popular 100 years ago come back into fashion), but may also be due to our fascination with nostalgia and tradition. Whatever the cause, it's nice to see some old favourites back in the game.

> Less than 1% of the UK's population changes their name by Deed Poll every year. Some recent UK deed poll name changes include Mr and Mrs Amazing, Sarge Metal Fatigue, and Pink Sparkly, whose real name before the change was actually Charlotte. Well, if you're going to change it you might as well go the whole hog, right?

In 2018, six new names entered the Top 100 for boys' names: Albie, Arlo, Ezra, Finn, Jasper and Jesse. These pushed Callum, Connor, Jamie, Kian, Seth and Sonny out of place. There were only four new entries in the girls' Top 100 list – Felicity, Iris, Luna and Lydia – and they forced Bethany, Hollie, Katie and Lacey down the charts. Keen eyes will notice that many of these new girls' names entries also appear in the Biggest Winners list for 2018.

The Disney Princess effect

You can't escape the impact of Disney anywhere these days, even in the world of baby names. Last year saw the massive release of the live action version of *Beauty and the Beast*, and the name Belle leapt all over the place. Funnily enough, it's even more popular as part of a hyphenated name, with options such as Tallulah-Belle, Ava-Belle, and Lily-Belle all popping up for the first time ever. A similar thing happened with *Frozen* and *Moana*, and Elsa and Moana have moved steadily up the charts. With a full-length *Frozen* sequel due in the near future, it's likely that we'll see our favourite freezing cold name appear in the Top 100, and it's currently at number 262.

Also – notice what happened to Aria. Compare Aria's current ranking (position 67) with where she was a decade ago, when a mere 22 babies in the UK were given that name. She jumped a whopping 33 places in a single year, which is tricky to do once you're battling with the other Top 100 names for competition. *Game of Thrones* has a lot to answer for …

Regional flavours and flairs

Another way to look at baby name trends is to look at regional variations. You'll find that, across the UK, each country favours different names. For example, parents in England are more likely than those in Wales to name their child Muhammad. However, Welsh parents choose Dylan more frequently than the English, and Scottish parents Like Harris far more both the English and the Welsh combined.

England's Top 10

Boys

1. Oliver	6. Noah
2. George	7. Charlie
3. Harry	8. Muhammad
4. Jack	9. Thomas
5. Jacob	10. Oscar

Girls

1. Olivia	6. Jessica
2. Amelia	7. Isabella
3. Emily	8. Lily
3. Isla	9. Ella
5. Ava	10. Mia

Wales' Top 10

Boys

1. Oliver	6. Harry
2. Jacob	7. Charlie
3. Noah	8. Alfie
4. Jack	9. George
5. Oscar	10. William

Girls

1. Olivia	6. Emily/Evie
2. Amelia	8. Mia
3. Ella	9. Lily
4. Ava	10. Isabelle
5. Isla	

Scotland's Top 10

Boys		Girls	
1. Jack	6. Logan	1. Olivia	6. Amelia
2. Oliver	7. Harris	2. Emily	7. Ava
3. James	8. Alexander	3. Isla	8. Ella
4. Lewis	9. Leo	4. Sophie	9. Charlotte
5. Noah	10. Harry	5. Jessica	10. Aria

Northern Ireland's Top 10

Boys		Girls	
1. James	6. Harry	1. Emily	6. Lily
2. Jack	7. Jacob	2. Grace	7. Amelia
3. Oliver	8. Daniel	3. Olivia	8. Ella
4. Charlie	9. Matthew	4. Anna	9. Ava
5. Noah	10. Alfie	5. Sophie	10. Sophia

When it comes to girls' names, parents from both England and Wales agree that Olivia is the favourite, followed by Amelia, as they appear in first and second place in both Top 10s. They also agree that Ava, Ella, Emily, Isla, Lily and Mia are excellent choices, as they also appear in both lists, but disagree on some others. English parents overwhelmingly liked Isabella and Jessica, while Welsh parents preferred Evie and Isabelle.

In Scotland and Northern Ireland, Jack, James and Oliver are the runaway hits for boys' names – names that have appeared all over the UK's Top 10 for years. In fact, Jack reigned supreme for a whopping 16 years before being toppled by Oliver and Harry a few years ago. As its popularity continues to dominate in Scotland, it's possible it could return to glory in the rest of the UK too. For girls, Olivia stands at the top of the heap in Scotland and Emily peaks in Northern Ireland – and in a neat little demonstration of just how important each registered baby name is for statistics, Amelia, Ava, Emily and Olivia are the only names that parents of little girls in the different regions agree on, showing up in all four lists around the UK. Parents of little boys, meanwhile, agree that Harry, Jack, Noah and Oliver are all great names for new babies, wherever they're born.

A Ukrainian man changed his name legally to iPhone 7 in 2016. Surprised he didn't pick Siri, actually.

The economics of baby names

While I've waxed lyrical so far about how we are finding comfort in the traditional and simple, now I'm going to give you a different perspective on what else is happening in the world of baby names.

There are always a few parents who break from the norm ... or at least a little bit ... but there are some interesting theories as to *why* that happens. The Top 10 names for both boys and girls account for only 11.5% of all registered names in the UK. This means that there is greater diversity in the names, or spellings, parents are choosing.

While the recession was in full swing and incomes were lower, there was a pattern in baby naming that moved towards conformity and tradition – and we're still seeing the lingering remnants of that today (see page 6). However, now that wages and house prices are stabilising again (well ... we'll see what happens with Brexit, as 2019 is our exit year), people are getting ready to push boundaries once more. Statistically we are more likely to choose unique and unusual names for our children when unemployment rates are low than when we're worried about making ends meet. Maybe from an evolutionary perspective we're afraid to stand out from the crowd when times are hard ... or maybe we're just too stressed and exhausted and lacking the creativity to spell Graham without a G.

The website 'Name of the Year" pronounced American NFL player Kobe Buffalomeat the winner of its annual competition. He beat Boats Botes, Sultan McDoom, and Aphrodite Bodycomb to win the top spot.

The idea of economic prosperity affecting baby name decisions is backed up by experts too – and not just plucked out of the air by our team. A Harvard sociologist suggested in 2017 that the pool of names we used to choose from was much smaller before the Industrial Revolution because it was important to keep money and influence – and therefore the names of the people with all the money and influence – in the same family. Think of all the Williams, Marys, Annes and Georges we used to have running around. However, once wealth began to be more evenly distributed (another discussion for another time), families no longer had to pay homage to the people holding the purse-strings, and began to branch out.

So how does this translate to for our modern society? Well, in simple terms it means that when we're feeling flush with cash we go wild with our baby names, and when we're counting the pennies we don't. Thanks, science!

Following tradition

So what do parents do if they really like a traditional or already-popular name but are afraid that everyone in their child's class will also be named that? Well, it seems they are picking a name they like and then adding their own unique spin on it. While it's definitely true that traditional names still dominate the charts, and the Top 10 for both boys and girls has been made up of pretty much the same (or similar) names for the last decade, there is a slight nudge towards the unique as well. Take a fairly conservative name like Alexandra, for example. It's definitely still popular – in the latest list it ranked 113th; but ten years ago it was 38th. The shortened versions, however, are popping up all over the Top 100, including Lexi in 85th place. Other options found in the ONS data include Alexis, Alexa, and Lexie.

> A recent study of names in Japan discovered that Japanese parents like to mix traditional Chinese characters with new and unusual pronunciations. It's an approach that works over here too, where we blend European-language names and characters with English ones – resulting in names such as Zoë.

All of this suggests that parents don't want to move away from the norm – but total conformity doesn't sit well with them either, so they add a little twist. The naming equivalent of a mullet perhaps, with business in the front and a little party in the back?

Other old-fashioned names, such as Alexander, Edward, Francesca and Harriet, have maintained their place in popularity ranks of the Top 100 lists, joining such stalwarts as Daniel, Grace, Michael and Victoria. However, their more unusual counterparts have recently started to join them, including Alexei, Eddie, Danny and Mikey, for boys, and Frankie, Gracie, Hattie and Vicky for girls.

Spelling options for traditional names

Boys		**Girls**	
You like …	**Try …**	**You like …**	**Try …**
Benjamin	Bennie	Charlotte	Lottie
Daniel	Danny	Jessica	Jessie
Joseph	Josef	Lucy	Lucie
Thomas	Tomaz	Molly	Mollie
William	Willem	Robin	Robyn

Some of Britain's quirky baby names

Boys	Girls
Axton	Bay
Blaze	Clover
Blue	Glory
Cosmo	Lux
Digby	Oceana
Forest	Peaches
Obi	Porsche
Ocean	Reign
Ren	Teddie
Royal	Venice

Giving a baby boy a shortened version of a traditional name as his complete first name is becoming increasingly popular. Take the second most popular boy's name, Harry, as an example. This in itself is a more familiar version of Henry (15th) or Harold (1,123rd), but it also lends itself to Harrie and Harri. The name James is also never far from the Top 10, and, in the most recent lists, its nickname Jamie just missed out on the Top 100 list at position 102. This has also happened with William (ranked 11th): Billy is 127th, Will is 585th, and Wil appears even further down – which for all the world just looks like a typo, doesn't it? Surprisingly, though, even the name Willie was given to four children last year!

How about a name without vowels? In 2018, Flynn, Gwyn, Sky and Vy all made their way onto the Births Register.

Heavenly hyphenation

One of the most common ways parents add twists to tradition is by hyphenating names. There are over 1,000 names with a hyphen in the most recent combined list of boys' and girls' names.

Popular hyphenations include: -Rose, -May/-Mae and -Leigh/-Lee, which make names such as Lily-Rose, Gracie-Mae, Demi-Leigh and Lacey-May. In fact, if you add all the spelling variations together, names

And how do you spell that?

A selection of the UK's original spellings for girls include Caitie (from Katy), Tiffanie (from Tiffany), Lejla (from Leila), and Zoi, Zoie, Zoey and Zoeya (from Zoe). The spelling of Emily as Emeli can also be attributed to the success of singer Emeli Sandé. Boys' names variations include Xzaviar (from Xavier), Juels (from Jules), Fynlee (from Finlay) and Rilee, Rileigh, Ryle, Rylea and Rylei (from Riley).

that end in -May or -Mae would be in the Top 25 and those that include Rose would be around position 60! The highest-ranking hyphenated girl's name is Amelia-Rose, in position 202, with almost 270 baby girls named that last year. Also popular are Lilly-May, Ellie-May, Ella-Rose and Ruby-Lee.

Boys are not exempt from this rule either, as it has become fashionable to add -James or -Lee to the end of a baby boy's name. The highest-ranking version is Alfie-Lee (in position 732), with 46 birth certificates to show for it. Also becoming more commonly used are Tommy-Lee, Abu-Bakr, Riley-James and Tyler-Jay.

French law prohibits all names other than those on an approved list. A French court ruled recently that Fraise was not an acceptable name for a baby girl because it translates to 'strawberry'. After the parents were ordered to change it, they picked Fraisine, which I suppose is abiding by the letter of the law if not the spirit. The same court also denied other parents the names 'Jihad' and 'Tilde'.

2 This year's predictions

Looking ahead to 2019, the trend for choosing comfortably familiar names, with or without a twist, is definitely going to continue. However, there's more out there than that! Take a look at some of the other latest and greatest ways to name a baby.

- Gender-neutral names. These are definitely hot stuff right now. Names like Max, Alex, Charlie and Andy are all going to be big winners in the coming years as parents move towards more fluid notions of gender and identity.

- Feminist names. With the 100th anniversary of the appointment of the UK's first female Member of Parliament, Lady Nancy Astor, combined with the current political climate both here and in the USA, many women are searching back into the world of women's history for inspiration for baby names. Emmeline, Ada, Nancy, Rosa and Frida could all make big surges in popularity in 2019.

- As we approach 2020 (can you believe it?), keep an eye out for names from the Roaring Twenties. If *Downton Abbey* has shown us anything, it's that Violet, Cora, Tom and Henry are all big hitters for baby names 100 years into the future.

- Ruh, Thuh and Vee names. Sometimes, names that look or sound similar hang around for a while. In 2019, names that start with R- or Th- will be big winners for boys, and names that end in -a or have a -v sound will dominate for girls. Look out for Reggie and Reuben, Theo and Thiago, Mia and Matilda, and Evelyn and Ivy.

> Iceland is so strict about its baby-naming laws that it has a committee that votes on whether to permit new additions to the approved list of names each year, and in 2017 it added Anjelína, Luna and Kiran.

Babies may be given literary names from children's books such as Hermione, Eloise, Sawyer or Danny in 2019. Other trends to hit include a move towards 'statement' names for babies, such as Justice, Royal, Gentry and Honor; and we may see a spike in popularity for water-based names, such as Ocean, Lake, River and Bay.

Predicted 2019 Top 10

Boys	Girls
1. Oliver	1. Olivia
2. Harry	2. Emily
3. George	3. Amelia
4. Noah	4. Isla
5. Jack	5. Isabella
6. Jacob	6. Lily
7. Muhammad	7. Ava
8. Thomas	8. Jessica
9. Charlie	9. Ella
10. Leo	10. Sophia

One trend that's coming to an end in 2019 is European names. With the separation of the UK from the European Union, parents may start to move away from continental choices and embrace names traditionally associated with our home country. This might include regal names such as Elizabeth, Victoria, James and Charles; geographical names such as London, Preston, Elan and Iona; or British folklore names as Robin, Britannia, Arthur or Bran.

Goings on in 2019

As well as getting ideas from the names that other parents choose, some influences on baby names in 2019 may come from the worlds of sport, politics and celebrity. Will tennis superstar Serena Williams and Internet entrepreneur Alexis Ohanian's baby girl Alexis Olympia may lead to a rise in Grecian names?

In 2019 there will be a number of major sporting events, and athletes who perform well at them will no doubt become inspirational for new parents. There's the Cricket World Cup and the FIFA Women's World Cup, followed by the Rugby Union World Cap later in the year. The athletics World Championship is also scheduled for 2019. Watch out for at least some sports-star names to pop up in 2018 if history is anything to go by.

The success of Great Britain's Olympic team in 2012 and 2016 led to an increase in babies being born with the names Victoria (after cyclist Victoria Pendleton), Alistair (after triathlete Alistair Brownlee), Charlotte (after dressage rider Charlotte Dujardin) and Lizzy (after Skeleton Winter Olympian Lizzy Yarnold). However, two years after each Olympics the names drop down again. Proof that sporting events really do have an impact.

Footballers have a strong tradition of influencing baby names. After the last FIFA World Cup in 2018, Neymar and Luis Suárez saw their names create waves on and off the pitch. Neymar jumped a staggering 2,300 places in three years, and Luis moved up 30 spots to the Top 350. With the Women's World Cup happening in 2019, it will be interesting to see which girls' names move up in the charts.

In terms of politics, politicians have an up and down relationship with baby name trends. During Barack Obama's term as US President his name never moved up more than a few places, so it's unlikely that Donald Trump's will be any different. However, American baby name statistics may see a leaning towards more Southern US 'redneck' names due to Trump's large voting bloc there. Suggestions include Brayden, Kynslee, McKenna and Royan, though frankly that's a trend I'd be happy to miss out on in the UK.

Also worth noting is that while Barack never trended either here or across the pond, the names of his daughters, Sasha and Malia, actually did, as did the children of David Cameron during his term as the nation's leader – particularly Florence. However, because Donald Trump kept the names of his children close to his own (another example of how wealthy families name their children; see page 15), we probably won't see the same effect from his. And we're willing to bet that the name Theresa won't gain traction any time soon, with only 19 babies so-named in 2018. But will we see Jeremy climbing the charts?

> According to American media outlet ABC News, the smash hit musical *Hamilton*, based on the life of US founding father Alexander Hamilton, has seen an increase in the number of babies given the name. This follows the trend of naming babies after US historical figures, such as Lincoln and Madison.

Anniversaries

There are a number of significant anniversaries in 2019 that might alert new parents to some names they haven't come across before. See if the anniversaries listed below provide you with any inspiration:

- 10th anniversary of the closing of Woolworths across the UK. Founded in 1909 by Frank Winfield Woolworth, this British High Street staple has been sorely missed by many. Especially the Pick n Mix section.

- 25th anniversary of the Church of England's decision to ordain female priests – starting with 32 women headed by Angela Berners-Wilson and Waveney Bishop. It's also been 25 years since the original *Lion King* film was released, so look out for Simba and Nala to become more popular again.

- 40th anniversary of the publication of Douglas Adams' The *Hitchhiker's Guide to the Galaxy*, and the 50th anniversary of the first time an episode of *Monty Python's Flying Circus* was broadcast on TV. Did you know Douglas Adams was also briefly part of the writing team for that infamous comedy series? Well, now you do.

- 80th anniversary of the start of the Second World War. Watch out for Neville and Winston to make an appearance again … although probably not Adolf.

- 100th anniversary of the the the passing of the Nineteenth Amendment in the USA, granting women the right to vote. You can thank Susan B. Anthony and Elizabeth Cady Stanton for helping our sisters across the pond catch up.

- 200 years since the birth of author and poet Walt Whitman, and 100 years for J.D. Salinger, the latter being the author of every angst-ridden teenage boy's favourite book *Catcher in the Rye*. It's also Sir Arthur Conan Doyle's 160th birthday.

Top anniversary names

Boys	Girls
Arthur	Angela
Douglas	Cady
Frank	Elizabeth
Henry	Nala
Monty	Susan
Neville	Susie
Walt	Waveney
Winston	Winnie

By royal decree

Did you know that the Queen gets a say in what new princes and princesses are called? In 1988, Princess Beatrice was going to be called Annabel but the Queen dismissed it as 'too yuppie', according to the *Sun*. She suggested the more traditional Beatrice and it stuck. Maybe she had the final say in Prince George's name – George was her father's name, after all – but we reckon it was probably her grandson Prince William who chose to use Elizabeth as a middle name for Princess Charlotte; and William paid heed to the Queen's choices for her own children by choosing Charles as a middle name for his third child.

3 The world of celebrity babies

Well, thank goodness for that! Finally, after a few years of celebrities picking the same ol' standard names that the rest of us go with, we've had a glorious return to the obscure and wacky. Hallelujah! Thank you, celebrities, for allowing us to sit back with a bowl of popcorn and watch the bizarre names roll on in.

Let's start with *Breaking Bad* actor Aaron Paul and his wife Lauren, who chose the rather bizarre but adorable name Story Annabelle. Or *Loose Women* star Jamelia, who decided True Winter was a great choice for her baby boy. Maybe she's a massive *Game of Thrones* fan? Khloe Kardashian must have followed Jamelia's lead, because she named her baby girl True Thompson. See? I was right about gender neutral names after all! Even odd celebrity choices aren't exempt. (See page 21 for more on this trend.) And not to be outdone (as usual), Kim Kardashian and Kanye West went for the extraordinary choice of Chicago for their newest arrival, beating sister Kylie Jenner's pick of Stormi in the game of unusual baby names.

> In June 2017 Beyoncé and Jay Z applied to trademark the names Rumi Carter and Sir Carter for their twin girl and boy, as they did for their daughter Blue Ivy Carter in 2012.

One theory behind these choices is that being a celebrity often demands a unique name, so that people know instantly to whom that news headline or BAFTA award belongs. Celebrities are probably just being smart in

Stars who still shine

One of the biggest celebrity trends right now is picking names of singers who have passed away. Geri Halliwell's son Montague George Hector was (partly) named after her good friend George Michael. Both Take That's Howard Donald and wife Katie Halil and Zoe Saldana and husband Marco Perego have sons named in honour of David Bowie: Bowie Taylan Howard and Bowie Ezio Perego.

this regard: give a baby a unique name from birth, and they'll never have to change their real name to a stage name later. Job done.

One recent theme has been to give new babies first names that are more traditionally used as surnames. Take Cooper Alf, the choice of McFly's Danny Jones, or Beckett Richard, the son of US Olympian swimmer Michael Phelps. There's also the trend of names that have been fairly common across the pond for some time, but haven't been as popular here in the UK: Grayson is JLS member Aston Merrygold's little boy, and Hayes belongs to Jessica Alba.

And finally, in a rather lovely exploration of how we can adopt new cultures in our baby-name choices, there's also been a celebrity trend for Hispanic names in the last few years. *Hamilton* composer Lin-Manuel Miranda, born in Puerto Rico, went for the name Francisco for his baby boy, and Adam Levine picked Gio Grace for his new daughter. And while the name Aurelia doesn't have roots in Latin America, being the feminine form of the Ancient Roman name

Old Hollywood names

Boys	Girls
Cary	Audrey
Clark	Ava
Clint	Grace
James	Elizabeth
Jimmy	Ingrid
Oliver	Judy
Marlon	Vivien

New arrivals

Alexis Olympia (Serena Williams and Alexis Ohanian)
Aurelia (Heidi Range and Alex Partakis)
Beckett Richard (Michael and Nicola Phelps)
Cass Mac (Wayne and Colleen Rooney)
Chicago (Kim Kardashian and Kanye West)
Colette Koala (Macklemore and Tricia Davis)
Cooper Alf (Danny and Izzy Jones)
Ennis Howard (Kirsten Dunst and Jesse Plemmons)
Francisco (Lin-Manuel Miranda and Vanessa Nadal)
Gio Grace (Adam Levine and Behati Prinsloo)
Grayson (Aston Merrygold and Sarah Richards)
Hayes (Jessica Alba and Cash Warren)
Jack (Rosie Huntington-Whiteley and Jason Statham)
Luke Richard (Eddie Redmayne and Hannah Bagshawe)
Louis Arthur Charles (Prince William and the Duchess of Cambridge)
Minnie Theodora (Jack and Lisa Osbourne)
Roman (Ore and Portia Oduba)
Romeo Alejandro David (Alec and Hillary Baldwin)
Santiago Enrique Bastón (Eva Longoria and Jose Bastón
Stevie (Andy Roddick and Brooklyn Decker)
Stormi (Kylie Jenner and Travis Scott)
Story Annabelle (Aaron and Lauren Paul)
Tiana Gia (Dwayne 'The Rock' Johnson and Lauren Hashian)
True (Khloe Kardashian and Tristan Thompson)
True Winter (Jamelia and mystery husband)
Violet Elizabeth (Tabitha Simmons and Topper Mortimer)

Aurelius, it has been popular in Hispanic communities for some time; so Atomic Kitten star Heidi Range should feel in good company for selecting it for her baby girl.

Despite some celebs choosing more 'interesting' names, there are still many who are following the general trend for choosing a traditional name. Most notable are Minnie Theodora, the daughter of reality star Jack Osbourne, and Violet Elizabeth, shoe designer Tabitha Simmons' baby girl.

Zooey Deschanel welcomed son Charlie Wolf in 2017, to join big sister Elsie Otter. When the actor was asked why she named her daughter so, she said, 'We just really loved the name Elsie and we both love otters. There are so many amazing things about otters. Who doesn't love otters?' She's got a point ...

Upcoming arrivals

Celebrity couples expecting new arrivals include Hugh Grant and Anna Eberstein, Tom Daley and Dustin Lance Black, and Rachel Weisz and Daniel Craig. If history is anything to go by, the names these couples pick will be highly scrutinised and influential on the rest of us.

With the arrival of Prince Louis Arthur Charles and another royal baby on the way for Zara and Mike Tindall, the world is sure to go a bit bonkers again for royal baby names. Remember the extraordinary spikes in popularity for George and Charlotte? ... Will Harry and Meghan be the next to make an announcement?

Celebrity bumps ahead

Michael Bublé and Luisana Lopilato
Daniel Craig and Rachel Weisz
Tom Daley and Dustin Lance Black
Claire Danes and Huigh Dancy
Cat Deeley and Patrick Kielty
Declan Donnelly and Ali Astall
Hilary Duff and Matthew Koma
Chris Evans and Natasha Shishmanian
Tom and Giovanna Fletcher
Kate Hudson and Danny Fujikawa
Rebecca Hall and Morgan Spector
Christine and Frank Lampard
Pippa Middleton and James Matthews
Joe Wicks and Rosie Jones

4 Big-screen inspiration

The impact of characters in movies, books and TV programmes has been huge on baby names in the last few years. There were some predictable trends, such as *Star Wars*, *Game of Thrones* and anything produced by Disney, but also some unexpected ones. Read on to discover if your love of binge watching Netflix during bouts of pregnancy-induced insomnia can technically be classified as research.

The biggest movie to hit screens recently was the newest instalment in the Star Wars franchise. *Solo: A Star Wars Story*, based on the backstory of to the orginal Star Wars character Han Solo, brought to our screens familiar character names, as well as some new ones. The names Han and Luke have both seen a rise in popularity since Episode VII, even though they had steadily declined since the 1990s; it's about time Han or Hans made a comeback. Incidentally, Rey is becoming a huge hit for parents seeking out middle names, and fits in nicely with the Freya-Audrey-Aubrey trend. The actor playing Rey in Episodes VII and VIII, Daisy Ridley, saw her name jump into the Top 25, and Finn, played by John Boyega, broke into the Top 100 last year. Clearly the Force is still strong.

> Suprisingly, the name Kylo is the fastest growing name in the US, jumping 2,368 places – this is attributed to the *Star Wars* villain Kylo Ren, and is highly unusual as, historically, baddies have the opposite effect on the baby name charts!

Saying goodbye to a princess

Carrie Fisher's sudden death at the tail end of 2016 left fans of the Star Wars actor reeling. One of the ways they chose to express their emotions was to name their baby girls after her character Princess Leia. The name moved up the charts to the Top 500 in 2017 – a position it hasn't held since the 1990s. Hope you're with the Force now, Leia.

Popular recent TV shows included *The Crown*, *Call the Midwife* and *Game of Thrones*.

Tell me you didn't fall in love with the gorgeous costuming and acting in *The Crown*? And now tell me you're not seriously considering the names George, Elizabeth, Philip, Margaret or Winston for your new baby. No one could blame you for being sucked into such a feast for the eyes. Anyway, continuing the theme of period dramas, *Call the Midwife* has allowed fun go-getter Trixie to swish up the charts and go from literally zero babies with that name to appearing in the Top 1,400. If you fancy a vintage name from everyone's favourite set of mid-century midwives, options include Cynthia, Jenny, Julienne, Lucille and Monica.

> The *Telegraph* reported a classic *Sherlock*-inspired name in their Marriages, Births and Deaths section recently: baby Rosamund Mary Watson made her appearance in 2017, and we can only hope she has Sherlock's brain and Watson's common sense.

But enough of the questionably historically accurate dramas; let's talk about the fantastical! *Game of Thrones* has had an astonishing impact on baby names here in the UK. The name Arya, for example, has gone from no babies named that before the show appeared on our screens, to one of the fastest-growing names for little girls (see page 7) – the spelling Aria is now in the Top 75 and will be ranked even higher in the next baby names chart. Its influence has even tipped over into boys' names, where it appeared in the charts for the first time a few years ago. The name Khaleesi, which is actually a royal title rather than a given name in *Game of Thrones*, was given to 69 British babies, according to the latest statistics, and Brienne has appeared in the charts for the third year in a row. 2019 sees the last series of the popular fantasy drama, so it will be interesting to see if the names drop out of fashion or if they're here to stay.

> Keira Knightley popularised the spelling of her first name when she first rose to fame – but it was actually an accident. Her first name was misspelled from Kiera on her birth certificate, and that little error has prompted thousands of parents to copy it.

Orange is the New Black has apparently been responsible for the sudden increase in the name Piper for baby girls. Bounty Baby Club surveyed readers of its website and reported that fans of the Netflix prison drama chose Piper 20% more often last year than in 2017. Other popular names from the series included Sophia, Gloria and Stella. Netflix might also be responsible for the names Nancy and Jonathon from sci-fi series *Stranger Things* jumping up the official nation's lists, as well as Harper and Patsy from comic-book series *Jessica Jones*.

Banned names around the world

@ – China
Chow Tow (meaning 'smelly head') – Malaysia
Lucifer – Germany
Messiah – New Zealand
Mona Lisa – Portugal
Monkey – Denmark
0 – Sweden
Osama Bin Laden – Germany
Stompy – Germany

An Israeli couple called their baby girl Like after the Facebook button. Their other children are called Pie and Vash, which means honey.

So what's next?

The year 2019 looks like being a pretty stonking one for new films. Disney is doubling-down on the success of the live-action remakes of *Cinderella, Beauty and the Beast*, and *The Jungle Book*, by releasing not one ..., not two ..., but three new versions of classic animations. Get set to relive your childhood (and probably cry your eyes out) through *Aladdin, Dumbo*, and *The Lion King*. The latter's release is being carefully timed to coincide with the 25th anniversary of the original cartoon – which makes me personally feel very old indeed. Disney is also crowning itself King of the Sequel again, by releasing *Toy Story 4*, *Frozen 2*, and what seem to be several thousand superhero films under their Marvel banner.

Big Screen Baby Names

Boys	Girls
Finn	Aria
George	Elizabeth
Graham	Elsa
Han	Jasmine
Jonathon	Khaleesi
Kylo	Nala
Lincoln	Piper
Philip	Rey
Ryan	Trixie
Winston	Yasmin

Names that are featured in these films stand a good chance of influencing baby names if past trends are repeated. *Frozen 2*, for example, will almost definitely spike interest in the names Elsa and Anna again. After the release of the original *Frozen* in late 2013, Elsa jumped 100 places into the Top 100, and Kristoff appeared in the charts for the first time ever! It's entirely possible the sequel will introduce us to a new cast of lovable characters whose names we just have to have for our children. And as for *Aladdin*, well. Jasmine was stuck in the middle of the charts for years and years before 1992, but since then it's remained steadfastly in the Top 100. 2019 could be the year it breaks the Top 25.

As for the influence the telly could wield on our collective baby-naming psyche, *Dr Who* is a good place to start. After the success of the first female Time Lord's series in 2018, another series is predicted to be equally as good in 2019. Maybe it's time for the names Graham, Ryan and Yasmin to break away from the rest of the pack?

And finally, everyone likes zombies … right? Well, according to newest data about American zombie series *The Walking Dead*, we at least love naming our babies after them. Walker, Abraham, Sasha and Maggie have all been big climbers since the show was first broadcast, and a new series in 2019 will have a similar impact. In fact, British actor Andrew Lincoln has seen his own name move up the charts recently – Lincoln is now in the Top 125 and has jumped over 1,000 spots in ten years.

Harry's back! (Sort of …)

Did you miss the Wizarding World of Harry Potter? You weren't alone. We turned out in droves to see the newest big screen addition to the Harry Potter/Fantastic Beasts universe in 2018, *Fantastic Beasts: The Crimes of Grindelwald*. While Newt Scamander might not be popping up on birth certificates any time soon, it did bring the delightful Albus Dumbledore back into our lives and the entire Harry Potter-naming phenomenon back into the charts.

5 How to choose a name

Your baby-naming checklist

- Fall in love with the name(s) you've chosen. Pick a name that makes you smile, because if you love it, hopefully your child will too – and won't grow up resenting and hating you with all their being. (That was a little joke.) Relax and get picking.

- Try it out. While you're pregnant, talk to your baby using their name to see if they respond. You can also try writing names down, practising a few signatures, or saying one out loud enough times to see if you ever get sick of it. Don't forget to say it aloud with the surname attached to make sure it feels right.

- Don't listen to other people. Sometimes grandparents and friends offer baby-naming advice, which may not always be welcome. If you've got your heart set on a name, keep it a secret until after the birth to avoid any unnecessary criticism. Trust your own instincts – they'll come in handy for parenting in general.

> Norwegians are only allowed to use names that appear on an approved list, which has led to parents being fined and even jailed for breaking the law! Banned names include Gesher (meaning bridge), and anything that could be mistaken for a surname.

- Also, don't steal ideas! One 2017 survey by the website Cafemom found that friends stealing baby names was a legitimate reason for the break down of adult friendships. Examples included a cousin who stole a whopping three baby names all in a row! If you really find it hard to come up with your own ideas, definitely talk to the other mum-to-be before using her favourite baby name.

- Find a name with meaning. Choosing a name that is rooted in history or folklore might just inspire your little one to be as great as their namesake. There's research to suggest this inspirational rub-off effect has real legs, so even if you pick a name out of the air, consider making something up to tell them later!

- Have fun. Picking out names should be fun. Laughing at the ones you'd never dream of choosing can really help you to narrow it down to the ones you would. There's time later for thinking through whether bizarre names will actually give your little one a headache when they have to spell it every time they say it. See page 48 for more on this.

- Expand your mind. Don't rule out the weird ones just yet! Be brave and bold if that's what you want, but just in case you get it massively wrong (definitely a possibility, let's face it) you might want to give them a simpler middle name so they can jump ship to that instead.

- Do *not* pick the name of an ex. No matter how lovely you think your ex's name is, it would take a very understanding partner to allow you to pick it for your kid. Just steer clear of any names you know will cause problems to other people, paying particular attention to your partner and loved ones.

> How's this for a 21st-century tip? Awesomebabyname.com will let you pick a name based on what domain names are available, in case you want to get ahead of your child's celebrity status and start their online visibility early.

• What if you can't agree? This is probably the trickiest problem to solve. Research a number of names that you and your partner both like, and make a point of discussing them long before the baby is due. Arguing about it in the delivery room isn't a great first impression to give to junior.

Posh names

Algernon	Araminta
Aubyn	Blanche
Cosmo	Jori
Horace	Milicent
Merlin	Octavia
Tybalt	Tansy
Zebedee	Tuppence

• Compromise is key. Pick two middle names so that you each have one in there that you love, or you could each have five names that you're allowed to veto – but no more. Whichever way you go about it, it's important that you eventually agree on the name you are giving your baby, even if it means losing out on the one you've had your heart set on for a while.

Finally: keep reading and re-reading this book – the answer is in here.

Think to the future

Let's go back to the future. Will the name you've chosen stand the test of time? Will names popular in 2019 remain popular in 2050? Will your son or daughter be able to enter a room and give a confident presentation with an awkward or unpronounceable name? Heck, can they survive the playgrounds of primary and secondary school with a name that could be embarrassing?

Buzzfeed.com recently ran an article on funny names of real people who were caught being interviewed for news stories and documentaries. Living among us are Dr Whet Faartz, horse-riding judge Willie Stroker, and shop district manager Rick Roll … which you might have to google

Emotional names

Destiny	Joy
Happy	Peace
Heaven	Serenity
Hope	Unique
Innocence	Unity

if that one passed you by. At the same time another article appeared, listing all the reasons why having an unusual name was a pain, such as never being able to find your name on novelty souvenirs, and other people giving you 'fun, new' nicknames because they can't be bothered with your actual name. Now obviously these are just silly articles and not meant to be taken seriously, … or are they?

Stereotypes: true or false?

Will the name you choose actually affect your child's life? Will names that seem clever mean that your child will be brainier? Will names with positive meanings make your child into a happier person? The answer is … possibly.

A study conducted by the Hebrew University of Jerusalem in 2017 found that we subconsciously act like stereotypes of our names, and that other people can pretty accurately guess what our names are as a result. They asked students to guess the names of faces they were shown, and the students were able to correctly match them twice as often as expected. So if you're choosing a name traditionally associated with a particular personality trait, it might be time to find out what the stereotype is. (But you can probably relax: Herbert was the name suggested to be most associated with a dimwit and only 52 baby boys were given that last year, so odds are you're safe.)

One thing you should consider is how your child's name will be perceived by the outside world. Typically, judgements are passed on names, even before meeting a person, in situations such as job interviews or at school.

Recently, teachers across the country were asked to decide from a list of names which children were more likely to be badly behaved than others. Topping the 'naughty' charts were Callum and Jack for boys, and Chelsea and Courtney for girls. On the other hand, the names in the 'clever' category were Alexander and Christopher for boys, and Elizabeth and Charlotte for girls.

Teachers were also asked to pick names that they felt were given to popular children and these included Jack, Daniel, Emma and Hannah – which means that little boys named Jack are naughty but popular!

William plays the clarinet?

Buzzfeed.com published a survey of opinions on British names. Responses included, 'Jennifers always have ponytails and exceptionally clear skin'; 'Maxes get in one fight in university and nearly get kicked out, but you still fancy them'; and 'Williams get good GCSE results, and they play the clarinet better than most.' You know … a highly scientific analysis of names. Thanks, Buzzfeed.

Around the same time, it was discovered that teenagers named Katherine and Duncan (or a variation, such as Kate) were up to eight times more likely to achieve high GCSE results than those named Wayne or Jermaine. Another study in 2015 analysed the number of stickers given to children as rewards for good behaviour. Those named Amy and Jacob are more likely to be praised for being well-behaved than children named Ella and Joseph; moreover, kids who do not shorten their name or go by nick-names are more likely to be better behaved, too.

> Actor Nigel Planer was quoted in the Guardian in 2017 as saying he's relieved parents don't want to call their baby Nigel anymore: "It was never a cool name, even before Farage helped consign it to the dustbin of history. It deserves to be no-platformed." Apprently he's spot on, as exactly zero babies were called Nigel last year!

Names that mean 'clever'		Names that sound 'clever'	
Abner	Shanahan	Alastair	Gabriel
Cassidy	Todd	Charles	Harriet
Haley	Ulysses	Christian	Sophia
Penelope	Washington	Elizabeth	Spencer
Portia	Wylie	Frances	William

Quirky names

While there are drawbacks to having an obviously out-there name, being different has advantages too. For one thing, other people will never forget your child's name, which means they won't be easily forgotten either. But does a quirky name demand a quirky personality? If you don't think your genes could stand up to a name like Satchel or Kerensa, perhaps it's time to think of one that's a little more run of the mill.

> The only names you can't change your name to by UK deed poll are those that indicate rank or title (such as Sir or Lord) and those that are deemed blasphemous – including Jesus and Satan. You also can't use numbers or symbols … so Sir Duke 1976 is a no-go. Sorry.

A survey carried out by the National Centre for Social Research found that the more unusual the name, the less likely a candidate is to be called for a job interview. Whether or not this fact would affect a child's development and future career is yet to be determined, but it is something to consider.

There is also new research from baby website Bounty, which says that as many as one in five parents regrets their choice of baby name. Of the 3,000 parents interviewed, 20% said they no longer thought the unusual choice of spelling or pronunciation was appropriate. Around 8% said they were tired of people mispronouncing their child's name and 10% thought the novelty of the original pick had worn off. They also said they would now pick a new name which had not occurred to them or been an option before. No pressure or anything, right?

Controversial names adopted by real people

Adolf Hitler	Jezebel
Beelzebub	Jihad
Desdemona	Mussolini
Hannibal	Stalin
Himmler	Voldemort

When it comes to the name Lucifer, America and Germany think differently. While German officials intervened in a request to name a child after Satan, in the US 13 babies were recorded as receiving that moniker in 2016.

New Zealand's Top 10

Boys	Girls
1. Oliver	1. Olivia
2. Jack	2. Charlotte
3. William	3. Isla
4. Mason	4. Harper
5. James	5. Ella
6. Hunter	6. Amelia
7. Noah	7. Emily
8. Lucas	8. Mia
9. Leo	9. Sophie
10. Max	10. Ava

Top 10 Māori Names

Boys	Girls
1. Nikau	1. Maia
2. Ari	2. Manaia
3. Manaia	3. Anahera
4. Wiremu	4. Ana
5. Aroha	5. Kauri
6. Kaia	6. Mikaere
7. Rawiri	7. Hana
8. Ihaia	8. Ataahua
9. Kai	9. Tia
10. Manaaki	10. Kora

New Zealand has a law that baby names, including first, middle and surnames, cannot exceed 99 characters.

Sex and gender

How do we define what makes a name masculine or feminine? Well, it may be connected to the sounds that the letters create when spoken. Harder-sounding combinations (-ter, -it, -ld, -id) tend to be found in masculine names, whereas softer-sounding combinations (-ie, -ay, -la) are generally associated with feminine names. You therefore end up with Sophie, Joanie and Bella, and Harold, Walter and David.

If you're planning on choosing a feminine-sounding name, approach with caution: recent research suggests that girls who are given particularly girly names – think Tiana, Kayla and Isabella – are much more likely to misbehave when they reach school age. These girls were also far less likely to choose subjects such as maths and science at school, while their sisters with more masculine names – for example, Morgan, Alexis and Ashley – were encouraged to excel in these courses. Which is fascinating and scary in equal measure.

Nowadays, names are becoming more androgynous and many appear in both boys' and girls' lists, including Hayden, Riley, Madison and, of course, Alex – some form of which appears in the Top 100 for both boys and girls every year. Therefore, if you want a more gender-neutral name for your new arrival, you won't be alone.

Popular gender-neutral names

Sam	Charlie
Riley	Morgan
Jamie	Alex
Kai	Andy
Bobby	Fran

But what about your own gender? Does the fact that you're a man or a woman mean you are more likely to pick certain names for your child? Well, in general, that's probably not the case, but there might be an element of truth to it. A study by Bounty found that mothers tend to win the argument over who gets to pick the final name of a newborn, with four in ten mums ignoring the choices selected by dads and one in ten dads simply backing down. However, four in ten couples don't make the final decision until after the baby is born, and a third will argue about it before settling.

Nicknames

Nicknames are unavoidable. They can range from the common – such as Mike from Michael or Sam from Samantha – to the trendy, funny or downright insulting. As we saw earlier, there's a growing trend of parents using simplified or shortened versions of their baby's full name and getting rid of the longer name altogether. If you're going to stick with the longer name, however, make sure that you'll be happy with any nicknames that emerge.

The first time your child encounters a nickname will probably be before they are even born – or at least within the first few months. Many older siblings find new names hard to remember or pronounce and your baby could end up with a nickname before you know it.

You can pre-empt problem nicknames to some extent by saying the name you've chosen out loud and trying to find rhymes for it. This is a clever way to avoid playground chants and nursery rhyme-type insults, such as Andy Pandy or Looby Lou. However, it's a disturbing fact that children will find a way to poke fun at literally anything, however carefully you plan, so maybe you should worry less about your child and their classmates, and more about what to do when your child discovers your own name rhymes with bum.

Using family names

This is a huge trend at the moment. It is very en vogue right now to choose a name from a grandparent or parent and then to make sure everyone else knows the reason you chose it!

Some families have a strong tradition of using names that come from the family tree and therefore there are instances where naming your baby boy Augustine VIII is simply not just an option: it's a rule. Admittedly, this doesn't seem to happen very often in the UK – outside nobility – but it is something to consider if it is one of your family's traditions. There are pros and cons with using family names.

- **Pro:** your child will feel part of a strong tradition, which will create a sense of security for them and help to make them feel a full member of the family.

- **Pro:** if you're struggling to select a name that you and your partner both agree on, this is an elegant solution that will make your new child's family very happy.

- **Con:** you might not actually like the name that's being passed down. Naming your child the 12th Thumbelina in a row might not actually hold the same attraction for you as for the generation before.

- **Con:** it could be that the cultural associations with that name have changed in your lifetime and it is no longer appropriate.

How about a compromise? You could use the family name as a middle name or refer to your baby by a nickname instead. You could also suggest using a name from the other parent's family: if the first name comes from your side, try finding a name you like from the other side for a middle name. If their argument is for tradition, this is an astonishingly effective counter-argument.

Whether or not you decide to use a family name, remember that this is your baby. Just as your parents got to decide what they named you, you get to decide this. If family and friends are disappointed, don't be alarmed. Once the baby is here, all they will see is how she has her grandmother's nose or he has his grandfather's ears, and the name will become far less important.

Bizarre US baby names	
Boys	**Girls**
Arrow	Footi
Chap	Kizzy
D'Artagnan	Madonna
Miggy	Psalm
Quest	Swayze

Spellings and pronunciation

Once you've finally agreed on a name, it's time to think about how you want it to be spelled and pronounced. Some parents love experimenting with unusual variations of traditional names, while others prefer names to be instantly recognisable. The only advice here is to use caution in your experiments so your kid isn't saddled with an unfortunate choice. And, as we have seen a growing trend in parents coming up with their own spellings, it's even more important that you take note if you are thinking of doing that!

Try to avoid making a common name too long or too unusual in its spelling, as this will be the first thing your child learns how to write. They will also be subjected to constantly correcting others during their lifetime, as people misspell or mispronounce their name in ever more frustrating ways. Also, make sure that the name isn't so long that it won't fit on forms or name badges, as they'll simply stop using it and take on a nickname instead. Substituting the odd 'i' for a 'y' isn't too bad, but turning the name Felicity into Philleysatee doesn't do anyone any favours.

A Swedish couple were banned from naming their child Brfxxccxxmnpcccclllmmnprxvclmnckssqlbbllll6, which they claimed was pronounced Albin. The law in Sweden also bans religious names that could cause offence, such as Allah and Jesus.

Historical names

Boys		Girls	
1918	*1998*	*1918*	*1998*
1. John	1. Jack	1. Mary	1. Chloe
2. William	2. Thomas	2. Margaret	2. Emily
3. George	3. James	3. Doris	3. Megan
4. Thomas	4. Daniel	4. Dorothy	4. Jessica
5. James	5. Joshua	5. Kathleen	5. Sophie
6. Arthur	6. Matthew	6. Florence	6. Charlotte
7. Frederick	7. Samuel	7. Elsie	7. Hannah
8. Albert	8. Callum	8. Edith	8. Lauren
9. Charles	9. Joseph	9. Elizabeth	9. Rebecca
10. Robert	10. Jordan	10. Winifred	10. Lucy

Middle names

Giving your child a middle name is pretty standard practice. In fact, it's fairly uncommon not to do so, although the use of second and third names only became popular around the turn of the twentieth century. Before then, giving a child a middle name was seen as a status symbol; it was only really used when a man married a higher-class woman and they wanted to keep the woman's maiden name as a reminder of that child's heritage. Once the fashion caught on, it became very popular to give more than one middle name to children of status. Since the 1900s a middle name has become pretty much standard for everyone. A recent study by Netmums found that three-quarters of parents chose a single middle name for the baby, and one in six parents chose two or more.

Medical terms used as names

The following list was provided by a midwife who has vivid recollections of parents thinking they were naming their children something unique and original, only to find out they'd used a medical term.

Chlamydia (pronounced cler-mid-EE-ya)
Eczema (pronounced ex-SEE-mah)
Female (pronounced fuh-MAH-lee)
Latrine (pronounced lah-TREE-nee)
Meconium (pronounced meh-COH-nee-um)
Syphilis (pronounced see-PHIL-iss)
Testicles (pronounced TESS-tee-clees)
Urine (pronounced yer-REE-nee)
Vagina (pronounced vaj-EE-nah)

In Spanish cultures, middle names are often the mother's surname or other name, to preserve the matriarchal lineage. Similarly, parents where one has chosen not to take the other's surname or who are not married may choose to give their child one surname as a middle name and one as a surname so that both parents are represented. However, be aware that doing either of these things can create some strange name combinations – as Richard Tiffany Gere, Billie Paul Piper and Courtney Bass Cox can testify. Other traditions may use an old family name, passed down to each first-born son or daughter, to encourage a sense of family pride and history. A decision about what middle name to pass on may therefore have already been made for you, even before your own birth.

If you are choosing a middle name, there are some common trends for 2019 to help you narrow it down.

- Names from the family tree. Parents frequently look back to their own lineage for interesting, unusual or influential names, and it is becoming increasingly popular to use a mother's surname as a middle name.

- Opposite-length names. It's pretty standard to give a child either a long first name and short middle name or a short first name and long middle name. Generally, if the first name has only one or two syllables (Owen, Steven, Yasmin, Zoe) then the middle name could have two, three or even four syllables (Owen Jonathan, Steven Michael, Yasmin Samantha, Zoe Jessica). And vice versa, so if the first name is three or four syllables long (Anthony, Jennifer, Nicholas, Rosemary) the middle name may be only one or two syllables (Anthony Kevin, Jennifer Ruth, Nicholas John, Rosemary Dawn).

> The shortest baby names are only two letters long (Al, Ed, Jo and Ty) but the longest could be any length imaginable. Popular 11-letter names include Bartholomew, Christopher, Constantine and Maximillian.

Long, longer and longest

How about trying to beat the record for the world's longest name? A woman from Hartlepool claims to have the longest name in the world, after changing it by deed poll in 2012. She went from Dawn McManus to Red Dreams (to raise money for her charity of the same name, set up after the death of her son) with no fewer than 159 middle names, including Wacky, Strange, Lunar, Sheep and Coalition! She beat the previous record-holder by a mile; he had won the title in 2011 with Barnaby Marmaduke Aloysius Benjy Cobweb Dartagnan Egbert Felix Gaspar Humbert Ignatius Jayden Kasper Leroy Maximilian Neddy Obiajulu Pepin Quilliam Rosencrantz Sexton Teddy Upwood Vivatma Wayland Xylon Yardley Zachary Usansky.

- Unusual names. Parents are beginning to choose more unusual middle names, which makes sense if they're sticking to tradition for the first name. They're using the middle name to show some individuality and creativity. So you might well come across Elizabeth Bronte, Katherine Keilyn or Thomas Titan.

Of course, you don't have to narrow down middle name choices to just one, particularly if you like more than one or want to include a family name as well. Be careful not to have too many, though, as this makes life very difficult when filling out official forms. Most institutions only recognise one middle name and some only recognise a middle initial.

Some famous examples of multiple middle names include British musician Brian Eno, whose full name is actually Brian Peter George St John le Baptiste de la Salle Eno, and Canadian actor Kiefer Sutherland, who has shortened his name considerably from Kiefer William Frederick Dempsey George Rufus Sutherland. The Royal Family also likes to give an abundance of middle names: Prince Charles's full name is Charles Philip Arthur George Mountbatten-Windsor and Prince William is William Arthur Philip Louis Mountbatten-Windsor. The newest member of the the royal family is, of course, Prince Louis Arthur Charles, named after Lord Louis Mountbatten and heir to the throne Prince Charles.

Many people choose to go by their middle name instead of their first name, so it could be seen as a safety net if you're worried your

Middle name predictions

Boys	Girls
Adam	Anne
Christopher	Elise
David	Grace
Jay	Leigh
James	Louise
Joseph	Mae
Lee	Marie
Michael	May
Steven	Rose
Thomas	Ruth

child won't like their name. For example, Alyson Hannigan and Alexis Denisof have given their daughters – Satyana Marie and Keeva Jane – more traditional middle names as a way of balancing their unusual first names, thus providing them options when they grow up.

Celebrities who go by middle names

Antonio Banderas (José Antonio Dominguez Banderas)
Ashton Kutcher (Christopher Ashton Kutcher)
Bob Marley (Nesta Robert Marley)
Brad Pitt (William Bradley Pitt)
Brooke Shields (Christa Brooke Camille Shields)
Dakota Fanning (Hannah Dakota Fanning)
Evangeline Lilly (Nicole Evangeline Lilly)
Hugh Laurie (James Hugh Calum Laurie)
Kelsey Grammer (Allen Kelsey Grammer)
Reese Witherspoon (Laura Jean Reese Witherspoon)
Rihanna (Robyn Rihanna Fenty)
Will Ferrell (John William Ferrell)

Initials

What surname will your baby have? Does its first letter already lend itself to amusing acronyms or initialisms? And would choosing certain first names only exacerbate the problem?

If your child will inherit a double-barrelled surname this becomes a bigger consideration still, as there are more funny four-letter words than there are three-letter ones. My brother-in-law was going to be called Andrew Steven Schmitt before he was born, until his parents realised at the last minute what his initials would spell …

It's worth taking the time to think about the acronyms or initialisms formed by initials in the real world too, such as how names are displayed

Amusing initialisms given to real people

David Vernon Durante – DVD
George Barry Holmes – GBH
Jake Clive Baxter – JCB
Neil Harvey Smith – NHS
Patricia Mary Simpson – PMS
Sally Theresa Donaghue – STD
Samuel Alan Spencer – SAS

on credit cards or imagining your child's name written out on a form. Nobody should have to go through life known as S Lugg because their parents didn't think that far ahead.

Across the UK, there are people whose initials spell out three-letter words – from RAT and FAG to FAB or POP – and some are better than others, so do check!

Your surname

Tied to your child's potential new initials is their new surname. Whether they are receiving their name from their mother, father or a hyphenated combination of both, matching their first name to their surname is key. Try writing down all the names you like alongside your child's surname and have someone else read them out loud. This second pair of eyes and ears might just spot something that you didn't.

The age of the internet has given parents a wonderful new weapon in their baby-naming arsenal: the search engine. Before you settle on anything final, try searching for any examples of the complete first name, middle name and surname of your new baby. You may find out that your baby has an axe-murderer namesake or, like one of my former colleagues, the same name as a well-known porn star.

Unfortunate first name/ surname combinations

Anna Sasin	Jenny Taylor
Barb Dwyer	Justin Thyme
Barry Code	Mary Christmas
Ben Dover	Oliver Sutton
Duane Pipe	Paige Turner
Grace Land	Russell Sprout
Harry Rump	Stan Still
Hazel Nutt	Teresa Green

There is also the possibility of your child having a spoonerism made out of their name, where the first letters or syllables get swapped around to form new words. Named after the Reverend Dr William Archibald Spooner (1844–1930), a spoonerism can be created out of almost anything to make clever, amusing or downright inappropriate phrases instead.

An unfortunate example of this would be Angelina Jolie and Brad Pitt's daughter Shiloh, whom they named Shiloh Jolie-Pitt to avoid the inevitable Shiloh Pitt spoonerism.

The 'Top 10 Worst Baby Names'?

Reddit users last year voted on a Top 10 Worst Baby Names list. Does your favourite make the top? What about your most hated?

Aliviyah (pronounced Olivia)
Baby
Beberly (yes, that spelling is correct)
Danger (surely that should always be a middle name?)
Elizabreth (again, that spelling is correct)
Harley Quinn
Little Sweetmeat
Mhavryck (pronounced Maverick)
Nevaeh (or, Heaven backwards)
North West (sorry, Kim and Kanye!)

Other entries included the dynamic Strawberry Rain (discussed as 'a great baby name if you were naming a shampoo'), Rhythm, and Diesel Duramax.

Naming twins, triplets and more

If you have discovered you are expecting multiples, congratulations! Naming multiples needn't be any different from naming one child … unless you want it to be. You could stick to the same process as everyone else by picking a unique name for each child.

Or you could choose a theme. During a caesarean section for premature triplets, Kimberly Fugate's doctor said 'More feet', and out popped a fourth baby! Kimberly and husband Craig are now the proud parents of identical quadruplet girls, called Kenleigh Rosa, Kristen Sue, Kayleigh Pearl and Kelsey Roxanne, who join big sister Katelyn. Channelling the Kardashians' penchant for the letter K perhaps?

Some parents do like to use a pattern, such as going down the alphabet (think Alastair, Benjamin, Christopher and David) or doing what the famous Phoenix acting clan did and giving each child a name to do with nature: River, Rain, Joaquin (Leaf), Liberty and Summer.

Twin names with the same meaning

Bernard and Brian (strong)
Daphne and Laura (laurel)
Deborah and Melissa (bee)
Dorcas and Tabitha (gazelle)
Elijah and Joel (God)
Eve and Zoe (life)
Irene and Salome (peace)
Lucius and Uri (light)
Lucy and Helen (light)
Sarah and Almira (princess)

> When Tress Montalvo gave birth to two sets of identical twin boys on the same day, the chances of which were one in 70 million, she named her miracles Ace, Blaine, Cash and Dylan (ABCD).

The UK's biggest-family title is currently held by the Radfords, though Sue and Noel Radford have not chosen to follow a theme when naming their 20 children. From oldest to youngest, they are: Christopher, Sophie, Chloe, Jack, Daniel, Luke, Millie, Katie, James, Ellie, Aimee, Josh, Max, Tilly May, Oscar, Caspar, Hallie, Phoebe, Archie and Alfie (sadly, they lost baby Alfie, born at 21 weeks, in 2014). They even have three grandchildren!

The official Guinness World Record for the most siblings baptised with the same initial is held by a Canadian family, who had 10 sons and six daughters all given names beginning with the letter E. However the unofficial challenger to this would be the notorious Duggar family from the USA, whose 19 children all have names starting with J.

Celebrity twin names

Alexander and Ella (Amal and George Clooney)
Amani and Aisha (Mo and Tania Farah)
Bowie and Cy (Zoe Saldana and Marco Perego)
Jacques and Gabriella (Prince Albert II and Princess Charlene of Monaco)
Jett and Jax (Caprice and Ty Comfort)
John and Gus (Julie Bowen and Scott Phillips)
Matteo and Valentino (Ricky Martin and unnamed surrogate)
Myla Rose and Charlene Riva *and* Leo and Lenny (two sets for Roger and Mirka Federer!)
Rumi and Sir (Beyoncé and Jay Z)
Tristan and Sasha (Chris Hemsworth and Elsa Pataky)

> Amal and George Clooney welcomed their twins into the world in June 2017 and chose the traditional names Alexander and Ella, surprising those who had expected some reference to Amal's Lebanese heritage.

There are a few things to keep in mind when naming twins or multiples, but they are at least pretty simple ones:

- Don't use very long names. You will often find yourself needing to write both names down, or calling both children for dinner, and very long names might get so bothersome you end up not using them. Instead, use shorter versions of the names you like, such as Max for Maximilian, or Eve for Evangeline.

- Don't get too complicated. Again, spelling out all the names and middle names you've given your multiples can be made a lot easier if you keep things simple. Stick with traditional spellings if possible, like Cameron instead of Kammeryn and Elizabeth instead of Alyzybeth.

- Don't forget that your babies are still individuals. If you use names that sound so similar you often mix them up, your children may get frustrated as they get older and other people confuse them. Instead, keep those nearly identical names you love as middle names and use this opportunity to explore more individual first names to match your babies' unique personalities.

Names for triplets

Aidan, Diana and Nadia (anagrams)
Amber, Jade and Ruby (jewels)
Amy, May and Mya (anagrams)
Ava, Eva and Iva (similar)
Daisy, Lily and Rose (flowers)
Ginger, Saffron and Rosemary (herbs)
Jay, Raven and Robin (birds)
Olive, Violet and Sage (colours)
River, Rain and Summer (nature)

Registering a baby's name

There are slightly different guidelines for registering births and names depending on where you live in the UK.

In England, Wales and Northern Ireland a birth must be recorded within 42 days of delivery and if not done at the hospital it requires a visit to a register office. The birth certificate will be written in English if a child is born in England or Northern Ireland, and can be in both English and Welsh if they are born in Wales.

If the birth is recorded at the hospital or registered in the same district, birth certificates are usually issued straight away but if you end up going to a different office, the certificate may be sent to you after a few days. This is important when applying for Child Benefit or registering your baby with a doctor, as you will need a copy of the short birth certificate to apply.

If the parents of a newborn are a heterosexual couple and married, either parent can register a birth. However, if the parents are not married there are several ways to ensure that both names are put on the birth certificate, including both parents being physically present at the registration or one parent submitting a declaration form in lieu of their presence. It's worth remembering that if the father's details were not recorded on the original certificate or if the natural parents have married since the registration, a new birth certificate will have to be generated.

If the parents are same-sex female and married or in a civil partnership, either parent can register the birth and both can be named on the birth certificate. However, if the parents aren't married or in a civil partnership, they will need a court order (or one of several other documentation options, such as a parenthood agreement) to be able to add both names. For same-sex male couples, a parental order must be granted before the birth can be registered, no matter what the married status.

If neither parent can be present to register a birth, someone who was present at the birth or someone who is now responsible for the child can also carry out the duty.

After the registration, the parents or those with parental responsibility also have the option of requesting a naming ceremony. These non-religious ceremonies are conducted by local authorities and can be a nice replacement for a baptism or christening, as adults outside the family can be nominated to act in secular roles similar to godparents. A birth certificate is also needed for this event to take place.

Registering a birth

Information you'll need to register a birth
Place and date of your baby's birth
Name, surname and sex of your baby
Places and dates of birth for both parents
The date of the marriage or civil partnership of the parents (if applicable)
Jobs of both parents
Former names of both parents (maiden name or deed poll, if applicable)

What to bring
Form of ID, such as a birth certificate, driving licence, or passport
Your baby's NHS personal health record or 'red book'
Proof of paternity (if applicable)

Useful websites
England and Wales: www.gov.uk
Northern Ireland: www.nidirect.gov.uk
Scotland: www.nrscotland.gov.uk

> While German law prohibits invented and androgynous names, the UK has some of the most liberal rules in the world on naming a baby. Only names that are deemed to be offensive make it onto the banned list here.

In Scotland, births need to be registered within 21 days, and this can take place in any district. As well as either married parent being allowed to register the birth, their relatives may also do this duty. If the parents are not married, the father may register the birth only if the mother is also present, or a declaration form is submitted or a court agrees that he has parental responsibility. Parents of newborns in Scotland should take a card given to them at the hospital and a copy of their marriage certificate to the birth registration.

If you are a British national and your baby is born abroad, you will have to register the birth in that country, following the appropriate rules and regulations. You should also register it at the local British Embassy or Consulate, or with UK authorities when you are back home, in order to obtain a British birth certificate, proof that the baby is a British citizen by birth, and to have the birth registered with the UK General Register Office. The name you choose won't be included in the official UK statistics, but it will instead be part of the statistics for the country where your baby was born ... which is kind of cool!

South Africa's Top 10

Boys	Girls
1. Junior	1. Precious
2. Blessing	2. Princess
3. Gift	3. Amahle
4. Bandile	4. Luthando
5. Prince	5. Thandolwethu
6. Melokuhle	6. Blessing
7. Siyabonga	7. Angel
8. Lethabo	8. Sisphesihle
9. Amogelang	9. Melokuhle
10. Lubanzi	10. Amogelang

Changing your mind

If you later decide that you want to change details on a birth certificate, there are procedures in place, although this can be a time-consuming process. In fact, even if the name was copied down incorrectly and is now misspelled, the burden is on the parents to prove it wasn't intentional. Documents showing the correct spelling at the time of the birth must be produced – and those can be tricky to find.

If you've just changed your mind about your baby's name, you only have about 12 months to act before it becomes an even bigger headache. Visit the Deed Poll Office's website for instructions on what to do, and remember that it can only be done once. The original name will still appear on the new birth certificate, with the new name listed underneath.

> The *Guardian* recently published a list of people who later regretted their choice of baby name. Examples included Tennessee, Bear, Rafferty and Astrid … who apparently gets called Asterisk a lot by mistake. Also included was the tale of one mother who changed her baby's name three times in 18 months because she couldn't make her mind up.

Changing the surname of your baby is only possible in two cases: either if the spelling is incorrect or if the details of the parents are being changed (such as the inclusion of the father or the parents now being married). A fee is usually incurred if a new certificate is required.

If you are in any way unsure about the choice you're about to make, keep in mind how difficult it may be for you to change your child's birth certificate at a later stage. On the bright side, though, bear in mind that if something unexpected happens and you need to make the change, it is possible.

Music to my baby's ears

In 2016 Classic FM had some fun with its Facebook followers by posting this 'helpful' list of baby name suggestions:

Cute music terms to name your children:

Viola	Oboe Player
Harmony	F Sharp
Melody	♮
Cadence	Barbaro
Carol	Plagal
Hymn	Smorzando
Celeste	Agitato
Clef	Canon in inversion and augmentation

Part two

Boys' names A–Z

Baby names vary widely in spelling and pronunciation. To simplify things, this book usually lists each name only once: under the most common initial and spelling. If a name has an alternative spelling with a different initial, it may be listed under that letter also.

Boys' names

Aaron

Hebrew, meaning 'mountain of strength'. In the Bible, Aaron was the older brother of Moses and the first high priest of Israel.

Abasi

Egyptian Arabic, meaning 'male'; Swahili, meaning 'stern'.

Abdiel

Hebrew, meaning 'servant of God'. Also the name of an important seraph in Milton's *Paradise Lost*.

Abdul

Arabic, meaning 'servant'. Often followed by a suffix indicating who Abdul is the servant of (e.g. Abdul-Basit, 'servant of the creator').

Abdullah
(alt. Abd-Allah, Abdallah, Abdollah)
Arabic, meaning 'servant of God'.

Abdur Rahman

Arabic, meaning 'one who serves a merciful man'.

Abel

Hebrew, meaning 'breath' or 'breathing spirit'. Associated with the biblical son of Adam and Eve, who was killed by his brother Cain.

Abelard

German, meaning 'resolute'.

Aberforth

Gaelic, meaning 'mouth of the river Forth'. The name of Dumbledore's younger brother in J.K. Rowling's 'Harry Potter' series.

Abhik
(alt. Abheek)
Sanskrit, meaning 'fearless'. Popular name for boys in India.

Abhishek

Sanskrit, meaning 'bath for a deity' or 'anointing'. Abhishek Bachchan is currently one of Bollywood's highest-paid and most popular actors.

Abner

Hebrew, meaning 'father of light'. Abner was the commander of Saul's army in the Bible.

Abraham

(alt. Abram; abbrev. Abe)
Hebrew, meaning 'father of the multitude'. Famous Abrahams include President Abraham Lincoln and Abraham Van Helsing – the vampire hunter and doctor in Bram Stoker's *Dracula*.

Absalom

(alt. Absalon)
Hebrew, meaning 'father/leader of peace'. The name of King David's favourite son in the Bible, and one of Chaucer's curly-haired characters in *The Canterbury Tales*.

Acacio

Greek, meaning 'thorny tree' or 'honourable'. Now widely used in Spain.

Ace

Latin, meaning 'unit'. Also used in English to mean 'number one' or 'the best'.

Achilles

Greek, mythological hero of the Trojan war, whose heel was his only weak spot.

Achim

Hebrew, meaning 'God will establish' or Polish, meaning 'the Lord exalts'. Also a shortened version of the name 'Joachim' in Germany.

Ackerley

Old English, meaning 'oak meadow'.

Adam

Hebrew, meaning 'man' or 'earth'. Found in the Bible, where the creation story names Adam as the first man on earth.

Adão

Portuguese variant of Adam, meaning 'earth'.

Addison

Old English, meaning 'son of Adam'. Also used as a female name in the USA.

Ade

Yoruba, meaning 'peak' or 'royal'. Ade is a common name in Nigeria.

Adelard

French or German, meaning 'brave' or 'noble'.

Adelbert

(alt. Adalberto)
Old German form of Albert. Popularity decreased in the nineteenth century, when Albert became more commonly used.

Adetokunbo

Yoruba, meaning 'the crown came from over the sea'.

Adin

Hebrew, meaning 'slender' or 'voluptuous'. Also Swahili, meaning 'ornamental'.

Aditya

Sanskrit, meaning 'belonging to the sun'. In Hindi, Aditya means 'sun god'. Aditya refers to the offspring of Aditi, the mother of the Gods.

Adlai

Hebrew, meaning 'God is just', or sometimes 'ornamental'.

Adler

Old German, meaning 'eagle'.

Adley

English, meaning 'son of Adam'.

Admon

Hebrew, variant of Adam meaning 'earth'. Also the name of a red peony.

Adolph
(alt. Adolf)

Old German, meaning 'noble majestic wolf'. Once popular before World War II, this name has now become deeply unpopular due to its association with Adolf Hitler, and several European nations have actually banned its use.

Adonis

Phoenician, meaning 'Lord'. Adonis was the god of beauty and desire in Greek mythology.

Adrian

Latin, meaning 'from Hadria', a town in northern Italy.

Adriel

Hebrew, meaning 'of God's flock'. Adriel was one of Saul's sons-in-law in the Bible.

Adyn
(alt. Ade)

Irish, meaning 'manly'. Also the name of a UK men's streetwear company (presumably because of its meaning).

Aeneas

Greek/Latin, meaning 'to praise'. Name of the hero who founded Rome in Virgil's *Aeneid*.

Aero

Greek, meaning 'air'.

Aeson
(alt. Aesion)

Greek, father of Jason in ancient Greek mythology.

Afonso

Portuguese, meaning 'eager noble warrior'.

Agamemnon

Greek, meaning 'leader of the assembly'. Figure in mythology, commanded the Greeks at the siege of Troy.

Agathon

Greek, meaning 'good' or 'superior'. The name of a tragic poet in ancient Greece.

Agustin

Latin/Spanish, meaning 'venerated'.

Ahab

Hebrew, meaning 'father's brother'. Name of the obsessed captain in *Moby-Dick*.

Ahijah

Hebrew, meaning 'brother of God' or 'friend of God'.

Ahmad

(alt. Ahmed)

Arabic/Turkish, meaning 'worthy of praise'. Ahmad is also one of the prophet Muhammad's many given names.

Aidan

(alt. Aiden, Aodhán)

Gaelic, meaning 'little fire'. Derives from Aodh, which is the name of a Celtic sun god.

Aidric

Old English, meaning 'oaken'. St Aidric was a bishop and court diplomat in the ninth century.

Ainsley

Old English, meaning 'meadow' or 'clearing'. Also a girls' name. Ainsley Harriott is a well-known TV chef.

Airyck

Old Norse, from Eric, meaning 'eternal ruler'.

Ajani

Swahili, meaning 'he fights for what he is'. Also Sanskrit, meaning 'of noble birth'.

Ajax

Greek, meaning 'mourner of the Earth'. A Greek hero from the siege of Troy.

Ajay

Hindi, meaning 'unconquerable'. One of the most popular names in India.

Ajit

Sanskrit, meaning 'invincible'. Alternative name for both Shiva and Vishnu in Hindu mythology.

Akeem

Arabic, meaning 'wise or insightful'. Popular name throughout Africa, particularly in Nigeria.

Akio

Japanese, meaning 'bright man'. Akio Morita was one of the co-founders of the electronics company Sony.

Akira

Japanese, meaning 'intelligent'. Name of a hugely influential animated Japanese film.

Akiva

Hebrew, meaning 'to protect' or 'to shelter'.

Akon

American, meaning 'flower'. Made popular by the rapper.

Aksel

Danish, meaning 'father of peace'. Its name day is 23 March, and babies with this name are sometimes celebrated in Nordic countries on this day.

Aladdin

Arabic, meaning 'servant of Allah'. From the medieval story in the *Arabian Nights*.

Alan

(alt. Allan, Allen, Allyn, Alun)

Gaelic or old French, meaning 'rock'. Alan is one of the oldest names still in popular use in the UK, and its roots can be traced back to the Norman invasion in the eleventh century.

Alaric

(alt. Aleric)

Old German, meaning 'noble regal ruler'. King Alaric I of the Visigoths played a key role in the downfall of the Roman Empire.

Alastair

(alt. Alasdair, Alastor, Alistair, Allister; abbrev. Ali, Allie)

Greek/Gaelic, meaning 'defending men'. Famous Alastairs include comedian and TV presenter Alistair McGowan, English cricketer Alastair Cook and Ali G, whose 'real name' is Alistair.

Alban

Latin, meaning 'from Alba'. Also the name of St Alban, the first British Christian martyr.

Alberic

Germanic, meaning 'Elfin king'.

Albert

(abbrev. Albie, Bert, Bertie)

Old German, meaning 'noble, bright,

Less common three-syllable names

Alastair	Elijah
Barnaby	Lancelot
Dominic	Roberto
Dorian	Theodore

---

famous'. Probably most commonly associated with Prince Albert, Queen Victoria's husband, who died in 1861.

Albin

Latin, variant of Albus, meaning 'white'. Popular in some areas including Scandinavia, Slovenia, Germany and Poland.

Albus

Latin, meaning 'white'. Made famous by Albus Dumbledore, the headmaster of Hogwarts in J.K. Rowling's 'Harry Potter' series.

Alcaeus

Greek, meaning 'strength'. Alcaeus of Mytilene was an influential ancient Greek poet.

Alden

Old English, meaning 'old friend'. More commonly used as a given name in the USA.

Aldis

English, meaning 'battle-seasoned'.

Aldo
(alt. Aldous)

Latin, meaning 'the tall one'. Aldo is the main gorilla character in the *Planet of the Apes* movie series.

Aldric

English, meaning 'old king'.

Aled

Welsh, meaning 'child' or 'offspring'. Aled Jones is a Welsh singer and TV presenter, who shot to fame as a choirboy for *Walking in the Air*.

Aleph
(alt. Alef)

Hebrew, meaning 'first letter of the alphabet', or 'leader'.

Aleron
(alt. Aileron, Alerun, Ailerun, Alejandro)

Latin, meaning 'child with wings'.

Alessio
(alt. Alejo)

Italian, meaning 'defender'.

Alexander
(alt. Alexandro, Alessandro, Alejandro; abbrev. Alec, Alex, Alexei, Sandy, Xander)

Greek, meaning 'defender of mankind'. Alexander the Great was an undefeated fourth-century king whose empire stretched from Greece to modern Pakistan. Sir Alec Guinness is the renowned actor whose illustrious career took him from Shakespeare on stage to Hollywood blockbusters.

Alfonso

Germanic/Spanish, meaning 'noble and prompt, ready to struggle'. Associated with *Gravity* director Alfonso Cuarón Orozco, and actor Alfonso Ribeiro.

Alford

Old English, meaning 'old river/ford'.

Alfred
(abbrev. Alf, Alfie)

English, meaning 'elf' or 'magical counsel'. Alfred the Great was a ninth-century king of England who defended the Anglo-Saxons against Viking invasion. *Alfie* is the name of a successful 1966 British film starring actor Michael Caine.

Algernon

French, meaning 'with a moustache'. A popular name among the nobility in eighteenth- and nineteenth-century England.

Alois

German, meaning 'famous warrior'.

Alok

Sanskrit, meaning 'cry of triumph'. Also the name of a style of singing in Javanese gamelan.

Alon

Hebrew, meaning 'oak tree'.

Alonso
(alt. Alonzo)

Germanic, meaning 'noble and ready'.

Aloysius

Old German, meaning 'fame and war'. Also the name of an Italian saint.

Alpha

First letter of the Greek alphabet.

Alphaeus

Hebrew, meaning 'changing'. Alphaeus is mentioned in the Bible as being the father of two of the twelve Apostles, Matthew and James.

Alpin

Gaelic, meaning 'related to the Alps'. The House of Alpin refers to a dynasty of Scottish kings.

Altair

Arabic, meaning 'flying' or 'bird'. Altair is one of the brightest stars seen in the night sky from Earth.

Alter
(alt. Altar)

Yiddish, meaning 'old man'.

Alton

Old English, meaning 'old town'.

Alva

Latin, meaning 'white'. Used more commonly for girls than boys.

Alvin
(alt. Alvie)

English, meaning 'friend of elves'. Alvin and the Chipmunks are a cartoon singing group, first created in 1958 and still making films today.

Alwyn

Welsh, meaning 'wise friend'. May also come from the River Alwen in Wales.

Amachi

Swahili, meaning 'who knows what God has brought us through this child'.

Amadeus

Latin, meaning 'God's love'. One of the given names of the composer Wolfgang Amadeus Mozart.

Amadi

Igbo, meaning 'appeared destined to die at birth'. Often given to babies who unexpectedly survive against the odds.

Amado

Spanish, meaning 'God's love'.

Amador

Spanish, meaning 'one who loves'.

Amari

Hebrew, meaning 'given by God'. Can be a boys' or girls' name.

Amarion

Arabic, meaning 'populous, flushing'.

Amasa

Hebrew, meaning 'burden'.

Ambrose

Greek, meaning 'undying, immortal'.

Americo

Germanic, meaning 'ever powerful in battle'. Popular in the nineteenth century, now this is an infrequently used baby name.

Amias
(alt. Amyas)

Latin, meaning 'loved'.

Amil

Sanskrit, meaning 'unavailable'. Popular name for boys in India.

Amir
(alt. Emir)

Arabic, meaning 'chieftain' or 'commander'. Emir or Amir is a title for a high-ranking sheikh, used in many Muslim communities.

Amit

Hindi, meaning 'infinite'. One of the 108 names for the Hindu God Shri Ganesha.

Ammon

Hebrew, meaning 'the hidden one'. The Ammonites were an ancient tribe of people mentioned in the Bible.

Amory

German/English, meaning 'work' and 'power'. Its popularity has waned since the nineteenth century, when it was a common name.

Amos

Hebrew, meaning 'encumbered' or 'burdened'. St Amos wrote the Book of Amos in the eighth century, which is part of the Hebrew Bible.

Anacletus

Latin, meaning 'called back' or 'invoked'. Pope Anacletus was the third pope in history, and served during the first century.

Anakin

American, meaning 'warrior'. Made famous by Anakin Skywalker in the *Star Wars* films.

Ananias

Greek/Italian, meaning 'answered by the Lord'. Ananias Dare was the first baby born to English parents in North America, making him the first-ever 'modern' American.

Anastasius
(alt. Anastasios)

Greek, meaning 'resurrection'. Popular name for popes, emperors, and saints – there are nearly 20 St Anastasiuses on record.

Anatole
(alt. Anatolius)

French, meaning 'sunrise'. Monsieur Anatole was an influential nineteenth-century French composer, master, and ballet dancer.

Anders

Scandinavian, meaning 'lion man'. A popular name for boys in Sweden.

Anderson

English, meaning 'male'.

Andrew
(alt. Andreas)
Greek, meaning 'man' or 'warrior'.
One of the Top 10 names for baby
boys during the 1980s and 1990s.

Androcles
Greek, meaning 'glory of a warrior'.
Androcles and the Lion was a well-
known folktale of the second century,
made famous in the twentieth
century by George Bernard Shaw's
play of the same title.

Angel
(alt. Angelo)
Greek, meaning 'messenger'. Angels
appear throughout the Bible and
modern culture, and the name Angel
is often used in Spanish-speaking
cultures as a name for both boys and
girls.

Angus
Gaelic, meaning 'one choice'. An
ancient name used especially in
Scotland. The name of Merida's
trusty Clydesdale horse in Disney
Pixar's *Brave*.

Anil
Sanskrit, meaning 'air' or 'wind'.
Anil Gupta is the producer (and for
some the creator) of many leading
television comedies, including
Goodness Gracious Me, *The Kumars
at No. 42* and *The Office*.

Anselm
German, meaning 'helmet of God'.
St Anselm was an archbishop of
Canterbury and influential figure in
the Christian religion.

Anson
English, meaning 'son of Agnes'.
Most commonly used in the USA.

Anthony
(alt. Antony; abbrev. Ant, Tony)
English, meaning 'invaluable
grace'. *Antony and Cleopatra* is
a Shakespearean play depicting
the romance between the Roman
general Mark Antony and Queen
Cleopatra of Eygpt.

Antipas
Israeli, meaning 'for all or against
all'. Herod Antipas was the leader
mentioned in the Bible as being
responsible for the executions of
John the Baptist and Jesus.

Antwan
(alt. Antoine)
Old English, meaning 'flower'.
Older and more unusual spelling of
Antoine.

Apollo
Greek, meaning 'to destroy'. Greek
god of poetry, music and the sun.

Apostolos
Greek, meaning 'apostle'. The
Apostolos book is a text believed
to have been written by one of the
twelve disciples of Jesus.

Ara
Arabic, meaning 'brings rain'.

Aragorn
Literary, a character in J.R.R. Tolkien's
The Lord of the Rings trilogy.

Aram

Hebrew, meaning 'royal highness'. Aram is an ancient region in modern-day Syria, mentioned in the Bible.

Aramis

Latin, meaning 'swordsman'. Aramis is one of the three musketeers in Alexandre Dumas's eponymous novel.

Arcadio

Greek/Spanish, from a place in ancient Greece. The word 'Arcadia' (meaning paradise) comes from this.

Archibald
(abbrev. Archie)

Old German, meaning 'genuine, bold, brave'. A popular name in Scotland.

Ardell

Latin, meaning 'eager, burning with enthusiasm'.

Arden

Celtic, meaning 'high'. A very early English motor car.

Ares

Greek, meaning 'ruin'. Son of Zeus and Hera, and the Greek god of war.

Ari

Hebrew, meaning 'lion' or 'eagle'. Can also be used in Hebrew to refer to an important or honourable man.

Arias

Germanic, meaning 'lion'.

Aric

English, meaning 'merciful ruler'. Alternative spelling of Eric.

Ariel

Hebrew, meaning 'lion of God'. One of the archangels, the angel of healing and new beginnings.

Arild

Old Norse, meaning 'battle commander'. Arild Andersen is an internationally popular Norwegian jazz musician.

Aris

Greek, meaning 'best figure'. Popular name in both ancient and modern Greece.

Ariston

Greek, meaning 'the best'. Ariston of Athens was the philosopher Plato's father.

Aristotle

Greek, meaning 'best'. Also an ancient Greek philosopher.

Arjun

Sanskrit, meaning 'bright and shining'. Name is derived from Arjuna, an ancient and legendary archer.

Arkady

Greek, a region of central Greece. Popular name for boys throughout Eastern Europe.

Arlan

Gaelic, meaning 'pledge' or 'oath'.

Arlie

Old English place name, meaning 'eagle wood'. Sometimes used as a shortened form of Arlan.

Arliss
(alt. Arlis)

Hebrew, meaning 'pledge'.

Arlo

Spanish, meaning 'barberry tree'. Can also be linked back to the Old Norse word for 'army of troops'.

Armand

Old German, meaning 'soldier'. Armand van Helden is a top American DJ and producer of electronic house music.

Armani

Same origin as Armand, meaning 'soldier'. Also the name of an Italian fashion house after designer Georgio Armani.

Arnaldo

Spanish, meaning 'eagle power'.

Arnav

Hindi, meaning 'the sea'. Can be pronounced as 'Arnav' or 'Arnaf'.

Arnold
(abbrev. Arnie)

Old German, meaning 'eagle ruler'. Also the name of actor, former bodybuilder and US politician Arnold Schwarzenegger.

Arrow

English, from the common word denoting weaponry.

Art

Irish, name of a warrior in Irish mythology, Art Oenfer (Art the Lonely). Also a shortened form of Arthur.

Arthur
(alt. Art, Arte, Artie, Artis)

Celtic, probably from 'artos', meaning 'bear'. Made famous by the tales of King Arthur and the Knights of the Round Table.

Arvel

From the Welsh 'Arwel', meaning 'wept over'. Used frequently as a name for mythical characters – for example, Arvel Crynyd in *Star Wars*, and Arvel the Swift in *The Elder Scrolls V: Skyrim*.

Arvid

Old Norse, meaning 'eagle in the woods'. Commonly used in Scandinavia.

Arvind
(alt. Aravind)

Sanskrit, meaning 'red lotus'. May also be derived from the word for 'white lotus', upon which the Hindu goddess Lakshmi sits.

Arvo

Finnish, meaning 'value' or 'worth'. Also used as slang term for 'afternoon' in Australia.

Asa

Hebrew, meaning 'doctor' or 'healer'.

Asante

Asante, meaning 'thank you'. Also refers to the language of the Ashanti people.

Asher

Hebrew, meaning 'fortunate' or 'lucky'. One of the twelve sons of Jacob in the Bible, and one of the brothers who sells Joseph into slavery in the story of Joseph and his multi-coloured coat.

Ashley

Old English, meaning 'ash meadow'. The name of several football players, including Ashley Cole and Ashley Young.

Ashok

Sanskrit, meaning 'not causing sorrow'. Popular in India and Sri Lanka.

Ashton

English, meaning 'settlement in the ash-tree grove'. Name has been popularised due to the American actor Ashton Kutcher – although his first name is actually Christopher.

Aslan

Turkish, meaning 'lion'. Strongly associated with the lion Aslan in C.S. Lewis's *The Lion, the Witch and the Wardrobe*.

Asriel

Hebrew, meaning 'help of God'. Lord Asriel is an important character in Philip Pullman's *His Dark Materials* trilogy.

Astrophel

Latin, meaning 'star lover'. *Astrophel and Stella* is the name of a group of sonnets by Philip Sidney, written in the 1590s, and the first time the name is recorded as being used.

Athanasios

(abbrev. Thanasis, Thanos)
Greek, meaning 'eternal life'.

Atílio

Portuguese, meaning 'father'. Can also be lengthened to Attilius.

Atlas

Greek, meaning 'to carry'. In Greek mythology Atlas was a Titan forced to carry the weight of the heavens.

Atlee

Hebrew, meaning 'God is just'.

Atticus

Latin, meaning 'from Athens'. Atticus Finch is one of the main characters in Harper Lee's influential novels *To Kill A Mockingbird* and *Go Set a Watchman*.

Auberon

Old German, meaning 'royal bear'. Also the name for a fairy king. It is the French spelling for Oberon.

Aubrey

French, meaning 'elf ruler'. Popular for boys during the Middle Ages; now more usually given to girls.

Auden

Old English, meaning 'old friend'. W.H. Auden is considered to be one of the most influential 20th-century poets.

Audie

Old English, meaning 'noble strength'. Audie L. Murphy was one of the most decorated and honoured American soldiers of World War II.

Augustus
(alt. Augustas)

Latin, meaning 'venerated'. The first Roman emperor. Also a character in Roald Dahl's Charlie and the Chocolate Factory.

Aurelien

French, meaning 'golden'. Also the name of a Roman emperor.

Austin

Latin, meaning 'venerated'. Austin Healey played rugby union for England. Also the name of a classic car.

Avery
(alt. Avrie, Averey, Averie)

English, meaning 'wise ruler'. Can also be derived from the name Alfred, or the ancient English word for elf.

Avi

Hebrew, meaning 'father of a multitude of nations'. Name of an author of popular children's and teens' fiction.

Awnan

Irish, meaning 'little Adam'.

Axel

German and Scandinavian, a Germanised form of the Hebrew Absalom, meaning 'father is peace'. Made famous by Guns 'n' Roses front man Axl Rose.

Ayers
(alt. Ayer, Aires, Aire)

English, meaning 'heir to a fortune'.

Azarel
(alt. Azaryah)

Hebrew, meaning 'helped by God'. Also the name of an evil spirit in the Bible.

Azriel

Hebrew, meaning 'God is my help'. Name is often used to describe the angel of death in many religions, including Christianity and Judaism.

Azuko

Igbo, meaning 'past glory'. Most commonly found in Japan.

B Boys' names

Baden

German, meaning 'battle'. Also the name of a city in Switzerland known for its hot springs.

Bailey

English, meaning 'bailiff'.

Baird

Scottish, meaning 'poet' or 'one who sings ballads'. John Logie Baird was a Scottish engineer credited with inventing the world's first working television.

Bakari

Swahili, meaning 'hope' or 'promise'.

Baker

English, from the word 'baker'.

Baldwin

Old French, meaning 'bold, brave friend'. The Baldwin family is a well-known acting dynasty in Hollywood, with brothers Alec, Stephen, William, and Daniel.

Balin

Old English. Balin was one of the Knights of the Round Table.

Balthazar

Babylonian, meaning 'protect the King'. A name commonly attributed to one of the Three Wise Men in the Christian Nativity story.

Balwinder
(alt. Balvinder)

Hindi, meaning 'merciful, compassionate'. Balwinder Singh Sandhu is a well-known former Indian Test cricketer.

Bannon

Irish, meaning 'descendant of O'Banain'. Also a river in Wales.

Barack

Contraction of the Swahili name Baruch and the Hebrew name Mubarak. Made popular by the 44th US President, Barack Obama.

Barclay

Old English, meaning 'birch tree meadow'.

Barker

Old English, meaning 'shepherd'.

Barnaby
(abbrev. Barney)

Greek, meaning 'son of consolation'. *Barnaby Rudge* is one of Charles Dickens's novels.

Barnard

English, meaning 'strong as a bear'.

Baron
(alt. Barron)

Old English, meaning 'young warrior'. Baron is a title given to men of nobility.

Barrett

English, meaning 'strong as a bear'.

Barry
(abbrev. Baz)

Irish Gaelic, meaning 'fair haired'. Famous Barrys include Barry Humphries, best known as the comedian behind Dame Edna Everage. Also Baz Luhrmann, the Australian film director.

Bartholomew
(abbrev. Bart)

Hebrew, meaning 'son of the farmer'. The name of one of Jesus' apostles. Bart is the name of the eldest child of the cartoon family the Simpsons.

Barton

Old English, meaning 'barley settlement'. One of the more popular names of towns in England, with at least 25 on record.

Baruch

Hebrew, meaning 'blessed'. Also a term for a Jewish blessing.

Barzillai

Hebrew, meaning 'made of iron'. A minor character in the Bible, Barzillai supposedly teaches youngsters not to be afraid of old age.

Bashir

Arabic, meaning 'well educated' and 'wise'.

Basil

Greek, meaning 'royal, kingly'. Basil is the lead character in the TV comedy *Fawlty Towers*. Also the name of a herb.

Basim

Arabic, meaning 'smile'.

Bastien

Greek, meaning 'revered'. Bastien Pagez was one of the most important servants to Mary, Queen of Scots.

Baxter

Old English, meaning 'baker'.

Bay

From the bay tree or the indentation in the coastline. Also a girls' name.

Bayard

French, meaning 'auburn haired'. Bayard Rustin was one of Martin Luther King Jr's mentors and advisors during the American Civil Rights movement.

Bayo
(alt. Baio)

Swahili, meaning 'to find joy'.

Bayre

American, meaning 'beautiful'.

Beau

French, meaning 'handsome'. Beau Bridges is an American actor. Beau Brummell was a fashionable figure in Regency England and friend of the future King George IV. Beau was not the given name of either man, but an adopted name.

Beck

Old Norse, meaning 'stream'.

Beckett

Old English, meaning 'beehive' or 'bee cottage'. Associated with the Irish writer Samuel Beckett.

Beckham

English, meaning 'homestead by the stream'. Made famous by David and Victoria Beckham.

Béla

Hungarian, meaning 'within'. Famously associated with the actor Bela Lugosi.

Belarius

Shakespearean, meaning 'a banished lord'. From Shakespeare's play *Cymbeline*.

Benedict
(abbrev. Ben)

Latin, meaning 'blessed'. Benedict Cumberbatch is currently enjoying mega stardom thanks to his role in *Sherlock*. Ben Ainslie is the most successful Olympic sailor ever.

Benicio

Spanish, meaning 'benevolent'. Benicio del Toro is an Oscar-winning actor from Puerto Rico.

Benjamin
(abbrev. Ben, Benjie, Bennie, Benny)

Hebrew, meaning 'son of the south'. Benjamin Franklin, American inventor and discoverer of electricity was one of the Founding Fathers of the United States. Ben Affleck, actor, and Ben Fogle, adventurer and TV personality, are both Benjamins.

Bennett

French/Latin vernacular form of Benedict, meaning 'blessed'.

Benoit

French form of Benedict, meaning 'blessed'.

Benson

English, meaning 'son of Ben'. Also linked to the village of Benson in Oxfordshire.

Bentley

Old English, meaning 'bent grass meadow'. Usually associated with the British luxury car company.

Benton

Old English, meaning 'town in the bent grass'. Derived from the towns of Long Benton and Little Benton in Northumberland.

Beriah

Hebrew, meaning 'in fellowship' or 'in envy'. Beriah was a son of Asher in the Bible.

Bernard

(abbrev. Bernie)

Germanic, meaning 'strong, brave bear'.

Berry

Old English, meaning 'berry'.

Berton

Old English, meaning 'bright settlement'. Guitartist Berton Averre was part of the band The Knack, known for its hit 'My Sharona'.

Bertrand

(alt. Bertram; abbrev. Bert, Bertie)

Old English, meaning 'illustrious'. Bertrand Russell was a British philosopher and social critic. Bertram (Bertie) Wooster was one of P.G. Wodehouse's most beloved characters. Bert is also a shortened form of Albert.

Bevan

Welsh, meaning 'son of Evan'.

Bilal

Arabic, meaning 'wetting, refreshing'. Popular in many Muslim communities.

Bill

(alt. Billy)

English, from William, meaning 'strong protector'.

Birch

Old English, meaning 'bright' or 'shining'. Also a type of tree.

Birger

Norwegian, meaning 'rescue'.

Bishop

Old English, meaning 'bishop'.

Bjorn

Old Norse, meaning 'bear'. Bjorn Ulvaeus was one of the founding members of Swedish pop supergroup ABBA, and is still a prolific songwriter with partner Benny Andersson.

Blaine

Irish Gaelic, meaning 'yellow'. Blaine Anderson is a fictional character from TV hit comedy *Glee*.

Blair

Scottish Gaelic, meaning 'plain'. Can be used as a boys' or a girls' name.

Blaise

French, meaning 'lisp' or 'stutter'. St Blaise was an Armenian bishop who was beaten and beheaded for his faith. Also commonly used as a girls' name.

Blake

Old English, meaning 'dark, black'.

Blas

(alt. *Blaze*)

German, meaning 'firebrand'. Also a mountain in the Alps.

Bo

Scandinavian, short form of Robert, meaning 'bright fame'. Rock and roll pioneer and musician Ellas Otha Bates was known by his stage name Bo Diddly.

Boaz

Hebrew, meaning 'swiftness' or 'strength'. A character in the Bible, found in the Book of Ruth.

Bob

(alt. *Bobby*)

Old German, from Robert, meaning 'bright fame'.

Boden

(alt. *Bodie*)

Scandinavian, meaning 'shelter'. In some translations Boden also means 'messenger'.

Bogumil

Slavic, meaning 'God's favour'. Usually associated with Bogomil Cove in the Shetland Islands.

Bolívar

Spanish, meaning 'the bank of the river'. Simón Bolívar was a leader in Latin America's struggle for independence from Spain. The bolívar is the currency of Venezuela.

Bond

Old English, meaning 'peasant farmer'. Usually associated with novel and film character James Bond.

Boris

Slavic, meaning 'battle glory'. Boris Johnson is the UK's Foreign Secretary.

Bosten

English, meaning 'town by the woods'.

Botolf

English, meaning 'wolf'. St Botwulf of Thorney is the patron saint of travellers and farming.

Bowen

Welsh, meaning 'son of Owen'. The Bowen knot is a common heraldic symbol, and looks like a square with loops at each corner.

Bowie

Gaelic, meaning 'long double-edged sword'.

Boyd

Scottish Gaelic, meaning 'yellow'. Famous Boyds include English historian Boyd Hilton, designer and star of *American Hot Rod* Boyd Coddington and cricketer Boyd Rankin.

Bradley

(abbrev. *Brad*)

Old English, meaning 'broad' or 'wide'. Brad Pitt is one of America's most famous modern actors. Sir Bradley Wiggins is the most famous modern cyclist, winner of both multiple Olympic medals and the Tour de France.

Brady

Irish, meaning 'large-chested'.

Bradyn

Gaelic, meaning 'descendant of Bradan'.

Bram

Gaelic, meaning 'raven'.

Brandon

(alt. Bran)

Old English, meaning 'gorse'. Brandon Stark is a character in the TV series *Game of Thrones*.

Brandt

(alt. Brant)

Old English, meaning 'beacon'.

Brannon

Gaelic, meaning 'raven'. Brannon Braga is a TV producer.

Branson

English, meaning 'son of Brand'. Sir Richard Branson is an entrepreneur and adventurer, the founder of the Virgin Group of companies.

Braulio

Spanish, meaning 'shining'.

Brendan

Gaelic, meaning 'prince'. Actor Brendan Fraser is known for his role in the 'Mummy' film series.

Brennan

Gaelic, meaning 'teardrop'. The Brennan family are Ireland's most successful musical family, selling over 100 million records worldwide.

Brenton

English, from Brent, meaning 'hill'. Actor Brenton Thwaites is known for his role in soap opera *Home and Away*.

Brett

English, meaning 'a brewer'. Singer Brett Michaels is the lead singer of rock group Poison, known for the hit 'Every Rose Has Its Thorn'.

Brewster

(alt. Brew, Brewer)

English, meaning 'a brewer'.

Brian

(alt. Bryan, Bryant)

Gaelic, meaning 'high' or 'noble'. Famous Brians include physicist and TV star Professor Brian Cox, actor Brian Blessed and Queen guitar legend Brian May.

Brice

(alt. Bryce)

Latin, meaning 'speckled'.

Brier

French, meaning 'heather'.

Brock

Old English dialect, meaning 'badger'.

Broderick

English, meaning 'ruler'.

Brody

Gaelic, meaning both 'ditch' and 'brother'. It can be used for girls but more commonly for boys.

Brogan

Irish, meaning 'sturdy shoe'. A very old name, being mentioned in texts from the ninth century.

Bronwyn

Welsh, meaning 'white breasted'. More commonly used as a girls' name.

Brook

English, meaning 'stream'.

Brooklyn

From the name of the New York borough. Commonly associated with David and Victoria Beckham's eldest child.

Bruce

Scottish, meaning 'high' or 'noble'. Television presenter Sir Bruce Forsyth holds the Guinness World Record for the longest television career for a male entertainer.

Bruno

Germanic, meaning 'brown'. Bruno Tonioli is a judge on *Strictly Come Dancing*, and its American counterpart *Dancing With The Stars*.

Brutus

Latin, meaning 'dim-wit'. The name of Julius Caesar's assassin.

Bryant

English variant of Brian, meaning 'high' or 'noble'.

Bryden

(*alt. Brydon*)

Irish, meaning 'strong one'.

Bryn

Welsh, meaning 'mount' or 'hill'.

Bryson

(*alt. Bryce, Brycen*)

Welsh, meaning 'descendant of Brice'.

Bubba

American, meaning 'boy'. Associated with the character Bubba in *Forrest Gump*.

Buck

American, meaning 'goat' or 'deer', specifically a male deer.

Bud

(*alt. Buddy*)

American, meaning 'friend'.

Burdett

Middle English, meaning 'bird'.

Burgess

(*alt. Burges, Burgiss, Berje*)

English, meaning 'business'.

Burke

French, meaning 'fortified settlement'.

Burl

French, meaning 'knotty wood'.

Buzz

American, shortened form of Busby, meaning 'village in the thicket'. The US astronaut Buzz Aldrin was the second person to set foot on the moon.

Byron

Old English, meaning 'barn'. Made famous by the poet Lord Byron.

C Boys' names

Cabot
Old English, meaning 'to sail'.

Cadby
(alt. Cadbey, Cadbee, Cadbie)
English, meaning 'soldiers' colony'.

Cade
(alt. Caben, Caden)
English, meaning 'round, lumpy'. A character in the novel *Gone With The Wind*.

Cadence
Latin, meaning 'with rhythm'. Can be used as a girls' or a boys' name.

Cadogan
Welsh, meaning 'battle glory and honour'. Sir Cadogan is a knight who constantly challenged Gryffindors to duels in J.K. Rowling's 'Harry Potter' series.

Caedmon
Celtic, meaning 'wise warrior'. An early English poet.

Caelan
Gaelic, meaning 'slender'.

Caerwyn
(alt. Carwyn, Gerwyn)
Welsh, meaning 'white fort' or 'settlement'. Carwyn Jones is the First Minister of Wales.

Caesar
Disputed origin. The Roman military leader and dictator Gaius Julius Caesar favoured the Moorish meaning 'elephant'.

Caetano
Portuguese, meaning 'from Gaeta, Italy'.

Cagney
Irish, meaning 'successor of the advocate'.

Caiden
Arabic, meaning 'companion'. A variant of the name Caden.

Caillou

French, meaning 'pebble'. Name of the main character in a Canadian children's cartoon.

Cain

Hebrew, meaning 'full of beauty'. Brother of Abel in the biblical Book of Genesis.

Cainan

Hebrew, meaning 'possessor' or 'purchaser'.

Cairo

Egypt's capital city. Located near Giza, home of the great pyramids.

Calder

Scottish, meaning 'rough waters'.

Caleb
(alt. Calen; abbrev. Cal)

Hebrew, meaning 'dog'. Caleb was one of twelve spies sent by Moses into Caanan.

Calhoun

Irish, meaning 'slight woods'.

Calix

Greek, meaning 'very handsome'.

Callahan

Irish, meaning 'contention' or 'strife'.

Callum
(alt. Calum)

Gaelic, meaning 'dove'. Often associated with St Columba, one of the Twelve Apostles of Ireland. Has seen a big rise in popularity outside of Scotland and Ireland in recent years.

Calvin
(alt. Kalvin)

French, meaning 'little bald one'. Name of popular fashion designer Calvin Klein.

Camden

Gaelic, meaning 'winding valley'. Also an area of north London.

Cameron

Scottish Gaelic, meaning 'crooked nose'. Name of a Scottish Clan.

Camillo

Latin, meaning 'free born' or 'noble'. A popular Italian name.

Campbell

Scottish Gaelic, meaning 'crooked mouth'. Was first used as a nickname.

Canaan

Hebrew, meaning 'to be humbled'. A region in the Middle East that existed during biblical times.

Candido

Latin, meaning 'candid' or 'honest'. Candido Jacuzzi is the inventor of the jacuzzi tub.

Canon
(alt. Cannon)

French, meaning 'of the church'.

Canton

French, meaning 'dweller of corner'.

Canute
(alt. Cnut, Cnute)
Scandinavian, meaning 'knot'. Name of an eleventh-century King of England.

Cappy
Italian, meaning 'lucky'. A nickname for someone with the rank of Captain.

Carden
Old English, meaning 'wool carder'. Carding is the process of combing raw wool fibres to remove tangles and impurities.

Carey
Gaelic, meaning 'love'. Becoming more popular as a girls' as well as a boys' name.

Carl
(alt. Carlo, Carlos)
Old Norse, variant of Charles, meaning 'free man'.

Carlton
Old English, meaning 'free peasant settlement'.

Carmelo
Latin, meaning 'garden' or 'orchard'. Its variant, Carmel, refers to Mount Carmel in Israel, which in biblical times was known for its fruitfulness.

Carmen
Latin/Spanish, meaning 'song'. Name of one of the most famous French operas.

Carmine
Latin, meaning 'song'. Also a bright red pigment used in the manufacture of ruby-red juice.

Carnell
English, meaning 'defender of the castle'.

Carson
(alt. Carsten)
Scottish, meaning 'marsh-dwellers'.

Carter
Old English, meaning 'transporter of goods'.

Cary
Old Celtic river name. Also means 'love'. Cary Grant was a legendary romantic lead actor in films; Cary Elwes is a modern British actor.

Case
(alt. Casey)
Irish Gaelic, meaning 'alert' or 'watchful'.

Casimer
Slavic, meaning 'famous destroyer of peace'.

Casper
Persian, meaning 'treasurer'. The name of a friendly ghost in a comic book.

Caspian
English, meaning 'of the Caspy people'. From the Caspian Sea. A literary character from the C.S. Lewis book Prince Caspian.

Cassidy

Irish, meaning 'clever' or 'curly haired'. Originated from the surname, Caiside.

Cassius

(alt. Cassio, Cason, Cash)

Latin, meaning 'empty, hollow'. A name popular during the Roman era. Cassius Clay was the original name of legendary American boxer Muhammad Ali.

Cathal

Celtic, meaning 'battle rule'.

Cato

Latin, meaning 'all-knowing'. Cato the Younger was a Roman politician who opposed Caesar.

Cecil

Latin, meaning 'blind'. Name of famous American movie director Cecil B. DeMille.

Cedar

English, from the name of an evergreen tree.

Cedric

Welsh, meaning 'spectacular bounty'. First appeared in Sir Walter Scott's 1819 novel, *Ivanhoe*.

Celesto

(alt. Celestino, Celindo)

Latin, meaning 'heaven sent'.

Chad

(alt. Chadrick)

Old English, meaning 'warlike, warrior'. Use of this name was rare until it sprang to popularity in the 1960s.

Chaim

(alt. Chayyim)

Hebrew, meaning 'life'.

Champion

English, from the word 'champion', meaning 'warrior'.

Chandler

Old English, meaning 'candle maker and seller'.

Charles

(abbrev. Chas, Charlie)

Old German, meaning 'free man'. Popularised by Charles the Great (a.k.a. Charlemagne). Prince Charles is heir to the throne of England. Charles Dickens was one of the finest and most enduringly popular English authors.

Chaska

Sioux name usually given to first son.

Chauncey

(alt. Chance)

English, from the word 'chance' meaning 'good fortune'.

Che

Spanish, shortened form of José. Made famous by Che Guevara.

Chesley

Old English, meaning 'camp on the meadow'.

Chesney

English, meaning 'place to camp'. Also used as a girls' name.

Chester

Latin, meaning 'camp of soldiers'. The name of an English city.

Chilton
(alt. Chillron, Chilly, Chilt)

English, meaning 'tranquil'.

Chima

Old English, meaning 'hilly land'.

Christian

English, from the word 'Christian'. Christian Bale is an actor and Christian Louboutin a famous shoe designer.

Christopher
(alt. Christophe; abbrev. Chris, Christy)

Greek, meaning 'Christ bearer'. Name of the famous explorer Christopher Columbus.

Cian

Irish, meaning 'ancient'. Father of Lug in Irish mythology.

Ciaran

Irish, meaning 'black'. Was the name of two Irish saints.

Cicero

Latin, meaning 'chickpea'. Famous Roman philosopher and orator.

Cimarron

City in western Kansas. Also the name of a novel by Edna Ferber.

Ciprian

Latin, meaning 'from Cyprus'. Popular in Romanian heritage.

Ciro

Spanish, meaning 'sun'. Name of an opera by Francesco Cavalli dating back to 1654.

Clancy

Old Irish, meaning 'red warrior'. Evolved from the surname Mac Fhlannchaidh.

Clarence

Latin, meaning 'one who lives near the river Clare'.

Clark

Latin, meaning 'clerk'. The human identity of the famed superhero Superman (Clark Kent).

Claude
(alt. Claudie, Claudio, Claudius)

Latin, meaning 'lame'. Has been in use since the Middle Ages.

Claus

Variant of Nicholas, meaning 'victorious'.

Clay

English, from the word 'clay'.

Clement
(alt. Clem)

Latin, meaning 'merciful'. Has been used as the name for 14 different popes.

Cleo

Greek, meaning 'glory'. Most commonly used as a name for girls, but also for boys.

Cletus

Greek, meaning 'illustrious'. Used to refer to the third pope, Anacletus.

Clifford
(alt. Clifton; abbrev. Cliff)

English, from the word 'cliff'.

Clint
(alt. Clinton)

Old English, meaning 'fenced settlement'. Name of famous actor/writer/director Clint Eastwood.

Clive

Old English, meaning 'cliff' or 'slope'. Famous Clives include actor Clive Owen and author and broadcaster Clive James.

Clyde

Scottish, from the river that passes through Glasgow. Name of famous American bank robber Clyde Barrow of the duo Bonnie and Clyde.

Coby
(alt. Cody, Colby)

Irish, meaning 'son of Oda'.

Cody

English, meaning 'pillow'. Also a girls' name.

Colden

Old English, meaning 'dark valley'.

Cole
(alt. Coley)

Old French, meaning 'coal black'.

Colin

Gaelic, meaning 'young creature'. Famous Colins include actor Colin Firth and champion rally driver Colin McRae.

Colson

Old English, meaning 'coal black'.

Colton

English, meaning 'swarthy'. Evolved from the Old English name, Cola.

Columbus

Latin, meaning 'dove'. Name of Italian explorer Christopher Columbus.

Colwyn

Welsh, from the river in Wales.

Conan

Gaelic, meaning 'wolf'. Middle name of 'Sherlock Holmes' author, Sir Arthur Conan Doyle.

Conley

Gaelic, meaning 'sensible'.

Connell
(alt. Connolly)

Irish, meaning 'high' or 'mighty'.

Connor
(alt. Conor, Conrad, Conroy)

Irish, meaning 'lover of hounds'. Evolved from the name Conchobhar (King of Ulster).

Constant
(alt. Constantine)

English, from the word 'constant'. A name widely used by Christians as early as the seventeenth century.

Cooper

Old English, meaning 'barrel maker'.

Corban

Hebrew, meaning 'dedicated and belonging to God'.

Corbett
(alt. Corbin, Corby)

Norman French, meaning 'young crow'.

Cordell

Old English, meaning 'cord maker'.

Corey
(alt. Cory)

Gaelic, meaning 'hill hollow'. Thought to have originated from the Old Norse name Kori.

Corin

Latin, meaning 'spear'. A variant of the German given name Quirin.

Corliss
(alt. Corlis, Corlyss, Corlys)

English, meaning 'benevolent'.

Cormac

Gaelic, meaning 'impure son'. Name given to a third-century Irish king.

Cornelius
(alt. Cornell)

Latin, meaning 'horn'. The head of the Ministry of Magic (Cornelius Fudge) in J.K. Rowling's 'Harry Potter' series.

Cortez

Spanish, meaning 'courteous'.

Corwin

Old English, meaning 'heart's friend' or 'companion'.

Cosimo
(alt. Cosme, Cosmo)

Italian, meaning 'order' or 'beauty'. Given name of Pope Innocent VII (1339–1406).

Coty

French, meaning 'riverbank'. Surname of people who lived near a coast.

Coulter

English, meaning 'young horse'.

Courtney

Old English, meaning 'domain of Curtis'. A given name that has been in use since the seventeenth century. Used for both boys and girls.

C

Covey

English, meaning 'flock of birds'.

Cowan

Gaelic, meaning 'hollow in the hill'.

Craig

Welsh, meaning 'rock'. Originally used as a surname by people who lived near a cliff. Craig David is a singer-songwriter and there are two famous sporting Craig Bellamys, one a Welsh footballer and the other an Australian rugby league star.

Crispin

Latin, meaning 'curly haired'. Name of a third-century saint, twin brother of St Crispinian. Patron saints of shoemakers.

Croix

French, meaning 'cross'.

Cruz

Spanish, meaning 'cross'. Made famous by David and Victoria Beckham's son.

Cullen

Gaelic, meaning 'handsome'. Made famous by the *Twilight* book series.

Curran

Gaelic, meaning 'dagger' or 'hero'.

Curtis
(alt. Curt)

Old French, meaning 'courteous'. Commonly used in the Middle Ages as a name of a courteous person.

Cutler

Old English, meaning 'knife maker'.

Cyprian

English, meaning 'from Cyprus'.

Cyril

Greek, meaning 'master' or 'Lord'. Name of St Cyril, one of the inventors of the Glagolitic alphabet, the precursor to the Cyrillic alphabet.

Cyrus

Persian, meaning 'Lord'. Cyrus the Great conquered Babylon in 539 BC.

D

Boys' names

Dabeel
(alt. Dabee, Dabie, Daby)
Sanskrit, meaning 'warrior'.

Daelan
English, meaning 'aware'. Also a girls' name.

Dafydd
(alt. Dai)
Welsh, meaning 'beloved'. Welsh version of David.

Daichi
Japanese, meaning 'great wisdom'.

Daire
(alt. Daer, Daere, Dair)
Irish, meaning 'wealthy'.

Daisuke
Japanese, meaning 'lionhearted'.

Dakari
Swahili, meaning 'happy'.

Dale
Old English, meaning 'valley'.

Dallin
English, meaning 'dweller in the valley'.

Dalton
English, meaning 'town in the valley'.

Daly
Gaelic, meaning 'assembly'.

Damarion
Greek, meaning 'gentle'.

Damian
(alt. Damien, Damon)
Greek, meaning 'to tame, subdue'. Name of a fourth-century patron saint of physicians. Damien is the name of the Devil's son in 'The Omen' series of films. Damon Hill is British champion racing driver and Damon Albarn is a musician and the lead singer of Blur.

Dane
Old English, meaning 'from Denmark'.

Daniel
(alt. Dan, Danny)

Hebrew, meaning 'God is my judge'. Daniel was a prophet during biblical times. An enduringly popular name for boys.

Dante

Latin, meaning 'lasting'. Associated with the thirteenth-century Italian poet Dante Alighieri, author of *The Divine Comedy*.

Darby

Irish, meaning 'without envy'.

Darcy

Gaelic, meaning 'dark'. Associated with Jane Austen's Mr Darcy, and the parody of this character in *Bridget Jones' Diary*. A name more commonly used for girls in modern times.

Dario
(alt. Darius)

Greek, meaning 'kingly'. Associated with Dario Argento, an Italian film director.

Darnell

Old English, meaning 'the hidden spot'.

Darragh
(alt. Dara)

Irish, meaning 'dark oak'. A popular name in Ireland, now being seen in England and Wales.

Darrell
(alt. Daryl)

Old English, meaning 'open'. Originated from the Norman French surname d'Airelle.

Darren
(alt. Darrian)

Gaelic, meaning 'great'. Darren Aronofsky is an American film-maker. In the UK the name is well connected with sport, including Darren Gough (cricket), Darren Bent and Darren Fletcher (football) and Darren Barker (boxing).

Darrick

Old German, meaning 'power of the tribe'.

Darshan

Hindi, meaning 'vision'.

Darwin

Old English, meaning 'dear friend'. Often associated with the naturalist Charles Darwin.

Dash
(alt. Dashawn)

American, meaning 'enlightened one'. Associated with one of the characters in Disney Pixar's *The Incredibles*.

Dashiell

French, meaning 'page boy'. Dashiell Hammett was an American author, famous for hard-boiled detective fiction.

Famous male drummers

Dave (Grohl)	Phil (Collins)
John (Bonham)	Ringo (Starr – real name Richard Starkey)
Keith (Moon)	Stewart (Copeland)
Lars (Ulrich)	Tommy (Lee)
Mick (Fleetwood)	Travis (Barker)

Dason

Native American, meaning 'chief'.

David

(alt. Dave, Davey, Davie, Davin)

Hebrew, meaning 'beloved'. Associated with the King of Israel who killed Goliath the giant as a boy.

Davis

Old English, meaning 'son of David'.

Dawson

Old English, meaning 'son of David'. Associated with the main character in the TV show *Dawson's Creek*.

Dax

(alt. Daxton)

French, once a town in south-western France.

Dayal

Sanskrit, meaning 'kind'.

Dayton

Old English, meaning 'David's place'. A city in the US state of Ohio.

Dean

Old English, meaning 'valley'. Dean Koontz is an American author and Dean Martin was a hugely popular singer and entertainer, known as the 'King of Cool'.

Declan

Irish, meaning 'full of goodness'. Associated with St Declan, who was born in the fifth century.

Dedric

Old English, meaning 'gifted ruler'.

Deepak

(alt. Deepan)

Sanskrit, meaning 'illumination'. Associated with doctor and spiritual author Deepak Chopra.

Del

(alt. Delano, Delbert, Dell)

Old English, meaning 'bright shining one'. Associated with the main character in *Only Fools and Horses*.

Delaney

Irish, meaning 'dark challenge'.

Demetrius

Greek, meaning 'harvest lover'. Name of a fourth-century Greek sculptor.

Dempsey

Irish, meaning 'proud'.

Denham

(alt. Denholm)

Old English, meaning 'valley settlement'.

Dennis

(alt. Denis, Denny, Denton)

English, meaning 'follower of Dionysius'. Associated with the boy in the comic strip *Dennis the Menace*. Other famous Dennises include actors Dennis Hopper and Dennis Quaid and footballer Dennis Bergkamp.

Denzil

(alt. Denzel)

English, meaning 'fort'. Most commonly associated with Oscar-winning actor Denzel Washington.

Deon

Greek, meaning 'of Zeus'.

Derek

English, meaning 'power of the tribe'. Short form for the given name Diderik.

Dermot

Irish, meaning 'free man'. Dermot Morgan portrayed Father Ted, and Dermot O'Leary is a prolific TV and radio presenter.

Desmond

Irish, meaning 'from south Munster'. Associated with South African social rights activist Archbishop Desmond Tutu.

Destin

French, meaning 'destiny'.

Deveraux

French, meaning 'from the town of Évreux'.

Devyn

(alt. Devin)

Irish, meaning 'poet'.

Dewey

Welsh, from Dewi (David). One of Disney character Donald Duck's three nephews.

Dexter

(alt. Dex)

Latin, meaning 'right-handed'.

Diallo

(alt. Dialo)

Swahili, meaning 'bold'.

Dick

(alt. Dickie, Dickon, Diccon)

From Richard, meaning 'powerful leader'. Dick is one of Enid Blyton's *Famous Five* and Dickon is a character in Frances Hodgson Burnett's *The Secret Garden*.

Didier

French, meaning 'much desired'. St Didier is a saint honoured in the Catholic Church. Famous Didiers include footballers Didier Deschamps and Didier Drogba.

Diego

Spanish, meaning 'supplanter'. Has been in use since the eleventh century.

Dietrich

Old German, meaning 'power of the tribe'.

Diggory

English, meaning 'dyke'.

Dilbert

English, meaning 'day bright'. Popularised by the American comic strip of the same name.

Dimitri

(alt. Dimitrios, Dimitris)

Greek, meaning 'prince'. A popular name in Russia.

Dino

Diminutive of Dean, meaning 'valley'. Used as short form for names ending with -dino.

Dion

Greek, short form of Dionysius, the Greek god of wine. Dionysius was the son of Zeus and Semele.

Dirk

Variant of Derek, meaning 'power of the tribe'. A name also used to refer to a dagger.

Divakar

Sanskrit, meaning 'the sun'.

Dominic

Latin, meaning 'Lord'.

Donald

(alt. Don, Donal, Donaldo)

Gaelic, meaning 'great chief'. Famous Donalds include actor Donald Sutherland, businessman turned politician Donald Trump and ever-popular Disney character Donald Duck.

Donato

Italian, meaning 'gift'. Given name of Italian sculptor Donatello.

Donnell

(alt. Donnie, Donny)

Gaelic, meaning 'world fighter'.

Donovan

Gaelic, meaning 'dark-haired chief'. Associated with Scottish singer Donovan.

Doran

Gaelic, meaning 'exile'.

Dorian

Greek, meaning 'descendant of Doris'. Name of the title character in Oscar Wilde's The Picture of Dorian Gray.

Douglas
(alt. Dougal, Dougie)

Scottish, meaning 'black river'. Douglas Adams was the author of *The Hitchhiker's Guide to the Galaxy*.

Doyle

Irish, meaning 'foreigner'.

Draco
(alt. Drake)

Latin, meaning 'dragon'. Made popular by the character Draco Malfoy in J.K. Rowling's 'Harry Potter' series.

Drew

Shortened form of Andrew, meaning 'man' or 'warrior'.

Dryden

English, meaning 'dry town'.

Dudley

Old English, meaning 'people's field'. Also the name of Harry Potter's cousin.

Duff

Gaelic, meaning 'swarthy'.

Duke

Latin, meaning 'leader'. The title of a nobleman ruling over a duchy.

Duncan

Scottish, meaning 'dark warrior'. King Duncan is a character in Shakespeare's *Macbeth*.

Dustin
(alt. Dusty)

French, meaning 'brave warrior'. Popularised by American actor Dustin Hoffman.

Dwayne
(alt. Duwayne, Duane)

Irish Gaelic, meaning 'swarthy'.

Dwight

Flemish, meaning 'blond'. Associated with the 34th President of the United States, Dwight D. Eisenhower.

Dwyer

Gaelic, meaning 'dark wise one'.

Dyani

Native American, meaning 'eagle'.

Dylan
(alt. Dillon)

Welsh, meaning 'son of the sea'. Name of the famous Welsh poet Dylan Thomas.

E Boys' names

Eagan
Irish, meaning 'fiery'.

Eamon
(alt. Eamonn, Eames)

Irish, meaning 'wealthy protector'. TV presenter Eamon Holmes is known for early-morning programmes.

Earl
(alt. Earle, Errol)

English, meaning 'nobleman, warrior, prince'. Earl is a title of nobility, used since Anglo-Saxon times.

Ebenezer
(abbrev. Ebb)

Hebrew, meaning 'stone of help'. Ebenezer Scrooge is the main character in Charles Dickens' novel *A Christmas Carol*.

Edgar
(alt. Elgar)

Old English, meaning 'wealthy spear'. Poet and writer Edgar Allan Poe is known for works such as *The Raven*.

Edison
English, meaning 'son of Edward'. Thomas Edison was one of America's greatest and most well-known inventors.

Edmund
(abbrev. Ed)

English, meaning 'wealthy protector'. Edmund Blackadder is the title character in the historical comedy series *Blackadder*, starring Rowan Atkinson.

Edric
Old English, meaning 'rich and powerful'.

Edsel

Old German, meaning 'noble'. Henry Ford, the automobile magnate, named his son Edsel.

Edward

(alt. Eduardo; abbrev. Ed, Edd, Eddie, Eddy)

Old English, meaning 'wealthy guard'. Edward has become extremely popular since the release of the *Twilight* series. Ed Miliband was the leader of the Labour Party.

Edwin

English, meaning 'wealthy friend'.

Efrain

Hebrew, meaning 'fruitful'. Normally used in Spanish-speaking cultures.

Egan

Irish, meaning 'fire'. Egan, derived from the name Aedhagan, is one of the oldest surnames in Europe.

Eilif

(alt. Elif, Eilyg, Elyf)

Norse, meaning 'immortal'. Eilif Paterssen was an influential Norwegian painter and artist in the early 20th century.

Einar

Old Norse, meaning 'battle leader'. Still a popular name in Iceland.

Eladio

Greek, meaning 'Greek'. Related to the name Heladio.

Elam

Hebrew, meaning 'eternal'. Elam is mentioned in the Bible as being a son of Shem, and son of Noah.

Elan

French, meaning 'energy and enthusiasm'. Also the name of a river valley in Wales.

Elbert

Old English, meaning 'famous'. Variation of the name Albert.

Eldon

Old English, meaning 'Ella's hill'. Also refers to the town in County Durham, England.

Eldred

(alt. Eldridge)

Old English, meaning 'old venerable counsel'.

Elgin

Old English, meaning 'high minded'. Also refers to the town of the same name in Scotland.

Eli

(alt. Eliah)

Hebrew, meaning 'high'. Eli is a character in the Old Testament of the Bible.

Elias

(alt. Elijah, Elio)

Hebrew, meaning 'the Lord is my God'. Walt Disney's father was Elias Disney. Actor Elijah Wood played Frodo Baggins in the *Lord of the Rings* films.

Ellery

Old English, meaning 'elder tree'.
Ellery Hanley is a former rugby league
player and coach for Great Britain.

Elliott

English variant of Elio, meaning 'the
Lord is my God'. Made popular by
the lead character in the film *E.T.*

Ellis

Welsh, variant of Elio, meaning 'the
Lord is my God'.

Ellison

English, meaning 'son of Ellis'.

Elmer

(alt. Elmo)

Old English, meaning 'noble'; Arabic,
meaning 'aristocratic'. Elmer the
elephant features in a number of
children's picture books by author
David McKee.

Elmo

(alt. Ellmo, Elmon)

Greek, meaning 'gregarious'. One of
the characters in the children's TV
series *Sesame Street*.

Elmore

Old English, meaning from 'elm tree'
and 'moor'. Elmore Leonard was an
American author.

Elon

(alt. Alon)

Hebrew, meaning 'oak tree'. A
very old name, it is now not used
much outside of Hebrew-speaking
communities.

Elroy

French, meaning 'king'. Elroy Jetson
was the youngest member of the
cartoon Jetson family.

Elton

Old English, meaning 'Ella's town'.
Singer and songwriter Sir Elton John's
real name is Reg Dwight.

Elvin

English, meaning 'elf-like'. Elvin Bale
was a big performer with circuses,
known for human cannonball acts
and high-wire daredevil work.

Elvis

Figure in Norse mythology. Made
famous by the singer Elvis Presley.

Emanuel

Hebrew, meaning 'God is with us'.
Features in hymns and carols.

Emeric

German, meaning 'work rule'.
St Emeric of Hungary was known for
a pure and pious life.

Emile

(alt. Emil, Emiliano, Emilio)

Latin, meaning 'eager'. Emile is
Remy the rat's older brother in
Disney's film *Ratatouille*.

Emlyn

Welsh. The name of a town,
Newcastle Emlyn, in west Wales.
Emlyn Hughes was a famous
footballer of the 1970s turned TV
presenter.

Emmett

English, meaning 'universal'. Emmett Scanlan played a villain in *Hollyoaks* for many years.

Emrys

Welsh, meaning 'immortal'. The legendary magician Merlin is said to have been given the name Emrys at birth, and only later adopted his more famous moniker.

Eneco

Spanish, meaning 'fiery one'.

Enoch

Hebrew, meaning 'dedicated'. Enoch was the great-great-grandfather of Noah in the Bible.

Enrico
(alt. Enrique)

Italian, form of Henry, meaning 'home ruler'. Extremely popular name in Italy for boys.

Enzo

Italian, short for Lorenzo, meaning 'laurel'. Enzo Ferrari was the founder of the Ferrari automobile company.

Eoghan
(alt. Eoin)

Irish form of Owen, meaning 'well born' or 'noble'. Eoghan was an Irish king in the fifth century. Eoin Colfer is the author of the young adult fiction series *Artemis Fowl*.

Ephron
(alt. Effron)

Hebrew, meaning 'dust'.

Erasmo
(alt. Erasmus)

Greek, meaning 'to love'. Erasmus was a Dutch humanist and theologian during the Renaissance period.

Eric

Old Norse, meaning 'ruler'. Often associated with singer and guitarist Eric Clapton.

Ernest
(alt. Ernesto, Ernie, Ernst)

Old German, meaning 'serious'. Author Ernest Hemingway is known for his influential novels *A Farewell to Arms* and *The Old Man and the Sea*.

Errol

English, meaning 'boar wolf'. Actor Errol Flynn is best known for his swashbuckler roles and the lead role in *The Adventures of Robin Hood*.

Erskine

Scottish, meaning 'high cliff'. Also a place in Scotland.

Erwin

Old English, meaning 'boar friend'.

Eryx

Greek, meaning 'boxer'. Sometimes used as an alternative spelling for Eric.

Ethan
(alt. Etienne)

Hebrew, meaning 'long lived'. Ethan Coen and Joel Coen are influential director brothers known for films such as *Fargo* and *Hail Caesar!* Ethan Hawke is an Oscar-nominated actor.

Eugene

Greek, meaning 'well born'.

Evan
(alt. Ifan)

Welsh, meaning 'God is gracious'.

Evelyn

German, meaning 'hazelnut'. Evelyn Waugh is the author of *Brideshead Revisited*, *Decline and Fall* and *Scoop*.

Everard
(alt. Everett)

Old English, meaning 'strong boar'. Also the name of an old English ale.

Everly
(alt. Everleigh, Everley)

English, meaning 'grazing meadow'. Used as a name for boys and girls.

Ewan
(alt. Euan, Ewald, Ewen, Ewell)

Old English, from Owen, meaning 'well born' or 'noble'. Actor Ewan McGregor is known for his roles in *Trainspotting*, *Moulin Rouge* and *Star Wars*.

Exton

English, meaning 'on the River Exe'.

Ezra

Hebrew, meaning 'helper'. Ezra Pound was an American poet.

Boys' names

Faber
(alt. Fabir)

Latin, meaning 'blacksmith'. Faber and Faber is a well-known UK publishing house.

Fabian
(alt. Fabien, Fabio)

Latin, meaning 'one who grows beans'. Also associated with the teen pop sensation Fabian in the 1950s and 1960s.

Fabrice
(alt. Fabrizio)

Latin, meaning 'works with his hands'. Popular in France. Fabrice Muamba is a former football player who survived an on-pitch heart attack.

Faisal

Arabic, meaning 'resolute'. Faisal II was the last King of Iraq, whose reign ended during the revolution of 1958.

Falco
(alt. Falcon, Falconer, Falke, Faulkner)

Latin, meaning 'falconer'.

Faron

Spanish, meaning 'pharaoh'. Also derived from a Gaelic word for 'thunder'.

Farrell

Gaelic, meaning 'hero'.

Faustino

Latin, meaning 'fortunate'.

Fela
(alt. Felah, Fella, Fellah)

Swahili, meaning 'a man who is warlike'. The name of the famous Nigerian musician Fela Kuti.

Felipe
(alt. Filippo)

Spanish, meaning 'lover of horses'. Formula One driver Felipe Massa has driven for Ferrari and Williams.

Felix
(alt. Felice)

Italian/Latin, meaning 'happy'. Felix the Cat was a popular twentieth-century cartoon character.

Fennel

Latin, name of a herb. More commonly used as a girls' name.

Ferdinand
(alt. Fernando)

Old German, meaning 'bold voyager'.

Fergus
(alt. Ferguson)

Gaelic, meaning 'supreme man'.

Ferris

Gaelic, meaning 'rock'. *Ferris Bueller's Day Off* was a runaway hit film during the 1980s.

Fiachra

Irish, meaning 'raven'. St Fiachra is the patron saint of gardeners.

Fidel

Latin, meaning 'faithful'. Fidel Castro was President of Cuba from 1976 to 2008.

Finbarr

Gaelic, meaning 'fair head'. St Finbarr is the patron saint of the City of Cork.

Finian
(alt. Finnian)

Gaelic, meaning 'fair'. St Finnian is an important Irish saint, and a founder of the theory of monasticism.

Finlay
(alt. Finley, Fynlee)

Gaelic, meaning 'fair-haired courageous one'.

Finn

Finnish, meaning 'from Finland'.

Finnegan

Gaelic, meaning 'fair'. Author James Joyce wrote *Finnegans Wake* as a complex work of comedy.

Fintan

Gaelic, meaning 'little fair one'. A seer in Irish mythology called Fintan supposedly saved one of Noah's granddaughters from the flood.

Fitzroy

English, meaning 'the king's son'. Usually associated with Vice-Admiral Robert Fitzroy, who accompanied Charles Darwin on his famous voyages.

Flavio

Latin, meaning 'yellow hair'. The opera *Flavio* was composed by Handel.

Florencio
(alt. Florentino)

Latin, meaning 'from Florence'.

Florian
(alt. Florin)

Slavic/Latin, meaning 'flower'. St Florian is the patron saint of chimney sweeps, soapmakers and firefighters.

Floyd
Welsh, meaning 'grey haired'.

Flynn
Gaelic, meaning 'with a ruddy complexion'.

Forbes
(alt. Forbs, Forb, Forbe)
Gaelic, meaning 'of the field'.

Fortunato
Italian, meaning 'lucky'.

Foster
Old English, meaning 'woodsman'.

Fotini
(alt. Fotis)
Greek, meaning 'light'.

Francis
(alt. Francesco, Francisco, Franco, François)
Latin, meaning 'from France'. After the election of Pope Francis, Francesco has become the most popular name for boys in Italy.

Frank
(alt. Frankie, Franklin, Franz)
Middle English, meaning 'free landholder'. Also a diminutive of Francis. Famous Franks include footballer Frank Lampard, crooner Frank Sinatra, and film director Frank Capra.

Fraser
(alt. Fraiser)
Scottish, meaning 'of the forest men'.

Frederick
(alt. Friedrich; abbrev. Freddie, Fred)
Old German, meaning 'peaceful ruler'. There is a spelling or pronunciation variation of Frederick in practically every European language.

Furman
Old German, meaning 'ferryman'.

Fyfe
(alt. Fife, Fyffes)
Scottish, meaning 'from Fifeshire'.

G

Boys' names

Gabino
Latin, meaning 'God is my strength'.

Gabriel
(abbrev. Gabe)

Hebrew, meaning 'hero of God'.
One of the archangels in the Bible.

Gael
(alt. Gale)

English, old reference to the Celts.
Gale has become a highly recognised
name since the release of 'The
Hunger Games' trilogy.

Gaius
(alt. Gaeus)

Latin, meaning 'rejoicing'. Julius
Caesar's full name was Gaius Julius
Caesar.

Galen
Greek, meaning 'healer'. Galen
of Pergamon was a well-respected
ancient Greek and Roman
philosopher and physician.

Galileo
Italian, meaning 'from Galilee'.
Galileo Galilei was an important and
influential physicist and astronomer
during the Scientific Revolution.

Ganesh
Hindi, meaning 'lord of the horde'.
One of the Hindu deities.

Gannon
Irish, meaning 'fair skinned'. More
commonly used as a surname,
particularly in Ireland.

Gareth
(alt. Garth, Garthe, Gart, Garte)

Welsh, meaning 'gentle'.

Garfield
Old English, meaning 'spear field'.
Also the name of the cartoon cat.

Garland
English, as in 'garland of flowers'.

Garnet

English, precious stone, red in colour. Occasionally used for boys, although not as frequently as for girls.

Garrett

Old German, meaning 'spear' or 'ruler'. Ireland's Garret the Great was known as 'the uncrowned King of Ireland' during his time of political power in the fifteenth century.

Gary
(alt. Garry, Geary)

Old English, meaning 'spear'. Some of Britain's best-loved Garys include Take That member Gary Barlow and football pundit Gary Lineker.

Gaspar
(alt. Gaspard)

Persian, meaning 'treasurer'. *Gaspar and Lisa* is a popular Disney children's television programme, about two dogs living in Paris.

Gaston

From the Gascony region in the south of France.

Gavin
(alt. Gawain)

Scottish/Welsh, meaning 'little falcon'.

Gene

Greek, shortened form of Eugene, meaning 'well born'. Famous Genes include actors Gene Kelly and Gene Hackman, and Kiss guitarist Gene Simmons.

Genkei

Japanese, meaning 'honoured'. One of Japan's most famous botanists is Genkei Masamune, who is credited with identifying hundreds of new species.

Gennaro

Italian, meaning 'of Janus'.

Geoffrey
(abbrev. Geoff)

Old German, meaning 'peace'.

George
(alt. Giorgio)

Greek, meaning 'farmer'. Chosen by the Duke and Duchess of Cambridge for their son, born in July 2013, and third in line to the throne.

Gerald
(alt. Geraldo, Gerard, Gerardo, Gerhard; abbrev. Gerry)

Old German, meaning 'spear ruler'. Former President of the United States Gerald Ford is the only person to have served as both President and Vice President without being elected to either position, thanks to two infamous resignations before him.

Geronimo

Italian, meaning 'sacred name'. Originally the name of a prominent Apache Indian, this has now become a word for 'go-get-'em!'

Gert

Old German, meaning 'strong spear'.

Gervase

Old German, meaning 'with honour'. Gervase Phinn is a widely read author of several humorous books describing his life as a school inspector in Yorkshire.

Giacomo

Italian, meaning 'God's son'. Legendary womaniser Casanova's full name was Giacomo Girolamo Casanova.

Gibson

English, meaning 'son of Gilbert'.

Gideon

Hebrew, meaning 'tree cutter'. Gideon is a figure in the Bible.

Gilbert

(alt. Gilberto)

French, meaning 'bright promise'.

Giles

Greek, meaning 'small goat'.

Gino

Italian, meaning 'well born'.

Giovanni

Italian form of John, meaning 'God is gracious'.

Giri

(alt. Gririe, Giry, Girey)

Sanskrit, meaning 'from the mountain'.

Giulio

Italian, meaning 'youthful'. Composer Giulio Caccini was active during the Baroque era.

Giuseppe

Italian form of Joseph, meaning 'Jehovah increases'.

Glen

(alt. Glenn, Glyn)

English, from the word 'glen'.

Godfrey

German, meaning 'peace of God'.

Gordon

Gaelic, meaning 'large fortification'. Famous Gordons include chef Gordon Ramsay, former England goalkeeper Gordon Banks, and former prime minister Gordon Brown.

Gottlieb

German, meaning 'good love'. One of Mozart's names at birth was Gottlieb; others included Johannes, Chrisostomus and Wolfgang.

Gower

Area of the Welsh coast, by the Bristol Channel.

Graeme

(alt. Graham)

English, meaning 'gravelled area'.

Grant

English, from the word 'grant'.

Granville

English, meaning 'gravelly town'. Probably the most famous Granville is the character portrayed by David Jason in sitcom *Open All Hours*.

Gray
(alt. Grey)
English, from the word 'grey'.

Grayson
English, meaning 'son of gray'. Grayson Perry is an artist who won the Turner Prize in 2003.

Green
English, from the word 'green'.

Gregory
(alt. Gregorio; abbrev. Greg, Greig)
English, from the word 'griffin'. Actor Gregory Peck was best known for his role in *To Kill A Mockingbird*.

Griffin
English. A griffin is a mythical creature with the body of a lion and the head and wings of an eagle.

Groves
English, meaning 'inhabits near grove of trees'.

Gruffudd
(alt. Griff, Gruff, Gruffydd)
Welsh, meaning 'strong prince'. It was a common name among medieval Welsh royalty.

Grylfi
(alt. Gylfie, Gylfee, Gylffi)
Scandinavian, meaning 'king'. Gylfi was the first Nordic king in Scandinavia.

Guido
Italian, meaning 'guide'.

Guillaume
French form of William, meaning 'strong protector'. William the Conqueror is known as Guillaume le Conquérant in France.

Gulliver
English, meaning 'glutton'. *Gulliver's Travels*, by Jonathan Swift, tells the story of a surgeon who sets sail for adventure.

Gunther
German, meaning 'warrior'.

Gurpreet
Sanskrit, meaning 'love of the teacher'. More commonly used in Punjabi-speaking communities.

Gustave
(abbrev. Gus)
Scandinavian, meaning 'royal staff'. Gustave Flaubert is the author of classics including *Madame Bovary*. Also the name given to a legendary crocodile in Burundi, whose length is said to be over 20ft and that has killed as many as 300 humans.

Guy
English, from the word 'guy'. Guy Fawkes is the character most associated with the Gunpowder Plot of 1605, which was an attempt to blow up the Houses of Parliament.

Gwyn
Welsh, meaning 'white'. Commonly used as a name for girls as well as for boys.

Boys' names

Habib
Arabic, meaning 'beloved one'.

Hackett
(alt. Hacket, Hackit, Hackitt)
German, meaning 'small hacker'.

Haden
(alt. Haiden)
English, meaning 'hedged valley'. Also a popular type of mango.

Hades
Greek, meaning 'sightless'. Name of the god of the underworld in Greek mythology.

Hadrian
From Hadria, a north Italian city. Hadrian's Wall in northern England is named after the Roman Emperor Hadrian.

Hadwin
Old English, meaning 'friend in war'.

Hakeem
Arabic, meaning 'wise and insightful'. Hakeem Lyon is a major character in the musical epic drama Empire.

Hal
(alt. Hale, Hallie)
English, nickname for Henry, meaning 'home ruler'. Used in this context in Shakespeare's Henry IV plays.

Halim
Arabic, meaning 'gentle'. Al-Halim is one the names of God in Islam.

Hallam
Old English, meaning 'the valley'.

Hamid
Arabic, meaning 'praiseworthy'. Hamid Karzai was the elected president of Afghanistan from 2001 to 2014.

Hamilton
Old English, meaning 'flat-topped hill'.

Hamish

Scottish form of James, meaning 'he who supplants'.

Hamlet

(alt. Hamlett, Hammet, Hamnet)

German, meaning 'village'. A variation of the Danish Amleth, and often associated with Shakespeare's tragedy *Hamlet*.

Hampus

Swedish form of Homer, meaning 'pledge'. Hampus Lindholm is an international ice hockey player, originally from Sweden.

Hamza

Arabic, meaning 'lamb'. Also a letter in the Arabic alphabet.

Han

(alt. Hannes, Hans)

Scandinavian, meaning 'the Lord is gracious'.

Hanif

(alt. Haneef, Haneaf, Haneif)

Arabic, meaning 'devout'. Usually refers to people who submitted entirely to their religion in Islam.

Hank

German, form of Henry, meaning 'home ruler'.

Hansel

German, meaning 'the Lord is gracious'. One of the most famous Grimm fairy tales is the story of Hansel and Gretel.

Hardy

English, meaning 'tough'. Often associated with the author Thomas Hardy, or comedic duo Laurel and Hardy.

Harlan

English, meaning 'dweller by the boundary wood'. Harlan Coben is the author of several mystery novels.

Harland

Old English, meaning 'army land'. Fast food chain KFC was founded by Colonel Harland David Sanders. The *Titanic* was built at Belfast shipyard Harland and Wolff.

Harley

Old English, meaning 'hare meadow'.

Harmon

Old German, meaning 'soldier'.

Harold

Scandinavian, meaning 'army ruler'. The last Anglo-Saxon King of England was Harold II, whose reign ended after he lost the Battle of Hastings.

Harris

Old English, meaning 'home ruler'.

Harry

Old German, form of Henry, meaning 'home ruler'. Famous Harrys include Prince Harry, Harry Potter and One Direction singer Harry Styles.

Hart

Old English, meaning 'stag'.

Harvey

Old English, meaning 'strong and worthy'. The film *Harvey*, starring Jimmy Stewart and Josephine Hull, is about a man whose best friend is an enormous invisible rabbit.

Haskell

Hebrew, meaning 'intellect'.

Hassan

Arabic, meaning 'handsome'. Hassan Rouhani is the current President of Iran.

Haydn
(alt. Hayden, Haydon)

Old English, meaning 'hedged valley'. Also a composer, Franz Joseph Haydn, was one of the most influential and popular of the classical period.

Heart

English, from the word 'heart'.

Heath

English, meaning 'heath' or 'moor'. Heath Ledger was a prolific actor, known for his roles in *A Knight's Tale*, *10 Things I Hate About You* and *The Dark Knight*.

Heathcliff

English, meaning 'cliff near a heath'. Made famous by Emily Brontë's novel *Wuthering Heights*.

Heber

Hebrew, meaning 'partner'.

Hector

Greek, meaning 'steadfast'. A Trojan prince and historic fighter in ancient Greek mythology.

Henry
(alt. Henri, Hendrik, Hendrix)

Old German, meaning 'home ruler'. There have been eight Kings of England named Henry, and in the unlikely event that Prince Harry found himself on the throne he would become Henry IX.

Henson

English, meaning 'son of Henry'.

Herbert
(alt. Heriberto; abbrev. Bert, Herb)

Old German, meaning 'illustrious warrior'. Herbert Hoover was a President of the United States and founder of the FBI.

Herman
(alt. Herminio, Hermon)

Old German, meaning 'soldier'.

Hermes

Greek, meaning 'messenger'. The messenger of the gods in Greek mythology.

Herschel
(alt. Hirsch)

Yiddish, meaning 'deer'.

Hezekiah

Hebrew, meaning 'God gives strength'. The 13th king of Judah was King Hezekiah.

Hideki

Japanese, meaning 'excellent trees'. The prime minister of Japan during World War II was Hideki Tojo.

Hideo

Japanese, meaning 'excellent name'. One of Japan's most prolific comedians is Hideo Higashikokubaru.

Hilario

Latin, meaning 'cheerful, happy'. Retired goalkeeper Henrique Hilario Meireles Sampaio is usually known just as Hilario.

Hilary

(alt. Hillary)

English, meaning 'cheerful'. Most used now as a girls' name although it can be used for boys, as with politician Hilary Benn.

Hildred

German, meaning 'battle counsellor'.

Hillel

Hebrew, meaning 'greatly praised'. Rabbi Hillel was an important leader in the Jewish faith.

Hilliard

Old German, meaning 'battle guard'.

Hilton

Old English, meaning 'hill settlement'.

Hiram

Hebrew, meaning 'exalted brother'.

Hiro

Spanish, meaning 'sacred name'.

Hiroshi

Japanese, meaning 'generous'.

Hobart

English, meaning 'bright and shining intellect'. Also the name of the capital of Tasmania.

Hodge

English, meaning 'son of Roger'.

Hogan

Gaelic, meaning 'youth'. Wrestling superstar Terry Bollea is better known as Hulk Hogan.

Holden

English, meaning 'deep valley'.

Hollis

Old English, meaning 'holly tree'.

Homer

Greek, meaning 'pledge'. Name of the Greek poet – and of the TV character Homer Simpson.

Honorius

Latin, meaning 'honourable'. Honorius was a Roman emperor in the fifth century BC.

Horace

Latin, common name of the Roman poet Quintus Horatius Flaccus.

Houston

Old English, meaning 'Hugh's town'. Also a city in the state of Texas, USA.

Howard

Old English, meaning 'noble watchman'. Howard Hughes was a businessman, film-maker and aviator and one of the wealthiest men on the planet. Howard Donald is a founder member of enduringly successful boy band Take That.

Howell

Welsh, meaning 'eminent and remarkable'. Also the name of a town in Lincolnshire.

Hoyt

Norse, meaning 'spirit' or 'soul'. Also believed to be an Old English name, meaning someone who lives on a hill.

Hristo

From Christo, meaning 'follower of Christ'. Hristo Stoichkov is acknowledged to be one of the best footballers of his generation, and the best Bulgarian footballer ever.

Hubbell

(alt. Hubble)

English, meaning 'brave hearted'.

Hubert

German, meaning 'bright and shining intellect'.

Hudson

Old English, meaning 'adventurous' or 'son of Hugh'. Also one of the largest rivers in the USA.

Hugh

(alt. Hubert, Hugo, Huw)

Old German, meaning 'soul, mind and intellect'. Famous Hughs include actors Hugh Grant, Hugh Laurie and Hugh Jackman. The founder of fashion house Givenchy was Count Hubert de Givenchy. Huw Stephens is a Welsh radio presenter.

Humbert

Old German, meaning 'famous giant'. Be warned: it's the name and surname of the paedophile protagonist of Vladimir Nabokov's novel *Lolita*.

Humphrey

Old German, meaning 'peaceful warrior'. Actor Humphrey Bogart is best known for his role in the film *Casablanca*.

Hunter

English, from the word 'hunter'. Popular name in the USA for boys, yet to take off in the UK.

Hurley

Gaelic, meaning 'sea tide'.

Huxley

Old English, meaning 'Hugh's meadow'.

Hyrum

(alt. Hiram, Hyram)

Hebrew, meaning 'exalted brother'. Hyrum Smith was one of the founders of the Church of Jesus Christ of Latter Day Saints; also known as the Mormons.

Boys' names

Iago

Spanish, meaning 'he who supplants'. Name of the villain in Shakespeare's *Othello*.

Ian
(alt. Ion, Iain)

Gaelic, variant of John, meaning 'God is gracious'. Famous Ians include former cricketer Sir Ian Botham, novelists Ian Fleming and Iain Banks and journalist and satirist Ian Hislop.

Ianto

Welsh, meaning 'gift of God'. Ianto Jones is a featured character in sci-fi drama series *Torchwood*.

Ibaad

Arabic, meaning 'a believer in God'.

Ibrahim

Arabic, meaning 'father of many'. Also the Arabic name for the prophet and father of Islam, Abraham.

Ichabod

Hebrew, meaning 'glory is good'. The protagonist in Washington Irving's short story 'The Legend of Sleepy Hollow' is called Ichabod Crane.

Ichiro

Japanese, meaning 'firstborn son'. A current Japanese superstar baseball player is Ichiro Suzuki.

Idan

Hebrew, meaning 'place in time'.

Idris

Welsh, meaning 'fiery leader'. Actor Idris Elba is known for his roles in *The Wire*, *Luther* and *Mandela: Long Walk to Freedom*.

Ieuan
(alt. Ioan)

Welsh variant of John, meaning 'God is gracious'.

Ignacio

Latin, meaning 'ardent' or 'burning'. More commonly found in South

America, particularly Uruguay and Argentina.

Ignatz

German, meaning 'fiery'.

Igor

Russian or Norse origin, meaning 'warrior'.

Ikaika

Hawaiian, meaning 'strong'.

Iku

Japanese, meaning 'nourishing'.

Ilan
(alt. Elan)

Hebrew, meaning 'tree'. Composer Ilan Eshkeri is known for his scores of several films, including *Layer Cake* and *Kick-Ass*.

Ilias

Greek variant of Hebrew Elijah, meaning 'the Lord is my God'.

Imanol

Basque-language variant of Immanuel, meaning 'God is with us'.

Indiana

Latin, meaning 'from India'. Also the film character Indiana Jones and the American state.

Indigo

English, describing a deep blue colour derived from a plant. Used as a boys' and girls' name.

Indio

Spanish, meaning 'indigenous people'.

Ingo

Danish, meaning 'meadow'. Also the name of a tropical plant.

Inigo

Spanish, meaning 'fiery'. Famous Inigos include the sixteenth-century English architect Inigo Jones and a character in the film *The Princess Bride*.

Ioannis

Greek, meaning 'the Lord is gracious'.

Iovianno

Native American, meaning 'yellow hawk'. More common as a spelling alternative for Giovanni.

Ira

Hebrew, meaning 'full grown and watchful'. In the Hindu faith, Ira-putra is Hanuman the monkey god. Ira Gershwin was a famous 20th-century American lyricist.

Irvin
(alt. Irving, Irwin)

Gaelic, meaning 'green and fresh water'. Composer Irving Berlin is known for songs such as 'White Christmas' and 'Alexander's Ragtime Band'.

Isaac
(alt. Isaak; abbrev. Ike)

Hebrew, meaning 'laughter'. Isaac was the son of Abraham and Sarah in the Bible and the Qur'an. Famous Ikes include singer Ike Turner and former US president Dwight D. Eisenhower (known as Ike).

Isadore
(alt. Isidore, Isidro)
Greek, meaning 'gift of Isis'. Popular name in both ancient Greece and ancient Egypt.

Isai
(alt. Isaiah, Isaias, Izaiah)
Arabic, meaning 'protection and security'.

Iser
Yiddish, meaning 'God wrestler'. Most common in Germany.

Ishedus
Native American, meaning 'on top'.

Ishmael
(alt. Ismael)
Hebrew, meaning 'God listens'. Ishmael was the son of the prophet Abraham and his wife Hagar.

Israel
Hebrew, meaning 'God perseveres'. Also the name of the country.

Istvan
Hungarian variant of Stephen, meaning 'crowned'. Very common in Eastern Europe.

Itai
Hebrew, meaning 'the Lord is with me'. One of the most common names in Israel.

Ivan
Hebrew, meaning 'God is gracious'. Russian Grand Prince Ivan the Terrible is credited with conquering so much land that Russia has ended up the size it is today.

Ivanhoe
Russian, meaning 'God is gracious'. Also name of the novel by Walter Scott.

Ivey
English, variant of Ivy usually reserved for boys.

Ivo
French, from the word 'yves', meaning 'yew tree'. Dr Ivo Robotnik is the villain in Sonic the Hedgehog video games.

Ivor
Scandinavian, meaning 'yew'. Composer Ivor Novello was such an influential performer that there is an entire awards series named after him: the Ivor Novello Awards (the Ivors) are given out for songwriting and composing.

Ivory
Latin, meaning 'white as elephant tusks'. More commonly used as a girls' name.

Izar
Basque, meaning 'star'. The izar is also a piece of Ihram clothing worn during the Islamic Hajj pilgrimage.

Boys' names

Jabari
Swahili, meaning 'valiant'.

Jabez
Hebrew, meaning 'borne in pain'.
Jabez is a well-respected ancestor of
Judah in the Bible.

Jabulani
(alt. Jabulanie, Jabulany, Jabulaney)
Swahili, meaning 'happy one'. The
Jabulani is also a name for a type
of Adidas football used in most
professional Association games.

Jace
(alt. Jaece, Jase, Jayce)
Hebrew, meaning 'healer'.
Sometimes used as a shortened
version of Jason.

Jacek
Polish, meaning 'hyacinth'. Derived
from the Greek name Hyakinthos,
which comes from an ancient myth
about a beautiful boy.

Jacinto
Spanish or Portuguese, meaning
'hyacinth'.

Jack
(alt. Jackie, Jacky)
From the Hebrew John, meaning
'God is gracious'. The UK's most
popular boys' name for 14 years
until fairly recently.

Jackson
(alt. Jaxon, Jaxson)
English, meaning 'son of Jack'.
Jackson Pollock was an abstract
expressionist artist, known for his
large-scale paintings of splashes and
drips.

Jacob
(alt. Jacobo, Jaco, Jago; abbrev.
Jake)
Hebrew, meaning 'he who
supplants'. Ancestor of the tribes of
Israel in the Bible.

Jacques
(alt. Jaquez)

French form of James, meaning 'he who supplants'. Famous Jacques include Jacques Cousteau, the marine explorer, writer and film-maker, and Jacques Villeneuve, the racing driver.

Jaden
(alt. Jadyn, Jaeden, Jaiden, Jaidyn, Jayden, Jaydin)

Hebrew, meaning 'Jehovah has heard'. Actor Will Smith's eldest child is called Jaden Smith, and has an acting career of his own.

Jaeger
(alt. Jager, Jaecer, Jaegar)

German, meaning 'mighty hunter'. Also the name of a designer clothing line in Britain.

Jafar

Arabic, meaning 'stream'. The name of the villain in Disney's *Aladdin*.

Jagger

Old English, meaning 'one who cuts'. Sir Mick Jagger is the lead singer of the Rolling Stones.

Jaheem
(alt. Jaheim)

Hebrew, meaning 'raised up'. R&B singer Jaheim Hoagland goes by the stage name Jaheim.

Jahir

Hindi, meaning 'jewel'.

Jair
(alt. Jairo)

Hebrew, meaning 'God enlightens'. Also the name of a minor character in the Bible.

Jalen
(alt. Jalon, Jaylon, Jaylan)

American, meaning 'healer' or 'tranquil'. The original spelling was probably Galen, in Greek.

Jali

Gujarati, meaning 'latticed screen'. Popular form of architectural detailing throughout India.

Jamar
(alt. Jamarcus, Jamari, Jamarion, Jamir)

Modern variant of Jamaal, meaning 'handsome'. More common in the USA than in Britain.

Jamel
(alt. Jamal, Jamaal, Jamil)

Arabic, meaning 'handsome'. Actor Jamel Debbouze is a French and Moroccan film star.

James
(alt. Jaime; abbrev. Jamie, Jamey, Jim, Jimmy)

English, meaning 'he who supplants'. An enduringly popular name. Famous actors with this name include James Coburn, James Franco, James Corden, Jamie Bell and Jamie Foxx.

Jameson
(alt. Jamison)

English, meaning 'son of James'.

Jamin
(alt. Yamin)
Hebrew, meaning 'son of the right hand'.

Jan
(alt. Janko, János)
Slavic, from John, meaning 'the Lord is gracious'. Jan is also a term of endearment in Arabic, meaning 'dear'. Used for boys and also girls.

Janesh
Hindi, meaning 'leader of people'.

Janus
Latin, meaning 'gateway'. The two-faced Roman god of doors, beginnings and endings.

Japheth
(alt. Japhet)
Hebrew, meaning 'comely'. One of the sons of Noah in the Bible.

Jared
(alt. Jarem, Jaren, Jaret, Jarod, Jarrod)
Hebrew, meaning 'descending'. Actor Jared Leto is known for his roles in Fight Club, American Psycho and Dallas Buyers Club.

Jarlath
Gaelic, from Iarlaith, from St Iarlaithe mac Loga.

Jarom
Greek, meaning 'to raise and exalt'. One of the prophets in the Book of Mormon.

Jarrell
Variant of Gerald, meaning 'spear ruler'.

Jarrett
Old English, meaning 'spear-brave'. Sometimes used as an alternative spelling to Garrett.

Jarvis
Old German, meaning 'with honour'. Jarvis Cocker is the singer with the band Pulp.

Jason
Greek, meaning 'healer'. Famous Jasons include actor Jason Statham, and the ancient Greek myth of Jason and the Argonauts.

Jasper
Greek, meaning 'treasure holder' or 'speckled stone'. The stone jasper has been used for thousands of years for carved ornaments and jewellery. Jasper Conran is a modern fashion designer.

Javen
(alt. Javan)
Arabic, meaning 'youth'. Javan was one of Noah's grandsons in the Bible.

Javier
Spanish, meaning 'bright'. Actor Javier Bardem is known for his roles in No Country for Old Men and the James Bond movie Skyfall.

Jay
Latin, meaning 'jaybird'. Jays are a group of bird species in the crow family.

Jeevan

Sanskrit, meaning 'life'. Often used with a prefix like 'har', to form other names (such as Harjeevan).

Jefferson

English, meaning 'son of Jeffrey'.

Jeffrey
(abbrev. Jeff)

Old German, meaning 'peace'. Famous Jeffreys include author Jeffrey Archer, and actors Jeff Bridges and Jeff Daniels.

Jensen
(alt. Jenson)

Scandinavian, meaning 'son of Jan'. Has increased in popularity in the UK in recent years, probably linked to the rise of Jenson Button, Formula One racing driver.

Jeremiah
(alt. Jeremia, Jeremias, Jeremiya)

Hebrew, meaning 'the Lord exalts'. One of the main prophets in the Bible.

Jeremy
(alt. Jem)

Hebrew, meaning 'the Lord exalts'. Famous Jeremys include actor Jeremy Irons, presenter Jeremy Clarkson and actor Jeremy Renner.

Jeriah

Hebrew, meaning 'Jehovah has seen'. Minor character in the Bible.

Jericho

Arabic, meaning 'city of the moon'. An ancient and religious city in the Palestinian West Bank.

Jermaine

Latin, meaning 'brotherly'. Jermaine Jackson was one of the original members of the Jackson 5.

Jerome

Greek, meaning 'sacred name'. Famous Jeromes include actor Jerome Flynn, and St Jerome, who was a medieval priest and theologian.

Jerry

English, from Gerald, meaning 'spear ruler'. Famous Jerrys include presenter Jerry Springer, comedian Jerry Seinfeld and the film *Jerry Maguire*.

Jesse

Hebrew, meaning 'the Lord exists'. Jesse James was a Wild West outlaw and train robber in the 1870s.

Jesus

Hebrew, meaning 'the Lord is Salvation' and the Son of God.

Jet
(alt. Jelt)

English, meaning 'black gemstone'. Jet is a minor gemstone, formed of fossilised wood.

Jethro

Hebrew, meaning 'eminent'. Famous Jethros include Jethro Tull, the agricultural pioineer, who gave his name to a 1970s rock band, and the father-in-law of Moses in the Bible.

Jim
(alt. Jimmy)

From James, meaning 'he who supplants'. Jim is one of the leading characters in Mark Twain's classic novel *Huckleberry Finn*.

Jiri
(alt. Jiro)

Czech, meaning 'farmer'. More commonly used in Czech-speaking communities as an alternative to George.

Joachim
(alt. Joaquin)

Hebrew, meaning 'established by God'. Also the name of the Virgin Mary's father in the Bible. Actor Joaquin Phoenix is known for his roles in *Gladiator*, *Walk the Line* and *Her*.

Joah
(alt. João)

Hebrew, meaning 'God is gracious'. The name of several minor characters in the Bible.

Joe
(alt. Joey, Jomar)

From Joseph, meaning 'Jehovah increases'. Usually used as a nickname for Joseph, Joel or Josiah, as well as a name in its own right.

Football players

Aaron (Lennon)

Alan (Shearer)

Ashley (Cole)

Daniel (Sturridge)

Darren (Fletcher)

David (Beckham)

Frank (Lampard)

Gareth (Bale)

Gary (Lineker)

Jack (Wilshere)

Joe (Cole)

Rio (Ferdinand)

Scott (Parker)

Steven (Gerrard)

Wayne (Rooney)

Joel

Hebrew, meaning 'Jehovah is the Lord'.

John
(alt. Johan, Johannes, Johnny)

Hebrew, meaning 'God is gracious'. John the Baptist and the apostle John are major characters in the New Testament of the Bible.

Jolyon

English, meaning 'young'. One of the more prominent characters in the 'Tintin' comic series is Jolyon Wagg.

Jonah
(alt. Jonas)

Hebrew, meaning 'dove'. A character in the Bible who was swallowed by a whale.

Jonathan
(alt. Johnathan, Johnathon, Jonathon; abbrev. Jon, Jonny, Jonty)

Hebrew, meaning 'God is gracious'. Famous Jonathans include comedian and TV presenter Jonathan Ross, author Jonathan Swift and actor Jonathan Pryce.

Jordan
(alt. Jory, Judd)

Hebrew, meaning 'down-flowing'. Can be used as a girls' name or a boys' name.

Jorge

Spanish or Portuguese version of George, meaning 'farmer'. Actor Jorge Garcia is known for his role as Hurley in Lost.

José

Spanish variant of Joseph, meaning 'God increases'. José Mourinho is the football manager known as 'the special one'.

Joseph
(alt. Josef, Joss)

Hebrew, meaning 'Jehovah increases'. Famous Josephs include two Biblical Josephs: the wearer of the many-coloured coat and the father of Jesus Christ. Others include actor Joseph Gordon-Levitt.

Joshua
(abbrev. Josh)

Hebrew, meaning 'God is salvation'. Joshua was the leader of the Israelites after Moses' death in the Bible.

Josiah

Hebrew, meaning 'God helps'. One of the kings of Judah in the Bible.

Josué

Spanish variant of Joshua, meaning 'God is salvation'.

Jovan

Latin, meaning 'the supreme God'. More commonly used in Serbia and Macedonia.

Joweese

Native American, meaning 'chirping bird'. Originally used more commonly for girls, it has now become a boys' name.

Joyce

Latin, meaning 'joy'. More commonly used as a girls' name but can be used for boys.

Juan

Spanish variant of John, meaning 'God is gracious'. It is also becoming a popular name for girls in China, with the meaning of 'chapter or scroll' in Mandarin.

Jubal

Hebrew, meaning 'ram's horn'. Also the name of the 'father of music' in the Bible.

Jude
(alt. Judson)

Hebrew, meaning 'praise' or 'thanks'. Famous Judes include St Jude, the patron saint of lost causes, actor Jude Law and Thomas Hardy's novel *Jude the Obscure*.

Julian
(alt. Julio, Julien; abbrev. Juels, Jules, Jools)

Greek, meaning 'belonging to Julius'. The original calendar in the Roman empire was called the Julian calendar. Famous Juleses include author Jules Verne, DJ Judge Jules and pianist/presenter Jools Holland.

Julius

Latin, meaning 'youthful'. Julius Caesar was dictator of Rome and the first Roman emperor, ruling in the first century BC.

Junior

Latin, meaning 'the younger one'. Can also be used as a suffix to names to denote a name that has been passed down from father to son (such as Steve Jones Sr and Steve Jones Jr).

Junius

Latin, meaning 'young'. The pseudonym of an anonymous and prolific political writer in the eighteenth century.

Jupiter

Latin, meaning 'the supreme God'. Jupiter was king of the Roman gods and the god of thunder. Jupiter is also the largest planet in the solar system.

Juraj

Hebrew, meaning 'God is my judge'. More popular in Eastern Europe.

Jurgen

German form of George, meaning 'farmer'. Former football player Jurgen Klinsmann is now the manager of the US national team.

Justice

English, from the word 'justice', meaning a set of moral values, ethics and law.

Justin
(alt. Justus)

Latin, meaning 'just and upright'. Famous Justins include singers Justin Timberlake and Justin Bieber, and children's TV presenter Justin Fletcher.

Juwan

Hebrew, meaning 'the Lord is gracious'.

Boys' names

Kabelo
Swahili, meaning 'gift'. Popular name in Botswana.

Kade
Scottish, meaning 'from the wetlands'. More commonly used as a spelling alternative to Cade.

Kadeem
Arabic, meaning 'one who serves'. Actor Kadeem Hardison is known for his role in *A Different World*.

Kaden
(alt. Kadin, Kaeden, Kaedin, Kaiden)
Arabic, meaning 'companion'. Also the name of a town in Germany.

Kadir
Arabic, meaning 'capable and competent'.

Kafka
Czech, meaning 'bird-like'. Often associated with the author Franz Kafka.

Kahekili
Hawaiian, meaning 'the thunder'. Also the name of several kings of Maui.

Kahlil
(alt. Kalil)
Arabic, meaning 'friend'. The Lebanese author Kahlil Gibran is known for his work *The Prophet*.

Kai
Greek, meaning 'keeper of the keys'. Kai has meanings in several languages, including 'dog' in Cornish, 'ocean water' in Hawaiian and 'food' in Maori.

Kaito
Japanese, a combination of the words 'sea, ocean' and 'soar, fly'.

Kalani
Hawaiian, meaning 'sky'.

Kale
German, meaning 'free man'. Also the name of a leafy green vegetable.

Kaleb
(alt. Caleb)

Hebrew, meaning 'dog' or 'aggressive'. Kaleb was also the most prominent King of Aksum, the capital of Abyssinia, in the sixth century.

Kalen

Gaelic, meaning 'uncertain'.

Kaleo

Hawaiian, meaning 'the voice'. Kaleo Kanahele is a silver medal-winning American paralympian in volleyball.

Kamari

Sanskrit, meaning 'the enemy of desire'. Also the name of a popular tourist destination in Greece.

Kamden

English, meaning 'winding valley'. Also a spelling alternative for Camden.

Kamil
(alt. Kaamil)

Arabic, meaning 'perfection'. Also a Polish and Slovak name meaning 'religious service attender'.

Kane

Gaelic, meaning 'little battler'.

Kani

Hawaiian, meaning 'sound'.

Kanye

A town in Botswana. Made popular by rapper Kanye West.

Kareem
(alt. Karim)

Arabic, meaning 'generous'.

Karl
(alt. Karson)

Old German, meaning 'free man'.

Kasey

Irish, meaning 'alert'.

Kaspar

Persian, meaning 'treasurer'.

Kavon

Gaelic, meaning 'handsome'. More commonly used in the USA.

Kayden

Arabic, meaning 'companion'. Also used as a spelling alternative for Caden.

Kazimierz

Polish, meaning 'declares peace'. Also the name of a town in Poland.

Kazuki

Japanese, meaning 'radiant hope'. Kazuki Takahashi is a well-known Japanese artist and video game creator.

Kazuo

Japanese, meaning 'harmonious man'. Depending on the characters/ spellings used, Kazuo can also mean 'first son' or 'first in leadership'.

Keagan
(alt. Keegan, Kegan)

Gaelic, meaning 'small flame'.

Keane

Gaelic, meaning 'fighter'.

Keanu

Hawaiian, meaning 'breeze'. Actor Keanu Reeves is known for his roles in *Bill & Ted's Excellent Adventure*, *Speed* and 'The Matrix' trilogy.

Keary

Gaelic, meaning 'black-haired'. Also used as a girls' name.

Keaton

English, meaning 'place of hawks'. Buster Keaton was a famous American actor and director of silent films.

Keefe
(alt. Keef, Keeffe, Kief, Kiefe)

Gaelic, meaning 'cherished, gentle and kind'.

Keeler

Middle English, meaning 'cool'. Also a term used for a small, shallow tub for bathing.

Keenan
(alt. Kenan)

Gaelic, meaning 'little ancient one'.

Keiji

Japanese, meaning 'govern with discretion'. Also a term sometimes used for police officers.

Keir

Gaelic, meaning 'dark-haired' or 'dark-skinned'. James Keir Hardie was a Scottish socialist and labour leader in the nineteenth and twentieth centuries.

Keith

Gaelic, meaning 'woodland'. Famous Keiths include Rolling Stones band member Keith Richards, presenter Keith Chegwin and chef Keith Floyd.

Kekoa

Hawaiian, meaning 'brave one' or 'soldier'.

Kelby

Old English, meaning 'farmhouse near the stream'.

Kell
(alt. Kellan, Kellen, Kelley, Kelly, Kiel)

Norse, meaning 'spring'. Usually associated with the ancient and lavishly illustrated Book of Kells (as well as the cartoon movie).

Kelsey

Old English, meaning 'victorious ship'. Actor Kelsey Grammer is known for his roles in *Cheers* and *Frasier*.

Kelton

Old English, meaning 'town of the keels'. Singer Roy Orbison (of 'Oh, Pretty Woman' fame) had the middle name Kelton.

Kelvin

Old English, meaning 'friend of ships'. A kelvin is a unit of measurement for temperature, using the Kelvin scale.

Kemenes

Hungarian, meaning 'maker of furnaces'. More commonly used in Eastern Europe.

Kendal

Old English, meaning 'the Kent river valley'.

Kendon

Old English, meaning 'brave guard'.

Kendrick

Gaelic, meaning 'royal ruler'. Fairly popular in the USA, including hip hop artist Kendrick Lamar and record producer Kendrick Dean.

Kenelm

Old English, meaning 'bold'. St Kenelm was a boy king and martyr, mentioned in *The Canterbury Tales*.

Kenji

Japanese, meaning 'intelligent second son'. Also the name of a period in Japanese history in the thirteenth century.

Kennedy

Gaelic, meaning 'helmet head'. The Kennedy family are a prominent American-Irish Catholic dynasty, whose members have included President John F. Kennedy. Used for girls as well as boys in the USA.

Kenneth
(abbrev, Ken, Kenny, Kenney)

Gaelic, meaning 'born of fire'. Famous Kenneths include actor Kenneth Branagh and designer brand Kenneth Cole.

Kennison

English, meaning 'son of Kenneth'.

Kent

English, meaning 'rim or border'. From the county of the same name in England.

Kenton

English, meaning 'town of Ken'. Kenton Cool is a British mountaineer and mountain guide. He has climbed Mount Everest 11 times.

Kenya

From the country and mountain in Africa.

Kenzo

Japanese, meaning 'wise'. Kenzo Takada is the Japanese designer who founded the fashion brand Kenzo.

Keola

Hawaiian, meaning 'life'.

Keon
(alt. Kean, Keoni)

Persian, meaning 'King of Kings'. In Hawaiian, the same spelling means 'God is gracious'.

Kepler

German, meaning 'hat maker'.

Kerr

English, meaning 'wetland'. Kerr Smith is an American actor.

Kerry

Irish, from the county of the same name. More commonly a girls' name.

Kerwin
(alt. Kermit)
Gaelic, meaning 'without envy'. Most popular in the USA.

Keshav
Sanskrit, meaning 'beautiful-haired'. One of the names for Vishnu in the Hindu religion.

Kevin
Gaelic, meaning 'handsome beloved'. Famous Kevins include former footballer Kevin Keegan and actors Kevin Kline and Kevin Bacon.

Khalid
(alt. Khaled, Khalif, Khalil)
Arabic, meaning 'immortal'. Actor Khalid Abdalla is known for his roles in *United 93* and *The Kite Runner*.

Kian
(alt. Keyon, Kyan)
Persian, meaning 'king or realm'. In Ireland, the same spelling means 'ancient'.

Kiefer
German, meaning 'barrel maker'. Actor Kiefer Sutherland is best known for his role in the series *24*.

Kieran
(alt. Kiaran, Kieron, Kyron)
Gaelic, meaning 'black'. Famous Kierans include gymnast Kieran Behan and actor Kieran Culkin.

Kijana
Swahili, meaning 'youth'.

Kilby
From the English 'Cilebi', a place in Leicestershire.

Kilian
Irish, meaning 'bright headed'. St Kilian was a bishop in Ireland in the seventh century.

Kimani
Swahili, meaning 'beautiful and sweet'. Kenyan Kimani Maruge held the Guinness World Record for being the oldest person to start primary school, at the ripe old age of 84.

King
English, from the word 'male ruler of state'.

Kingsley
English, meaning 'the king's meadow'. Sir Kingsley Amis was an English novelist.

Kirby
German, meaning 'settlement by a church'. Also the name of a small, pink, bubble-like video game character.

Kirk
Old German, meaning 'church'.

Klaus
German, meaning 'victorious'. Also a shortened form of Nikolaus.

Knightley
(alt. Knightly)
English, meaning 'of the knight's meadows'. An English place name in Staffordshire.

Kobe
(alt. Koda, Kody)
Japanese, meaning 'a Japanese city'.

Kofi
Akan, meaning 'born on Friday'. Kofi Annan was Secretary General of the United Nations from 1997 to 2006.

Kohana
Japanese, meaning 'little flower'. The Kohana cat is a hairless breed of cat.

Kojo
Akan, meaning 'Monday'. Kojo is also a type of computer programming language.

Kolby
Norse, meaning 'settlement'. Often used as a spelling alternative for Colby.

Komal
Hindi, meaning 'soft and tender'.

Korben
(alt. Korbin)
Gaelic, meaning 'a steep hill'. Korben Dallas is the protagonist in the sci-fi film *The Fifth Element*.

Kramer
German, meaning 'shopkeeper'. Usually associated with the character Kramer in the 1990s sitcom *Seinfeld*.

Kris
(alt. Krish, Kristoff)
From Christopher, meaning 'Christ bearer'. Can be a short form of Kristopher, Kristian or (for girls) Kristen.

Kurt
German, meaning 'courageous advice'. Famous Kurts include *Glee* character Kurt, actor Kurt Russell and singer Kurt Cobain.

Kurtis
French, meaning 'courtier'.

Kwame
Akan, meaning 'born on Saturday'. Kwame Nkrumah was the first president of Ghana.

Kyden
English, meaning 'narrow little fire'. Sometimes used as a spelling alternative for Caden.

Kyle
(alt. Kylan, Kyleb, Kyler)
Scottish Gaelic, meaning 'narrow and straight'. Originated from the place name in Scotland.

Kyllion
Irish, meaning 'war'.

Kyree
From Cree, a Canadian tribe. More commonly used in the USA.

Kyros
Greek, meaning 'legitimate power'. Kyros of Constantinople was an important figure in the Orthodox Church in the eighth century.

L Boys' names

Laban
Hebrew, meaning 'white'. Laban is the brother of Rebekah in the Bible.

Lachlan
Gaelic, meaning 'from the land of lakes'. A popular name in Australia.

Lacy
Old French, after the place in France. The feminine equivalent is Lacey.

Laertes
English, meaning 'adventurous'. Ophelia's brother in Shakespeare's *Hamlet*.

Lalit
Hindi, meaning 'beautiful'. The Lalit is one of the melodic aspects of Indian classical music.

Lamar
(alt. Lemar)

Old German, meaning 'water'. Singer Lemar is known for his songs 'Dance (With U)' and 'If There's Any Justice'.

Lambert
(alt. Lambros)

Scandinavian, two elements meaning 'land' and 'brilliant'. The name has been in use since Roman times.

Lamont
Old Norse, meaning 'law man'.

Lancelot
(abbrev. Lance)

Variant of Lance, meaning 'land'. The name of one of the Knights of the Round Table. Cyclist Lance Armstrong won the Tour de France seven times before being stripped of his titles for cheating.

Landen
(alt. Lando, Landon, Langdon, Landen)
English, meaning 'long hill'. Also the name of a town in Belgium.

Lane
(alt. Layne)
English, from the common word meaning 'narrow road'.

Lang
(alt. Langston)
Norse, meaning 'long meadow'.

Lannie
(alt. Lanny)
German, meaning 'precious'. Sometimes used as a nickname for Roland or Orlando, as well as a name in its own right.

Larkin
Gaelic, meaning 'rough' or 'fierce'. Poet Philip Larkin was known for his works *The Whitsun Weddings* and *High Windows*.

Laron
French, meaning 'thief'.

Larry
Latin, variant of Laurence, meaning 'man from Laurentum'. Famous Larrys include actor Larry Hagman, presenter Larry King and comedian Larry Grayson.

Lars
Scandinavian variant of Laurence, meaning 'man from Laurentum'. The founder of Swedish electronics brand Ericsson was called Lars Magnus Ericsson.

Lasse
Finnish, meaning 'girl'. (Still, ironically, a boy's name.) Men with the name Lars are sometimes called Lasse as a nickname in Scandinavia. Finn Lasse Viren was one of the greatest long-distance runners of all time. Lasse Hallström is a Swedish film director.

Laszlo
Hungarian, meaning 'glorious rule'. Derived from the name of King/St Ladislaus I of Hungary.

Lathyn
Latin, meaning 'fighter'. Sometimes also used as a name for girls.

Latif
Arabic, meaning 'gentle'. The female equivalent for girls is Latifa.

Laurel
Latin, meaning 'bay'. One of the founders of Jamaican ska music was Laurel Aitken.

Laurence
(alt. Lawrence; abbrev. Larry)
Latin, meaning 'man from Laurentum'. Actor Laurence Olivier was known for his roles in dozens of Shakespeare productions and Hollywood films.

Laurent
French form of Laurence, meaning 'man from Laurentum'. Laurent-Perrier is a champagne brand.

Lazarus

Hebrew, meaning 'God is my help'. Also the name of a minor character in the Bible, said to have been raised from the dead by Jesus Christ.

Leandro

Spanish, meaning 'lion man'. More commonly used in South America.

Lear

German, meaning 'of the meadow'. Shakespeare's play *King Lear* tells the story of a wealthy king decending into madness.

Lee
(alt. Leigh)

English, meaning 'pasture' or 'meadow'. Famous Lees include comedian Lee Mack, 'Harry Potter' character Lee Jordan and assassin Lee Harvey Oswald.

Leib

Yiddish, meaning 'lion'.

Leif
(alt. Liev)

Scandinavian, meaning 'heir'. Actor Liev Schreiber is known for his roles in *X-Men Origins: Wolverine*, the 'Scream' trilogy and *Ray Donovan*.

Leith

From the name of a busy port town in Scotland.

Lennox

Gaelic, meaning 'with many elm trees'. Lennox Lewis is a retired world heavyweight boxing champion.

Lenny

Shortened form of Lennox or Leonard, as well as a name in its own right. Lenny Kravitz is a musician and Lenny Godber was a much-loved character in the classic TV series *Porridge*.

Leo
(alt. Leon)

Latin, meaning 'lion'. Also the star sign.

Leonard
(alt. Leonardo)

Old German, meaning 'lion strength'. Famous Leonards and Leonardos include actor Leonardo DiCaprio and artist and inventor Leonardo da Vinci.

Leopold

German, meaning 'brave people'. Prince Leopold was Queen Victoria and Prince Albert's eighth child, who was known to suffer from the blood disorder haemophilia.

Leroy

French, meaning 'king'. The song 'Bad Bad Leroy Brown' was a hit for R&B singer Jim Croce in 1973.

Leslie
(abbrev. Les)

Scottish Gaelic, from the name of the prominent clan. Also meaning 'holly garden'. Used as a name for girls (more commonly spelt Lesley) and for boys equally.

Lester

English, meaning 'from Leicester'. Lester Piggott is one of England's most successful jockeys.

Lewis

English form of French Louis, meaning 'famous warrior'. Famous Lewises include the Formula One racing driver Lewis Hamilton, comedian Lewis Black and *Alice in Wonderland* author Lewis Carroll.

Lex

English variant of Alexander, meaning 'defending men'. Lex Luthor is the villain of the *Superman* stories.

Liam

German, meaning 'helmet'. Famous Liams include actor Liam Neeson, singer Liam Gallagher and One Direction member Liam Payne.

Lincoln

English, meaning 'lake colony'.

Linden

European, from the tree of the same name. Less commonly used for girls.

Lindsay

Scottish, meaning 'linden tree'. In recent times used more for girls than for boys.

Linus

Latin, meaning 'lion'. Usually associated with the *Peanuts* cartoon strip character, who is known for carrying a blanket everywhere.

Lionel

English, meaning 'lion'. Famous Lionels include dancer/actor Lionel Blair, singer Lionel Richie and composer Lionel Bart.

Llewellyn

Welsh, meaning 'like a lion'.

Lloyd

Welsh, meaning 'grey-haired and sacred'. Famous Lloyds include actor Roger Lloyd Pack, former prime minister David Lloyd George and composer Andrew Lloyd Webber.

Logan

Gaelic, meaning 'hollow'. Usually associated with sci-fi novel *Logan's Run*. Has risen in popularity in recent years. Logan Lerman is the American actor playing the title role in the *Percy Jackson* films.

London

Pre-Celtic, meaning 'place at the navigable or unfordable river'.

Lonnie

English, meaning 'lion strength'.

Lorcan

Gaelic, meaning 'little fierce one'. Also the name of several kings of Leinster in Ireland.

Louis

(alt. Lou, Louie, Luigi, Luis)

French, meaning 'famous warrior'. The given name of the latest heir to the throne, Prince Louis Arthur Charles, as well as One Direction's Louis Tomlinson, music manager Louis Walsh and designer brand Louis Vuitton.

Lucas

(alt. Lukas, Luca)

English, meaning 'man from Luciana'. Popular in Brazil – there are several Brazilian footballers with this first name.

Lucian

(alt. Lucio)

Latin, meaning 'light'. Lucian of Samosata was an ancient Greek writer. Lucian Freud was a painter.

Ludwig

German, meaning 'famous warrior'. Ludwig van Beethoven was a hugely influential Classical and Romantic composer.

Luke

(alt. Luc, Luka)

Latin, meaning 'from Lucanus'. Famous Lukes include a primary character in the Bible, the author of the Gospel of Luke, *Star Wars* protagonist Luke Skywalker and actor Luke Perry.

Lupe

Latin, meaning 'wolf'. Rapper Lupe Fiasco is known for his songs 'Superstar' and 'The Show Goes On'.

Luther

German, meaning 'soldier of the people'. Famous Luthers include the German church reformer Martin Luther, US civil rights activist Martin Luther King Jr and Luther Vandross, the multi-award-winning singer.

Lyle

French, meaning 'the island'. Lyle Lovett is an American country singer.

Lyn

(alt. Lyndon)

Spanish, meaning 'pretty'. More commonly used as a name for girls.

Lynton

English, meaning 'town of lime trees'. Also a girls' name.

Boys' names

Mabon
(alt. Maban, Mabery)
Welsh, meaning 'our son'. A character in the King Arthur legend.

Mac
(alt. Mack, Mackie)
Scottish, meaning 'son of'.

Macaulay
Scottish, meaning 'son of the phantom'. Actor Macaulay Culkin shot to fame as a child actor in the *Home Alone* films.

Mace
English, meaning 'heavy staff' or 'club'. Can also be a nickname for Mason.

Mackenzie
Scottish, meaning 'the fair one'. Actor Mackenzie Crook is known for his roles in *The Office*, *Pirates of the Caribbean*, and *Game of Thrones*.

Mackland
Scottish, meaning 'land of Mac'.

Macon
French, name of towns in France and Georgia (USA).

Macsen
Scottish, meaning 'son of Mac'.

Madden
(abbrev. Mads)
Irish, meaning 'descendant of the hound'.

Maddox
English, meaning 'good' or 'generous'. Derived from Madoc, a legendary Welsh prince who supposedly discovered America years before Christopher Columbus. Maddox Jolie-Pitt is the eldest son of Angelina and Brad.

Madison
(alt. Madsen)
Irish, meaning 'son of Madden'.

Magnus
(alt. Manus)

Latin, meaning 'great'. Famous Magnuses include Magnus Carlsen the chess grand master and TV presenter Magnus Magnusson.

Maguire

Gaelic, meaning 'son of the beige one'.

Mahabala

Sanskrit, meaning 'great strength'. Also the name of a Buddhist guardian.

Mahesh

Hindi, meaning 'great ruler'. Also one of the names of Lord Shiva in the Hindu faith.

Mahir

Arabic, meaning 'skilful'.

Mahlon

Hebrew, meaning 'sickness'. Found in the Bible.

Mahmoud

Arabic, meaning 'praiseworthy'. Mahmoud Ahmadinejad was the president of Iran until 2013.

Mahoney

Irish, meaning 'bear'.

Major

English, from the word 'major'.

Makal

Alternative to Michael or Mikael, meaning 'close to God'.

Makani

Hawaiian, meaning 'wind'. Also a popular name in Arabic-speaking communities.

Makis

Hebrew, meaning 'gift from God'.

Mako

Hebrew, meaning 'God is with us'. Mako Iwamatsu was a prominent voice-over artist known for his roles in *Avatar: The Last Airbender* and *Conan the Barbarian*.

Malachi
(alt. Malachy)

Hebrew, meaning 'messenger of God', the name of a Jewish prophet in the Bible. Also an Irish name.

Malcolm

English, meaning 'Columba's servant'. Famous Malcolms include activist Malcolm X, actor Malcolm McDowell and bestselling author and journalist Malcolm Gladwell.

Mali

Arabic, meaning 'full and rich'. Also the name of a West African republic.

Manfred

Old German, meaning 'man of peace'. The band Manfred Mann is known for the song 'Blinded by the Light'.

Manish
(alt. Manesh)

English, meaning 'manly'. Extremely popular name in large parts of India.

Manley

English, meaning 'manly and brave'. Also the name of a Cornish village.

Mannix

Gaelic, meaning 'little monk'. Usually associated with the detective series *Mannix*.

Manoi
(alt. Manos)

Japanese, meaning 'love springing from intellect'. Also the name of a Laotian king.

Manuel

Spanish variation of Hebrew Emanuel, meaning 'God is with us'. Usually associated with the character of Manuel in the sitcom *Fawlty Towers*.

Manzi

Italian, meaning 'steer'. Also the old name for parts of southern China.

Marc
(alt. Marco, Marcos, Marcus, Markel)

French, meaning 'from the god Mars'. Famous Marcs include designer brand Marc Jacobs, singer Marc Bolan and drummer Marc Bell.

Marcel
(alt. Marcelino, Marcello)

French, meaning 'little warrior'. One of the most famous mimes of all time was Frenchman Marcel Marceau.

Marek

Polish variant of Mark, meaning 'from the god Mars'.

Mariano

Latin, meaning 'from the god Mars'. Other theories suggest that Mariano is a tribute to the Virgin Mary.

Mario
(alt. Marius)

Latin, meaning 'manly'. Mario is a popular Nintendo video game character, alongside his brother Luigi. Mario Andretti is a retired Formula One world champion racing driver.

Mark
(alt. Markus)

English, meaning 'from the god Mars'. Famous Marks include the Gospel of Mark from the Bible, actors Mark Hamill and Mark Wahlberg and author Mark Twain.

Marley
(alt. Marlin)

Old English, meaning 'meadow near the lake'. Sometimes used as a short form of Marlon. Famous Marleys include singer Bob Marley.

Marlo

American, meaning 'bitter'.

Marlon

English, meaning 'like little hawk'. Famous Marlons include actor Marlon Brando, singer Marlon Jackson and comedian Marlon Wayans.

Marshall

Old French, meaning 'caretaker of horses'. Also the name of a group of islands in the Pacific Ocean.

Martin
(abbrev. Marty)

Latin, meaning 'dedicated to Mars'. Famous Martins include actors Martin Freeman and Martin Sheen and director Martin Scorsese.

Marvel

English, from the word 'marvel'. Also the name of the long-running comic book company.

Marvin

Welsh, meaning 'sea friend'. Famous Marvins include singer Marvin Gaye, composer Marvin Hamlish and cartoon character Marvin the Martian.

Mason

English; a mason is a craftsman in either stonework or brickwork.

Massimo

Italian, meaning 'greatest'. The Massimo family were an ancient Roman family with great influence.

Mathias
(alt. Matthias)

Hebrew, meaning 'gift of the Lord'. Matthias was the apostle chosen to replace Judas in the Bible.

Mathieu

French form of Matthew, meaning 'gift of God'.

Matthew
(alt. Mathew)

Hebrew, meaning 'gift of the Lord'. Famous Matthews include the Gospel of Matthew and actors Matthew McConaughey and Matthew Lewis.

Maurice
(alt. Mauricio)

Latin, meaning 'dark skinned' or 'Moorish'. Children's author Maurice Sendak was best known for his work *Where the Wild Things Are*.

Maverick

American, meaning 'non-conformist leader'. Usually associated with the character Maverick from the film *Top Gun*.

Maximillian
(alt. Maximilian; abbrev. Max, Maxie, Maxim)

Latin, meaning 'greatest'. The name of several Roman emperors. Famous Maxes include actor Max Greenfield, the film *Mad Max: Fury Road*, and cosmetics brand Max Factor.

Maximino

Latin, meaning 'little Max'. More commonly used in Spanish-speaking communities.

Maxwell

Latin, meaning 'Maccus' stream'.

Maynard

Old German, meaning 'brave'. John Maynard Keynes was a highly influential British economist.

Mearl

English, meaning 'my earl'. Was used widely in the nineteenth century.

Mederic

French, meaning 'doctor'. Most commonly used in Quebec, Canada.

Mekhi

Swahili, meaning 'who is God?' Actor Mekhi Phifer is known for his roles in *ER*, *8 Mile* and *Divergent*.

Melbourne

From the city of the same name in Victoria, Australia.

Melchior

Persian, meaning 'king of the city'. The name of one of the three kings in the biblical story of the birth of Jesus.

Melton

English, meaning 'town of Mel'.

Melville

Scottish, meaning 'town of Mel'.

Melvin

(alt. Melvyn; abbrev. Mel)

English, meaning 'smooth brow'. Famous Melvins include DJ Melvin O'Doom, presenter Melvyn Bragg and actor Melvyn Douglas. Famous Mels include director Mel Brooks and comedian Mel Smith.

Memphis

Greek, meaning 'established and beautiful'. Also the name of a city in Tennessee, USA.

Mercer

English; a mercer was a man who traded or dealt in textiles.

Meredith

Welsh, meaning 'great ruler'. Used equally for girls and boys.

Merle

(alt. Merl, Murl)

French, meaning 'blackbird'.

Merlin

Welsh, meaning 'sea fortress'. Merlin was a magician and wise man in the King Arthur legend.

Merrick

Welsh, meaning 'Moorish'.

Merrill

Gaelic, meaning 'shining sea'.

Merritt

English, from the word 'merit'. Can be used for both boys and girls.

Merton

Old English, meaning 'town by the lake'. Also the name of a London borough.

Meyer

(alt. Mayer)

Hebrew, meaning 'bright farmer'.

Michael
(abbrev. Mick, Micky, Mickey, Mike)
Hebrew, meaning 'resembles God'.
Famous Michaels include one of
the archangels, Formula One racing
legend Michael Schumacher, singer
Michael Jackson and, reportedly the
highest-paid comedian in the world,
Michael McIntyre.

Michalis
Greek form of Michael, meaning
'resembles God'. Singer Michalis
Hatzigiannis is popular in Greece
and Cyprus.

Michel
French form of Michael, meaning
'resembles God'. Deutscher
Michel is also the cartoon
personification of Germany (in
the same way that Uncle Sam
represents the USA).

Michelangelo
Italian, meaning 'Michael's angel'.
Name of the famous painter whose
work can still be seen in the Sistine
Chapel in Rome.

Michele
Italian form of Michael, meaning
'resembles God'. Elsewhere, more
commonly used as a girls' name.

Michio
Japanese, meaning 'a man with the
strength of three thousand men'.
Michio Kaku is a leading theoretical
physicist.

Miguel
Spanish form of Michael, meaning
'resembles God'.

Miklos
Greek form of Nicholas, meaning
'victorious'. Sometimes used as an
alternative to Michael as well.

Milan
From the name of the Italian city.
Also the name of singer-songwriter
Shakira's son.

Miles
(alt. Milo, Milos, Myles)
English, from the word 'miles'.
Famous Mileses include trumpeter
Miles Davies, singer Miles Kane and
Star Trek: Next Generation character
Miles O'Brien.

Milton
English, meaning 'miller's town'.

Miro
Slavic, meaning 'peace'.

Misha
Russian, meaning 'resembles God'.
Its English equivalent is often thought
to be Mike, and the feminine version
is Mischa.

Mitchell
(abbrev. Mitch)
English, meaning 'who is like God'.
Mitchell Mark was a pioneer in
motion picture technology.

Modesto

Italian, meaning 'modest'. Also the name of a town in California, USA.

Mohandas

Sanskrit, meaning 'servant'.

Monroe

Gaelic, meaning 'mouth of the river Rotha'.

Monserrate

Latin, meaning 'jagged mountain'. A mountain in Colombia.

Montague
(abbrev. Monty)

French, meaning 'pointed hill'.

Montana

Latin, meaning 'mountain'. Also a state in the USA.

Monte

Italian, meaning 'mountain'. Also the name of a popular card game.

Montgomery
(abbrev. Monty)

Variant of Montague, meaning 'pointed hill'. Actor Montgomery Clift was known for his roles in *From Here to Eternity*, *A Place in the Sun* and *The Misfits*.

Moody

English, from the word 'moody'. Mad Eye Moody is a prominent character in J.K. Rowling's 'Harry Potter' series.

Mordecai

Hebrew, meaning 'little man'. Also a character in the Bible.

Morgan

Welsh, meaning 'great and bright'. Can be used for both boys and girls. Famous Morgans include actor Morgan Freeman, film maker Morgan Spurlock and musician Morgan Nicholls.

Moritz

Latin, meaning 'dark skinned and Moorish'. Also the German equivalent of Maurice.

Moroccan

Arabic, meaning 'from Morocco'. Also the name of one of Mariah Carey's twins.

Morpheus

Greek, meaning 'shape'. The name of the god of dreams in the epic poem *Metamorphoses* by Roman poet Ovid. Also a character in *The Matrix*.

Morris

Welsh, meaning 'dark skinned and Moorish'.

Morrison

English, meaning 'son of Morris'.

Mortimer

French, meaning 'dead sea'.

Morton

Old English, meaning 'moor town'. The name of several English towns.

Moses

(alt. Moshe, Moshon)

Hebrew, meaning 'saviour'. In the Bible, Moses receives the Ten Commandments from God.

Moss

English, meaning 'near a peat bog'.

Muhammad

(alt. Mohamed, Mohamet, Mohammad, Mohammed; abbrev. Mo)

Arabic, meaning 'praiseworthy'. Acknowledged as the prophet and founder of Islam. The name is extremely popular in large parts of the world. British runner Mo Farah is the Olympic and world record holder for the 5,000 and 10,000 metres.

Muir

Gaelic, meaning 'of the moor'.

Mungo

Gaelic, meaning 'most dear'.

Murphy

Irish, meaning 'sea warrior'.

Murray

Gaelic, meaning 'lord and master'. Famous Murrays include legendary Formula One commentator Murray Walker and Nobel Prize-winning physicist Murray Gell-Mann.

Mustafa

Arabic, meaning 'chosen'. Also a name for the prophet Muhammad in the Muslim faith.

Mwita

Swahili, meaning 'humorous one'.

Myron

Greek, meaning 'myrrh'. Myron was a popular sculptor in ancient Greece.

Boys' names

Nairn

Scottish, meaning 'alder-tree river'. From the Scottish town of the same name.

Najee

Arabic, meaning 'dear companion'. Also the name of an influential jazz musician.

Nakia

Arabic, meaning 'pure'. Also used as a name for girls.

Nakul

Sanskrit, meaning 'mongoose'. Choreographer Nakul Dev Mahajan has made a name for himself choreographing both Bollywood and Hollywood films.

Naphtali
(alt. Naftali)

Hebrew, meaning 'wrestling'. One of Joseph's brothers in the Bible.

Napoleon

Italian, meaning 'man from Naples'. The French general Napoleon Bonaparte became emperor of France.

Narciso

Latin, from the myth of Narcissus, who drowned after falling in love with his own reflection.

Nash

English, meaning 'at the ash tree'.

Nasir

Arabic, meaning 'helper'.

Nathan
(alt. Nathaniel; abbrev. Nat, Nate)

Hebrew, meaning 'God has given'. Name of many characters in the Bible.

Naval

Sanskrit, meaning 'wonder'.

Naveen

Sanskrit, meaning 'new'. Actor Naveen Andrews is known for his roles in *Lost*, *The English Patient* and *Rollerball*.

Ned

Used as a short form of Edward, meaning 'wealthy guard', but can be used in its own right. A character in *Game of Thrones* and *The Simpsons* and the chosen name of Ned Rocknroll, most famous for being married to Kate Winslet.

Prime ministers' names

Alexander (Alec) (Douglas-Home)

Andrew (Bonar Law)

Anthony (Eden, Blair)

Arthur (Wellesley, Balfour, Chamberlain)

Benjamin (Disraeli)

Clement (Attlee)

David (Lloyd George, Cameron)

Edward (Heath)

Gordon (Brown)

Harold (Macmillan, Wilson – though neither of their first names was Harold)

James (Callaghan – whose first name was Leonard)

John (Stuart, Russell, Major)

Neville (Chamberlain)

Ramsay (MacDonald – whose first name was James)

Spencer (Crompton, Perceval)

Stanley (Baldwin)

William (Cavendish, Pitt (Elder and Younger), Wyndham, Lamb, Gladstone)

Winston (Churchill)

– and Margaret (Thatcher) and Theresa (May) for girls.

Nehemiah

Hebrew, meaning 'comforter'. A prominent character in the Bible.

Neil

(alt. Neal, Niall)

Irish, meaning 'champion'.

Neilson

Irish, meaning 'son of Neil'. Also the name of a prominent train manufacturer in Scotland.

Nelson

Variant of Neil, meaning 'champion'. Admiral Horatio Nelson commanded the British navy at the Battle of Trafalgar. Nelson Mandela was the first black president of South Africa.

Nemo

Latin, meaning 'nobody'. Made famous by the Disney animation Finding Nemo.

Neo

Latin, meaning 'new'. Neo is the protagonist in The Matrix trilogy.

Nephi

Greek, meaning 'cloud'. The Books of Nephi are some of the subdivisions of the Book of Mormon.

Nessim

(alt. Nasim)

Arabic, meaning 'breeze'. Sham el-Nessim is also the first day of spring in Egypt.

Nestor

Greek, meaning 'traveller'. Nestor was the king of Pylos in ancient Greek mythology.

Neville

Old French, meaning 'new village'. Famous Nevilles include former prime minister Neville Chamberlain and Harry Potter character Neville Longbottom.

Newland

(alt. Newlands, Newland, Neuland)

English, meaning 'from a new land'. Also the name of several towns in the UK.

Newton

English, meaning 'new town'.

Neymar

Portuguese contraction of Latin names Netuno and Mars. Made popular by Brazilian footballer Neymar de Silva Santos.

Nicholas

(alt. Nicolas, Niklas; abbrev. Nick, Nicky, Niko, Nikos, Nico)

Greek, meaning 'victorious'. An enduringly popular name. Famous Nicholases include St Nicholas (the original Santa Claus), actor Nicolas Cage and the alchemist Nicholas Flamel.

Nigel

Gaelic, meaning 'champion'. Famous Nigels include actor Nigel Hawthorne, photographer Nigel Barker and producer/presenter Nigel Lythgoe.

Nikhil

Sanskrit, meaning 'whole' or 'entire'. Often associated with former *Emmerdale* character Nikhil Sharma.

Nikita

Greek, meaning 'unconquered', also Russian. Nikita Khrushchev was leader of the Soviet Union from 1953 to 1964. Also used as a girls' name.

Nikolai

(alt. Nikolay)

Russian variant of Nicholas, meaning 'victorious'. Several Russian emperors were known as either Nicholas or Nikolai.

Nimrod

Hebrew, meaning 'we will rebel'. Character in the Bible. Also the title of a piece of music by Elgar and the name of a type of aircraft.

Ninian

Gaelic, associated with the fifth-century saint of the same name.

Nissim

Hebrew, meaning 'wonderful things'.

Noah

Hebrew, meaning 'peaceful'. In the Bible, Noah is said to have built an ark to save two of every animal from a flood that covered the earth.

Noel

French, meaning 'Christmas'. Famous Noels include actor/composer Noel Coward and musician Noel Gallagher.

Nolan

Gaelic, meaning 'champion'.

Norbert

Old German, meaning 'Northern brightness'. Norbert is also the name of Hagrid's pet dragon in J.K. Rowling's 'Harry Potter' series.

Norman

Old German, meaning 'Northerner'.

Normand

French, meaning 'from Normandy'.

Norris

Old French, meaning 'Northerner'. Norris McWhirter was the co-author with his brother, Ross, of *The Guiness Book of Records*.

Norton

English, meaning 'Northern town'.

Norval

French, meaning 'Northern town'.

Norwood

English, meaning 'Northern forest'. Also the name of several towns in the UK.

Nova

Latin, meaning 'new'.

Nuno

Latin, meaning 'ninth'.

Nunzio

Italian, meaning 'messenger'. A fairly popular name in Italy.

Boys' names

Oakley

English, meaning 'from the oak meadow'. Also the name of a clothing brand.

Obadiah

Hebrew, meaning 'God's worker'. Used throughout the Bible to indicate a servant of God.

Obama

Swahili, meaning 'crooked'. Made famous by the 44th President of the USA, Barack Obama.

Obed

Hebrew, meaning 'servant of God'. Obed was the grandfather of David in the Bible.

Oberon
(abbrev. Obie)

Old German, meaning 'royal bear'. The Fairy King in Shakespeare's *A Midsummer Night's Dream*.

Obijulu
(alt. Obiajulu)

Swahili, meaning 'one who has been consoled'.

Octave
(alt. Octavian, Octavio)

Latin, meaning 'eight'. An octave is a group of eight notes in a musical scale.

Oda
(alt. Odell, Odie, Odis)

Hebrew, meaning 'praise God'. Oda of Canterbury was archbishop in the tenth century.

Ogden

Old English, meaning 'oak valley'. Ogden Nash was an American humorous poet.

Oisin
(alt. Ossian)

Celtic, meaning 'fawn'. The name of an ancient Irish poet.

Ola

Norse, meaning 'precious'. Ola Nordmann is the personification of Norway, in the same way Uncle Sam represents the USA.

Olaf

(alt. Olan)

Old Norse, meaning 'ancestor'. Also the name of the snowman in Disney's *Frozen*.

Oleander

Hawaiian, meaning 'joyous'. Also the name of a highly poisonous flowering shrub.

Oleg

(alt. Olen)

Russian, meaning 'holy'. Oleg the Seer was a Grand Prince of Rus', who ruled large parts of eastern Europe in the tenth century.

Olin

Russian, meaning 'rock'.

Oliver

(abbrev. Ollie)

Latin, meaning 'olive tree'. The UK's most popular boys' name in several recent years.

Olivier

French form of Oliver, meaning 'olive tree'.

Omar

(alt. Omari, Omarion)

Arabic, meaning 'speaker'. Extremely popular name in Sunni communities.

Ondrej

Czech, meaning 'manly'. The English equivalent is Andrew.

Ora

Latin, meaning 'hour'.

Oran

(alt. Oren, Orrin)

Gaelic, meaning 'light and pale'.

Orange

English, from the word 'orange', applied to both the fruit and the colour.

Orion

Greek, from the legend of a massive hunter, who was sent to spend eternity as a star constellation.

Orlando

(alt. Orlo)

Old German, meaning 'old land'. Famous Orlandos include actor Orlando Bloom, the Shakespearean character Orlando in *As You Like It* and the city of Orlando in Florida, USA.

Orpheus

Greek, meaning 'beautiful voice'. Orpheus was an ancient Greek musician and charmer, who tried to rescue his wife from the underworld.

Orrick

English, meaning 'sword ruler'.

Orson

Latin, meaning 'bear'. Film director Orson Welles was known for his radio play *The War of the Worlds*, and films *Citizen Kane* and *Touch of Evil*.

Orville

Old French, meaning 'gold town'. Orville and Wilbur Wright were the American brothers credited with building the first successful aeroplane.

Osaka

From the Japanese city.

Osborne
(alt. Osbourne)

Norse, meaning 'bear god'.

Oscar

Old English, meaning 'spear of the Gods'. Oscar Wilde was an Irish poet and writer, best known for his ready wit.

Osias

Hebrew, meaning 'salvation'. Osias Beert was an influential still-life painter in the seventeenth century.

Oswald

German, meaning 'God's power'. Oswald the Lucky Rabbit was Walt Disney's original cartoon creation before Mickey Mouse was born.

Othello

Old German, meaning 'wealth'. From the character in Shakespeare's play *Othello*.

Otis

German, meaning 'wealth'. Singer Otis Redding was known for his songs '(Sittin' on) The Dock of the Bay', 'Respect' and 'Try A Little Tenderness'.

Otten

German, meaning 'son of Otto'.

Otto
(alt. Otha, Otho)

German, meaning 'wealthy'. Famous Ottos include Anne Frank's father, Otto Frank, and Prussian leader Otto von Bismarck.

Ovid

Latin, meaning 'sheep'. Associated with the Roman poet, author of *Metamorphoses*.

Owain
(alt. Owen)

Welsh, meaning 'noble-born'. Owain Ddantgwyn was a prince of Wales and a contender to be the real King Arthur.

Oz

Hebrew, meaning 'strength'. As well as the fictional land of Oz in the story *The Wizard of Oz*, this is also a slang term for Australia.

Boys' names

Pablo

Spanish, meaning 'little'. Spanish painter and sculptor Pablo Picasso was one of the most influential artists of the twentieth century.

Paco

Native American, meaning 'eagle'. Also a Spanish alternative for Francisco.

Padma

Sanskrit, meaning 'lotus'. Also used as a name for girls.

Padraig

Irish, meaning 'noble'. The English equivalent is Patrick.

Panos

Greek, meaning 'all holy'.

Paolo
(alt. Paulo)

Italian, meaning 'little'. Paolo Nutini is a singer and Paulo Coelho is a Brazilian author.

Paresh

Sanskrit, meaning 'supreme spirit'.

Paris

From France's capital city. Also the Trojan prince in Homer's *Iliad* and Juliet's suitor in Shakespeare's *Romeo and Juliet*. Originally a boys' name, but now also used as a name for girls.

Pascal

Latin, meaning 'Easter child'.

Patrice

French form of Patrick, meaning 'noble'. Also a name given to girls.

Patrick
(abbrev. Pat, Paddy)

Irish, meaning 'noble'. The patron saint of Ireland. Patrick Stewart is an English actor whose long and distinguished career has included many spells with the Royal Shakespeare Company and playing Captain Jean-Luc Picard in *Star Trek*.

Patten

English, meaning 'noble'.

Paul

Hebrew, meaning 'small'. Paul the Apostle is a key character in the Bible. Famous Pauls include singers Paul Simon and Paul McCartney and artist Paul Cézanne.

Pavel

Latin, meaning 'small'. The English equivalent is Paul.

Pax

Latin, meaning 'peace'. From the Roman goddess of peace.

Paxton

English, meaning 'town of peace'.

Payne

Latin, meaning 'peasant'.

Payton

Latin, meaning 'peasant's town'.

Pedro

Spanish form of Peter, meaning 'rock'. Several kings of Portugal and Aragon have been named Pedro.

Penn

English, meaning 'hill'. Famous Penns include magician Penn Jillette. English Quaker William Penn was the founder of the state of Pennsylvania in the USA.

Percival
(abbrev. Percy)

French, meaning 'pierce the valley'. One of the Knights of the Round Table.

Perez

Hebrew, meaning 'breach'. One of Judah's sons in the Bible.

Pericles

Greek, meaning 'far-famed'. Pericles was an influential ancient Greek general and statesman.

Perrin

Greek, meaning 'rock'.

Perry

English, meaning 'rock'. Perry is an alcoholic drink made from pears.

Pervis

English, meaning 'purveyor'.

Pesah
(alt. Pesach, Pesasch)

Hebrew, meaning 'spared'. Pesach is the Hebrew name for the Jewish festival of Passover.

Peter
(abbrev. Pete)

Greek, meaning 'rock'. St Peter was one of Jesus's disciples in the Bible. Famous Peters include Peter Pan, film director Sir Peter Jackson, actor Peter Sellers and Russian emperor Peter the Great.

Petros

Greek form of Peter, meaning 'rock'.

Peyton

Old English, meaning 'fighting man's estate'.

Philemon

Greek, meaning 'affectionate'. A character in the New Testament of the Bible.

Philip

(alt. Phillip; abbrev. Phil, Phill, Pip)

Greek, meaning 'lover of horses'. Famous Philips include Prince Philip, Philip the Apostle in the Bible and author Philip Pullman. Pip is usually associated with the character of the same name in Charles Dickens' novel *Great Expectations*.

Philo

Greek, meaning 'love'. Philo of Alexandria was an ancient Roman Jewish philosopher.

Phineas

(alt. Pinchas)

Hebrew, meaning 'oracle'. Phineas was an ancient Greek king of Thrace.

Phoenix

Greek, meaning 'dark red'. In ancient Greek mythology, a phoenix is a bird that has the power to regenerate itself from its ashes.

Pierre

French form of Peter, meaning 'rock'. A popular French name.

Piers

Old English form of Peter, meaning 'rock'. Journalist and TV presenter Piers Morgan is known for his work with various tabloid newspapers and *Britain's Got Talent*.

Pierson

Variant of Piers, meaning 'son of Piers'.

Placido

Latin, meaning 'placid'. Tenor opera singer Placido Domingo is known for his vast array of operatic roles and performances with Luciano Pavarotti and José Carreras.

Pradeep

Hindi, meaning 'light'.

Pranav

Sanskrit, meaning 'spiritual leader'. Pranava is another way of saying 'Om' in Sanskrit.

Presley

Old English, meaning 'priest's meadow'. Usually associated with legend Elvis Presley.

Preston

Old English, meaning 'priest's town'. Also the name of a city in England. Preston Sturges was an Oscar-winning playwright.

Primo

Italian, meaning 'first'. Also used as a slang term for 'good' or 'excellent'.

Primus

Latin, meaning 'first'. Primus is often used in cartoons and comic books as a name for villains or superheroes, including in *Transformers* and Marvel comics.

Prince

English, from the word 'prince'. As well as a title of nobility, this name is often associated with the singer Prince.

Proctor

(alt. Prockter, Procter)

Latin, meaning 'steward'.

Prospero

Latin, meaning 'prosperous'. Prospero is the protagonist in Shakespeare's play *The Tempest*.

Pryor

English, meaning 'first'.

Ptolemy

Greek, meaning 'aggressive' or 'warlike'. Claudius Ptolemy was an ancient Greek mathematician and astronomer.

Purvis

(alt. Purves, Purviss)

French, meaning 'purveyor'.

Boys' names

Qabil
(alt. Quabil)
Arabic, meaning 'accepter'. Qabil is the Arabic name for Cain, who was one of the sons of Adam and Eve in the Bible.

Qadim
(alt. Qaadim, Qadem, Qadeem, Quadim)
Arabic, meaning 'organiser, convenor'. Often used with the prefix 'al', to form Al-Qadim.

Qadir
(alt. Quadir)
Arabic, meaning 'powerful'.

Qino
(alt. Quino)
Chinese, meaning 'handsome'. Also used in Spanish-speaking communities.

Quaid
Irish, meaning 'fourth'.

Qued
Old English, meaning 'bad or ugly'. Also an old name for the devil.

Quemby
Norse, meaning 'from the woman's estate'.

Quentin
(alt. Quinten, Quintin, Quinton, Quintus)
Latin, meaning 'fifth'. Famous Quentins include illustrator Quentin Blake and film director Quentin Tarantino.

Quillan
Gaelic, meaning 'sword'.

Quillon
Gaelic, meaning 'club'. The quillon is the bar on a sword where the handle meets the blade.

Quincy

Old French, meaning 'estate of the fifth son'. Jazz and soul legend Quincy Jones is known for his long career of music production, songwriting and performing.

Quinlan

Gaelic, meaning 'fit, shapely and strong'.

Quinn

Gaelic, meaning 'counsel'. Usually associated with the character from *Glee*.

Quinton

English, meaning 'queen's community'.

Boys' names

Radames

Slavic, meaning 'famous joy'. A character in the Verdi opera *Aïda*.

Rafael

(alt. Raphael; abbrev. Rafa, Rafe, Rafer, Raffi)

Hebrew, meaning 'God has healed'. One of the archangels in the Bible. Rafael Nadal is a Spanish tennis player who has held the world No. 1 ranking.

Ragnar

Old Norse, meaning 'strong counsellor'. Very popular name in Scandinavia and Germany.

Raheem

(alt. Rahim)

Arabic, meaning 'merciful and kind'.

Rahm

Hebrew, meaning 'mercy'.

Rahul

(alt. Raoul, Raul)

Sanskrit, meaning 'efficient'. Rahul was Buddha's son.

Raiden

(alt. Rainen)

From the Japanese god of thunder. It also refers to the combination of lightning and thunder.

Rainer

Old German, meaning 'warrior from the gods'. Rainer Hersch is a British classical music comedian.

Raj

Sanskrit, meaning 'kingdom'. Also a Polish term for 'heaven'.

Rajesh

(alt. Ramesh)

Sanskrit, meaning 'ruler of kings'. Popular in both India and Nepal.

Raleigh

Old English, meaning 'deer's meadow'. Sir Walter Raleigh was an Elizabethan explorer and politician.

Ralph

Old English, meaning 'wolf'. Famous Ralphs include actor Ralph Fiennes, fashion brand Ralph Lauren and cartoon character Ralph from *The Simpsons*.

Ram

English, from the word for a male sheep.

Ramiro

Spanish, meaning 'judicious'. A popular name for boys in Argentina.

Ramone

Spanish, meaning 'wise supporter' or 'romantic'. The Ramones were an American rock band who all had the stage surname Ramone.

Ramsey
(alt. Ramsay)

Old English, meaning 'wild garlic island'. Ramsay MacDonald was the UK's first-ever Labour prime minister.

Randall
(alt. Randal, Randolph; abbrev. Randy)

Old German, meaning 'wolf shield'. Randy Newman is an American singer-songwriter and film composer. In modern English, randy can also mean amorous.

Raniel

English, meaning 'God is my happiness'. Can also be used as an alternative to Daniel.

Ranjit

Sanskrit, meaning 'influenced by charm'. Several Indian cricketers have been called Ranjit.

Rannoch

Gaelic, meaning 'fern'. Also an area in the Scottish Highlands.

Rashad

Arabic, meaning 'good judgement'.

Rashid
(alt. Rasheed)

Sanskrit, meaning 'rightly guided'. Ar-Rashid, meaning The Guide, is one of God's names in the Islamic tradition.

Rasmus

Greek, meaning 'beloved'. Usually used as a shortened form of Erasmus.

Raven

English, from the word 'raven', referring to the black bird.

Ravi

Hindi, meaning 'sun'. Ravivar is the Hindi word for Sunday.

Rawlins

French alternative of Roland, meaning 'renowned land'.

Ray

English, from the word 'ray'. Also a short form of Raymond. Famous Rays include singer Ray Charles and actors Ray Liotta and Ray Winstone.

Raymond

(alt. Rayner; abbrev. Ray)

English, meaning 'adviser'. Illustrator and author Raymond Briggs is known for *The Snowman*.

Raz

Hebrew, meaning 'secret' or 'mystery'.

Reagan

Irish, meaning 'little king'.

Reginald

(abbrev. Reggie)

Latin, meaning 'regal'. Singer Elton John's birth name was Reginald Kenneth Dwight. Reggie Yates is a British actor and TV and radio presenter.

Regis

Latin, meaning 'of the king'.

Reid

Old English, meaning 'by the reeds'.

Reilly

(alt. Rilee, Rileigh, Riley, Ryle, Rylea, Rylei)

Irish, meaning 'courageous'. A very common first name and surname in Ireland.

Remington

English, meaning 'ridge town'.

Remus

Latin, meaning 'swift'. Famous Remuses include the ancient Roman myth of Romulus and Remus, and the character of Remus Lupin in J.K. Rowling's 'Harry Potter' series.

Rémy

French, meaning 'from Rheims'.

Ren

Shortened form of Reginald, meaning 'regal'. According to Confucianism, Ren is also the feeling of satisfaction or pleasure after doing something nice for someone else.

Renato

Latin, meaning 'rebirth'.

René

French, meaning 'rebirth'. Traditionally only a name for boys, René is now often given to girls as well – in place of Renée.

Reno

Latin, meaning 'renewed'. Also a gambling city in Nevada, USA.

Reuben

(alt. Ruben)

Spanish, meaning 'a son'. The son of Jacob and eldest brother of Joseph in the Bible.

Reuel

Hebrew, meaning 'friend of God'. The name of several characters in the Bible.

Rex
Latin, meaning 'king'.

Rey
Spanish, meaning 'king'. In Telugu, Rey also means 'friend'.

Reynold
Latin, meaning 'king's adviser'. As a surname, Reynold can be traced back to pre-Norman times.

Rhodes
German, meaning 'where the roses grow'. Also the name of the Greek island and city.

Rhodri
Welsh, meaning 'ruler of the circle'. Rhodri the Great was a Welsh king in the ninth century.

Rhys
(alt. Reece)

Welsh, meaning 'enthusiasm'. Famous Rhyses include actors Rhys Ifans, Griff Rhys Jones and Jonathan Rhys Meyers.

Ricardo
Spanish form of Richard, meaning 'powerful leader'.

Richard
(abbrev. Rich, Richie, Ritchie, Rick, Ricki, Ricky, Dick, Dicky)

Old German, meaning 'powerful leader'. A popular name through many decades, it has dropped off in usage in recent years. Famous Richards include three kings of England, and the most famous Ritchie has to be singer Ritchie Valens.

Ridley
English, meaning 'cleared wood'. Film director Sir Ridley Scott is known for his films *Alien*, *Thelma & Louise* and *Gladiator*.

Rigby
English, meaning 'valley of the ruler'.

Ringo
English, meaning 'ring'. Usually associated with Beatles drummer Ringo Starr, whose birth name is Richard Starkey.

Rio
Spanish, meaning 'river'. Footballer Rio Ferdinand has played for Manchester United and England.

Riordan
Gaelic, meaning 'bard'.

Rishi
Sanskrit, meaning 'scribe'. In ancient India, Rishis were the scribes who kept records of hymns and scientific advancement.

River
English, from the body of water. Actor River Phoenix was known for his roles in *Stand By Me*, *Indiana Jones and the Last Crusade* and *My Own Private Idaho*.

Roald
Scandinavian, meaning 'ruler'. Author Roald Dahl is one of the best-loved children's authors of all time, penning books such as *Charlie and the Chocolate Factory*, *Matilda* and *The Witches*.

Robbie

Shortened form of Robert, meaning 'bright fame'. Famous Robbies include singer Robbie Wiliams, actor Robbie Coltrane and poet Robert 'Robbie' Burns.

Robert
(abbrev. Rob, Robbie, Bob, Bobby, Dobbin)

Old German, meaning 'bright fame'. Famous Roberts include Scottish king Robert the Bruce and actors Robert Pattinson and Robert de Niro. Famous Robs include actor Rob Lowe and comedian Rob Brydon.

Roberto

Italian form of Robert, meaning 'bright fame'.

Robin

English, from the word for the small, flame-breasted bird. Famous Robins include comedian Robin Williams, singer Robin Thicke and outlaw legend Robin Hood.

Robinson

English, meaning 'son of Robin'. Usually associated with the novel and title character *Robinson Crusoe*, by Daniel Defoe.

Rocco
(alt. Rocky)

Italian, meaning 'rest'. Famous Roccos include Madonna's son Rocco Ritchie.

Rockwell

English, meaning 'of the rock well'.

Rod

Shortened form of Rhodri, Roderick and Rodney. Famous Rods include singer Rod Stewart and journalist Rod Liddle.

Roderick
(abbrev. Rod, Roddy)

German, meaning 'famous power'. Impressionist Rory Bremner's real name is Roderick Bremner.

Rodney
(abbrev. Rod, Roddy)

Old German, meaning 'island near the clearing'. Also a much-loved character in *Only Fools And Horses*.

Rodrigo

Spanish form of Roderick, meaning 'famous power'.

Roger

Old German, meaning 'spear man'. Famous Rogers include athlete Roger Bannister, The Who singer Roger Daltrey and tennis player Roger Federer.

Roland
(alt. Rowland)

Old German, meaning 'renowned land'. Also puppet character Roland Rat.

Rolf

Old German, meaning 'wolf'.

Rollie
(alt. Rollo)

Old German, meaning 'renowned land'. Often used as a shortened version of Rolf or Roland.

Roman

Latin, meaning 'from Rome'.

Romeo

Latin, meaning 'pilgrim to Rome'. Made famous by Shakespeare's play *Romeo and Juliet*. Romeo is the second son of David and Victoria Beckham.

Ronald

(abbrev. Ron, Ronnie)

Norse, meaning 'mountain of strength'. Hollywood actor Ronald Reagan became the 40th president of the United States.

Ronan

Gaelic, meaning 'little seal'. Singer Ronan Keating is known for his career with boy band Boyzone.

Rory

English, meaning 'red king'. Famous Rorys include comedian Rory Bremner, actor Rory MacGregor and comedian Rory McGrath.

Ross

(alt. Russ)

Scottish, meaning 'cape'. Famous Rosses include actor Ross Kemp and comedian Ross Noble.

Rowan

(alt. Roan)

Gaelic, meaning 'little red one'. Also reference to the rowan tree. Rowan Atkinson is the comedian, writer and actor best known for his roles in *Blackadder* and as *Mr Bean*.

Roy

Gaelic, meaning 'red'. Famous Roys include England football manager Roy Hodgson and singer Roy Orbison.

Rudolph

(abbrev. Rudy)

Old German, meaning 'famous wolf'. Usually associated with the Christmas reindeer with a shiny red nose.

Rufus

Latin, meaning 'red-haired'. Famous Rufuses include presenter Rufus Hound, actor Rufus Sewell and singer Rufus Wainwright.

Rupert

Variant of Robert, meaning 'bright fame'.

Ruslan

Russian, meaning 'like a lion'.

Russell

Old French, meaning 'little red one'. Famous Russells include comedian Russell Brand, screenwriter Russell T. Davies and astrologer Russell Grant.

Rusty

English, meaning 'ruddy'. Most commonly used in the USA as a name for boys.

Ryan

Gaelic, meaning 'little king'. Famous Ryans include actor Ryan Gosling, footballer Ryan Giggs and comedian Ryan Stiles.

Ryder

English, meaning 'horseman'.

Rye

English, from the word 'rye'. Also a type of grain.

Ryker

From Richard, meaning 'powerful leader'.

Rylan

English, meaning 'land where rye is grown'. Presenter Rylan Clark is known for several reality TV programmes, including *Celebrity Big Brother*.

Ryley

Old English, meaning 'rye clearing'. More commonly used as a spelling alternative to Riley.

Rym

Arabic, meaning 'antelope'.

Ryu

Japanese, meaning 'dragon'. A Ryu can also refer to a discipline, such as a martial art, or school of thought.

Boys' names

Saar
Hebrew, meaning 'tempest'.

Saber
(alt. Sabre)
French, meaning 'sword'.

Sagar
Bengali, meaning 'sea'.

Sage
English, meaning 'wise'. Also a herb.

Sakari
Native American, meaning 'sweet'. Most commonly used in Finnish-speaking communities.

Salil
Sanskrit, meaning 'from the water'. Salil Shetty is the current Secretary General of Amnesty International.

Salim
(alt. Saleem)
Arabic, meaning 'secure'. The Salim Khan family are a Bollywood dynasty, with dozens of members involved as actors, directors, producers or writers.

Salvador
Spanish, meaning 'saviour'. Artist Salvador Dali was known for his surrealist paintings.

Salvatore
Italian, meaning 'saviour'.

Samir
Arabic, meaning 'pleasant companion'.

Samson
Hebrew, meaning 'son of Sam'. Character with supernatural strength in the Bible.

Samuel
(abbrev. Sam, Sama, Sammie, Sammy)
Hebrew, meaning 'God is heard'. Famous Samuels include a prophet in the Bible, author Samuel Langhorne Clemens (known as Mark Twain) and actor Samuel L. Jackson.

Sandeep
(alt. Sundeep)

Hindi, meaning 'lighting the way'. Popular in Hindu and Sikh communities.

Sandro

Italian, a shortened form of Alessandro, meaning 'defending men'.

Sandy

Shortened form of Alexander, meaning 'defender of mankind'. Famous Sandys include TV presenter Sandy Gall and pro golfer Sandy Lyle.

Sanjay

Hindi, meaning 'victory'. Famous Sanjays include *The Simpsons* character Sanjay, politician Sanjay Gandhi and Hindu narrative *Mahabharata* character Sanjaya.

Santiago

Spanish, meaning 'St James'. Also the name of the capital city of Chile.

Santino

Spanish, meaning 'little St James'. Santino was also the name of the first chimpanzee recognised to have forward-planning skills, in 2009.

Santo
(alt. Santos)

Latin, meaning 'saint'. Also the name of at least 10 separate football clubs around the world, including in Brazil, Mexico and Cape Town.

Sasha
(alt. Sacha)

Shortened Russian form of Alexander, meaning 'defending men'. DJ Sasha is known for his remixes of popular songs by Madonna and The Chemical Brothers.

Scott
(alt. Scottie)

English, meaning 'from Scotland'. Scott Mills is a radio DJ and TV presenter.

Seamus

Irish variant of James, meaning 'he who supplants'. Irish poet and playwright Seamus Heaney was awarded the Nobel Prize for literature.

Sean
(alt. Shaun, Shawn)

Variant of John, meaning 'God is gracious'. The name originated in the Middle Ages, when French invaders reached Ireland and the Irish began pronouncing the French name Jean as Sean. Famous Seans include legendary Bond actor Sean Connery.

Sebastian
(alt. Sébastien; abbrev. Seb)

Greek, meaning 'revered'. Famous Sebastians include the crab character in Disney's *The Little Mermaid*, novelist Sebastian Faulks and Sebastian Vettel, the Formula One world champion racing driver.

Sergio

(alt. Serge)

Latin, meaning 'servant'. Popular name for boys in parts of Cameroon, Belgium and Haiti.

Seth

Hebrew, meaning 'appointed'. Famous Seths include the third son of Adam and Eve in the Bible, and actors Seth MacFarlane and Seth Greene.

Severus

Latin, meaning 'severe'. Best known now as the character Severus Snape in J.K. Rowling's 'Harry Potter' series.

Seymour

English, from Saint-Maur in northern France. Famous fictional Seymours include Seymour of *The Little Shop of Horrors* and Principal Seymour Skinner in *The Simpsons*.

Shalen

Arabic, meaning 'tribal leader'.

Shane

Variant of Sean, meaning 'God is gracious'. Famous Shanes include presenter Shane Richie, novelist Shane Briant and film director Shane Meadows.

Sharif

Arabic, meaning 'honoured'. Also a name for descendants of one of Muhammad's grandchildren.

Shea

Gaelic, meaning 'admirable'.

Shelby

Norse, meaning 'willow'. Also the name of a type of Mustang car.

Sherlock

English, meaning 'fair haired'. Usually associated with the character Sherlock Holmes.

Sherman

Old English, meaning 'shear man'. Also a type of World War II tank.

Shmuel

Hebrew, meaning 'his name is God'. The English equivalent is Samuel.

Shola

Arabic, meaning 'energetic'. Can be used for boys and girls. Shola Ameobi is a footballer who has played for Fleetwood Town and for Nigeria.

Sidney

(alt. Sydney; abbrev. Sid)

English, meaning 'wide meadow'. Actor Sidney Poitier is known for his roles in *Guess Who's Coming to Dinner* and *In The Heat of the Night*, as well as his work as a Bahamas diplomat.

Sigmund

Old German, meaning 'victorious hand'. Neurologist Sigmund Freud was known for his vast work of psychoanalysis.

Silvanus
(alt. Silvio)

Latin, meaning 'woods'. Silvanus was an ancient Roman deity of woods and fields.

Simba
(abbrev. Sim)

Swahili, meaning 'lion'. Usually associated with the character of Simba in Disney's *The Lion King*.

Simon
(alt. Simeon)

Hebrew, meaning 'to hear'. Famous Simons include music producer Simon Cowell and actor Simon Pegg.

Sinbad
(alt. Sindbad)

Persian, meaning 'Lord of Sages'. Also a literary merchant adventurer.

Sindri

Norse, meaning 'dwarf', from ancient Norse mythology.

Sipho

Swahili, meaning 'the unknown one'.

Sire

English, from the word 'sire'. Used as a form of address or title for reigning kings.

Sirius

Hebrew, meaning 'brightest star'. Name of Harry Potter's godfather, Sirius Black, in J.K. Rowling's 'Harry Potter' series.

Skipper

English, meaning 'ship captain'.

Skyler
(alt. Skylar)

English, meaning 'scholar'. Can be a boys' or girls' name. Now often associated with female *Breaking Bad* character Skyler White.

Solomon
(alt. Shlomo)

Hebrew, meaning 'peace'. One of the most important kings in the Bible and Torah.

Sonny

American English, meaning 'son'. Singer Sonny Bono was half of the duo Sonny and Cher.

Soren

Scandinavian, meaning 'brightest star'. Also the name of a town in Germany.

Spencer

English, meaning 'guardian'. Actor Spencer Tracy was a star of Hollywood's golden era.

Spike

English, from the word 'spike'. Famous Spikes include film director Spike Lee and comedian and writer Spike Milligan (though neither was actually given the name Spike).

Stamos

Greek, meaning 'reasonable'.

Stanford

English, meaning 'stone ford'.
Stanford University in the USA is one
of the most well-known Ivy League
universities.

Stanley
(abbrev. Stan)

English, meaning 'stony meadow'.
Famous Stanleys include children's
character Flat Stanley, film director
Stanley Kubrick and actor Stanley
Tucci.

Stavros

Greek, meaning 'cross'.

Stellan

Latin, meaning 'starred'. More
commonly used in Swedish-speaking
communities.

Steno

German, meaning 'stone'.

Stephen
*(alt. Steven, Stefan, Stefano, Steffan;
abbrev. Steve, Stevie)*

English, meaning 'crowned'. Famous
Stephens include actor Stephen
Fry, physicist Stephen Hawking and
author Stephen King, while the
Stevens include film director Steven
Spielberg, Apple founder Steve Jobs
and actor Steve Coogan.

Stewart
(alt. Stuart)

English, meaning 'steward'. The
House of Stewart was the longest-
surviving royal line in the Scottish
monarchy. Stewart Lee is a British
stand-up comedian. Famous Stuarts
include DJ Stuart Maconie, football
manager Stuart Pearce and film
director Stuart Townsend.

Stoney

English, meaning 'stone like'. More
commonly used as a surname.

Storm

English, from the word 'storm'.

Sven

Norse, meaning 'boy'. In the UK,
Sven is usually associated with former
England football manager Sven-
Goran Eriksson.

Syed
(alt. Sayyid)

Arabic, meaning 'lucky'. Also a way
of describing decendants of one of
Muhammad's grandchildren.

Sylvester

Latin, meaning 'wooded'. Usually
associated with the cartoon cat or
actor Sylvester Stallone.

Syon

Sanskrit, meaning 'followed by
good'. Also the name of a large
historical stately home in England.

Boys' names

Tacitus

Latin, meaning 'silent, calm'. From the ancient Roman historian and senator.

Tad

English, from the word 'tadpole'. Also a shortened form of Thaddeus.

Taine

Gaelic, meaning 'river'.

Taj

Sanskrit, meaning 'crown'. Usually associated with the Indian palace the Taj Mahal.

Takashi

Japanese, meaning 'praiseworthy'.

Takoda

Sioux, meaning 'friend to everyone'. Most commonly used in the USA.

Talbot
(alt. Tal)

English, meaning 'command of the valley'. An aristocratic name.

Tamir

Arabic, meaning 'tall and wealthy'.

Taras
(alt. Tarez)

Scottish, meaning 'crag'. Taras was the son of Poseidon in ancient Greek mythology.

Tarek
(alt. Tarik, Tariq)

Arabic, meaning 'to strike'.

Tarian

Welsh, meaning 'shield'. Also the name of a breed of Welsh pony.

Tarquin

Latin, from the Roman clan name. Author Tarquin Hall is known for his works *To the Elephant Graveyard* and *Salaam Brick Lane*.

171

Tarun

Hindi, meaning 'young'. Bollywood star Tarun Kumar Bhatti is known simply as Tarun.

Tatanka

Lakota, meaning 'buffalo'. Legendary Native American leader Sitting Bull's Western name was Tatanka Lyotake.

Tate

English, meaning 'cheerful'.

Taurean

English, meaning 'bull like'. Also used as a term for people born under the Taurus star sign.

Tavares

English, meaning 'descendant of the hermit'. Also found as a last name in Portuguese-speaking communities.

Tave
(alt. Tavian, Tavis, Tavish)

French, from Gustave, meaning 'royal staff'. In Nordic cultures the name also means 'guarantor'.

Tavor

Hebrew, meaning 'misfortunate'. Also the name given to a type of assault rifle.

Taylor

English, meaning 'tailor'. Actor Taylor Lautner appeared in the *Twilight* films. Now used as often for girls as for boys.

Names of poets

Andrew (Marvell)

Benjamin (Zephaniah)

Geoffrey (Chaucer)

Hugo (Williams)

John (Donne, Keats, Milton, Cooper Clarke)

Percy (Bysshe Shelley)

Robert (Burns)

Ted (Hughes)

Walt (Whitman)

William (Blake, Wordsworth)

Ted
(alt. Teddy)

Shortened form of Edward, meaning 'wealthy guard'. Famous Teds include *Father Ted*, and the *Ted* films.

Tennessee

Native American, meaning 'river town'. Also the name of a state in the USA.

Terence
(alt. Terrill, Terrence; abbrev. Terry)

English, meaning 'tender'. Terence was an ancient Roman playwright of comedies. Actor Terrence Howard is known for his roles in *Hustle & Flow* and *Empire*.

Tex

English, meaning 'Texan'. More commonly used in the USA.

Thabo

Swahili, meaning 'filled with happiness'. Thabo Mbeki was the president of South Africa from 1999 to 2008.

Thane
(alt. Thayer)

Scottish, meaning 'landholder'.

Thelonious

Latin, meaning 'ruler of the people'. Thelonious Monk was an influential jazz pianist and composer.

Theodore
(abbrev. Theo)

Greek, meaning 'God's gift'. St Theodore was a warrior and martyr of the Eastern Orthodox Church.

Theophile
(alt. Theophilus)

Latin, meaning 'God's love'.

Theron

Greek, meaning 'hunter'.

Thierry

French variant of Terence, meaning 'tender'. Striker Thierry Henry played for Arsenal and France.

Thomas
(abbrev. Thom, Tom, Tomaz, Tommy)

Aramaic, meaning 'twin'. An enduringly popular name. Thomas the Tank Engine is one of the most long-standing popular children's characters of book and screen.

Thomson
(alt. Thomsen)

English, meaning 'son of Thomas'. The spelling Thomsen also means 'twin' in Aramaic.

Thor

Norse, meaning 'thunder'. Thor was an ancient Nordic god of thunder and lightning.

Tiago

From Santiago, meaning 'St James'. Used as a shortened form of Santiago as often as a name in its own right, particularly in Portuguese-speaking communities.

Tibor

Latin, from the river Tiber. In Hungary, the name can also mean 'a short meeting'.

Tieman
(alt. Tiemann)

Gaelic, meaning 'lord'.

Tien

Vietnamese, meaning 'first'.

Timothy
(abbrev. Tim, Timmy)

Greek, meaning 'God's honour'. Famous Timothys include actors Timothy Spall, Timothy Olyphant and Timothy Dalton.

Tito
(alt. Titus)

Latin, meaning 'defender'. Usually associated with Tito Jackson, an original member of the Jackson 5.

Tobias
(alt. Toby)

Hebrew, meaning 'God is good'. Several characters in the Bible are named Tobias.

Tod
(alt. Todd)

English, meaning 'fox'. Several fictional characters are called Tod or Todd, including Todd Flanders in *The Simpsons*, Todd Alquist in *Breaking Bad* and Todd Grimshaw in *Coronation Street*.

Tonneau

French, meaning 'barrel'. A tonneau is also a word used for the rear section of a car, particularly old-fashioned cars.

Tony

Shortened form of Anthony, from the old Roman family name. Famous Tonys include footballer Tony Adams, former prime minister Tony Blair and comedian, historian and TV presenter Tony Robinson.

Torin

Gaelic, meaning 'chief'. Actor Torin Thatcher was known for his numerous stage roles and films, including *Great Expectations* and *Mutiny on the Bounty*.

Torquil

Gaelic, meaning 'helmet'. In Scandinavia the name is also derived from Thor, the god of thunder and lightning.

Tory
(alt. Torey)

Norse, meaning 'Thor'.

Toshi

Japanese, meaning 'reflection'. More commonly used in Japanese-speaking communities.

Travis

French, meaning 'crossroads'.

Trevelyan

Cornish, meaning 'of the house of Eden'.

Trevor

Welsh, meaning 'great settlement'. Famous Trevors include inventor Trevor Baylis, DJ Trevor Nelson and politician and presenter Trevor Phillips.

Trey
(alt. Tyree)

French, meaning 'three'. Sometimes used as a nickname for a third-born child or person whose name ends in III, such as Microsoft founder Bill Gates, whose birth name is William Henry Gates III.

Tristan
(alt. Tristram)

Celtic, from the Celtic hero. One of the knights of the Round Table.

Troy

Gaelic, meaning 'descended from the soldier'. Troy was a legendary city in ancient Greece.

Tudor

Variant of Theodore, 'God's gift'. The Tudors were a family dynasty who ruled England during the sixteenth century, including Henry VIII and Elizabeth I.

Tyler

English, meaning 'tile maker'. The name can be traced back to the fourteenth century and English rebel Wat Tyler, leader of the Peasants' Revolt.

Tyrell

French, meaning 'puller'. Usually associated with the House Tyrell from *Game of Thrones*.

Tyrone

Gaelic, meaning 'Owen's county'. Also the name of a county in Northern Ireland.

Tyson

English, meaning 'son of Tyrone'. Became popular after the rise of Mike Tyson, the boxer known for his aggressive fighting style.

Boys' names

Uberto
(alt. Umberto)
Italian, variant of Hubert, meaning 'bright or shining intellect'. Several kings of Italy were called Umberto.

Udath
(alt. Udathel)
Sanskrit, meaning 'noble'. More commonly used in Sanskrit-speaking communities.

Udo
German, meaning 'power of the wolf'.

Ugo
Italian form of Hugo, meaning 'soul, mind and intellect'. Also the name of a town in Japan.

Ulf
German, meaning 'wolf'. Also the name of a Danish Viking chief.

Ulrich
German, meaning 'noble ruler'.

Ultan
Irish, meaning 'from Ulster'. St Ultan was an Irish monk in the seventh century.

Ulysses
Greek, meaning 'wrathful'. Made famous by the mythological voyager of ancient Greece.

Unwyn
(alt. Unwin, Unwine)
English, meaning 'unfriendly'.

Old name, new fashion

Bertrand	Norris
Dexter	Pierce
Felix	Reginald
Hector	Ulysses
Jefferson	Winston

Upton

English, meaning 'high town'.

Urho

Finnish, meaning 'brave'.

Uri
(alt. Uriah, Urias)

Hebrew, meaning 'my light'. Magician Uri Geller is known for his illusions of psychokinesis and telepathy.

Uriel

Hebrew, meaning 'angel of light'. One of the archangels in the Bible.

Usher

English, from the word 'usher'. Made famous by the American R&B star.

Uttam

Sanskrit, meaning 'best'. Actor Uttam Kumar is known as one of the great Bollywood actors of the twentieth century.

Uzi
(alt. Uzzi, Uzziah)

Hebrew, meaning 'God is my strength'. The name of several characters in the Bible. Also the name of an Israeli type of submachine gun.

Boys' names

Vaclav

Czech, meaning 'receives glory'. The English form is Wenceslaus.

Vadim

Russian, meaning 'scandal maker'. Vadim the Bold was a legendary warrior in Eastern Europe during the ninth century.

Valdemar

German, meaning 'renowned leader'. Valdemar was a king of Sweden during the thirteenth century.

Valente

Latin, meaning 'valiant'. More commonly used as a surname, particularly in Italy and Portugal.

Valentine

(alt. Valentin, Valentino; abbrev. Val)

English, from the word 'valentine'. St Valentine was a Roman saint associated with the tradition of courtly love, and whose day is celebrated on 14 February. The Spanish variant is Valentin and the Italian Valentino.

Valerio

Italian, meaning 'to be strong'. Originally a surname in Italy, Valerio is now also being given as a first name to boys.

Valia

Sanskrit, meaning 'king of the monkeys'. Also used as a girls' name.

Van

Dutch, meaning 'son of'. Also a shortened form of Ivan, as with singer Van Morrison.

Vance

English, meaning 'marshland'. Usually associated with the comic book hero Justice, whose real name is Vance Astrovik.

Vangelis

Greek, meaning 'good news'. Vangelis is a modern Greek composer of various music, and is known for his work on films such as *Chariots of Fire*, *Blade Runner* and *Alexander*.

Varro

Latin, meaning 'strong'. There are several ancient Roman generals and poets known as Varro, most of whom were related to each other.

Varun

Hindi, meaning 'water god'. Shortened form of Varuna, who is the Hindu god of all water.

Vasilis

Greek, meaning 'kingly'.

Vaughan
(alt. Vaughn)

Welsh, meaning 'little'.

Vernell

French, meaning 'green and flourishing'. More commonly used in the USA.

Verner

Scandinavian form of the German Werner, meaning 'army defender'.

Vernon
(alt. Vernie)

French, meaning 'alder grove'.

Versilius

Latin, meaning 'flier'. Also the name of a fashionable part of Tuscany, Italy.

Vester

Latin, meaning 'wooded'. Also the name of a manufacturer of guitars.

Vibol

Cambodian, meaning 'man of plenty'.

Victor
(alt. Viktor)

Latin, meaning 'champion'. Author Victor Hugo is known for his novels *Les Miserables* and *The Hunchback of Notre-Dame*.

Vidal
(alt. Vidar)

Spanish, meaning 'life giving'. Hairdresser Vidal Sassoon owned a chain of salons and a range of styling products.

Vijay

Hindi, meaning 'conquering'. Bollywood star Joseph Vijay Chandrasekhar is known simply as Vijay.

Vikram

Hindi, meaning 'sun'. Bollywood star Vikram Kennedy Vinod Raj is known simply as Vikram.

Ville

French, meaning 'town'. The word is used to describe towns or cities throughout France and the UK, usually as a suffix – such as Carville in Yorkshire.

Vincent
(abbrev. Vin, Vince, Vinnie)
English, meaning 'victorious'.
Famous Vincents include actor Vince
Vaughn, artist Vincent van Gogh and
footballer-turned-actor Vinnie Jones.

Virgil
Latin, meaning 'staff bearer'. Ancient
Roman poet of the same name.

Vito
Spanish, meaning 'life'. Usually
associated with the character Vito
Corleone from *The Godfather*.

Vittorio
Italian, meaning 'victory'. The English
equivalent is Victor.

Vitus
Latin, meaning 'life'. St Vitus's day
was traditionally celebrated with
dancing, which led to naming a
neurological condition that looks
like uncontrolled dancing as 'St Vitus
Dance'.

Vivek
Sanskrit, meaning 'wisdom'.
Bollywood star Vivekananthan is
known simply as Vivek.

Vivian
Latin, meaning 'lively'. Commonly
given to both boys and girls.

Vladimir
(abbrev. Vlad)
Slavic, meaning 'prince'. Famous
Vladimirs include Russian President
Vladimir Putin and legendary warrior
Vlad the Impaler – who was also
known as Dracula.

Volker
German, meaning 'defender of the
people'.

Von
Norse, meaning 'hope'. In Germany,
'von' also means 'of' or 'from', and is
used in names to denote origin, such
as Ulrich von Liechtenstein.

Boys' names

Wade

English, meaning 'to move forward' or 'to go'. Wade Robson is a prolific choreographer of contemporary dance.

Waldemar

German, meaning 'famous ruler'. A common name for German princes during the Middle Ages.

Walden

English, meaning 'valley of the Britons'. Title of Henry Thoreau's famous book reflecting on simple living off the land.

Waldo

Old German, meaning 'rule'. Famous in the USA for the line of 'Where's Waldo?' books, known as 'Where's Wally?' in the UK.

Walker

English, meaning 'a fuller'. Most common in late 1800s and early 1900s in America.

Wallace

English, meaning 'foreigner' or 'stranger'. The man of the man-and-dog duo known to children everywhere as Wallace and Gromit.

Walter
(abbrev. Walt, Wally)

German, meaning 'ruler of the army'.

Ward

English, meaning 'guardian'.

Wardell

Old English, meaning 'watchman's hill'.

Warner

German, meaning 'army guard'. Best known for the movie studio Warner Brothers Entertainment, which has released blockbusters such as *Batman* and *Superman*.

Warren

German, meaning 'guard' or 'the game park'. Warren Buffett, an American businessman and philanthropist, is known as one of the richest people in the world.

Warwick

English, meaning 'farm near the weir'. The name of a historic town in England with a castle and a university.

Washington

English, meaning 'clever' or 'clever man's settlement'. The surname of the first president of the USA.

Wasim

Arabic, meaning 'attractive' or 'full of grace'.

Wassily

Greek, meaning 'royal' or 'kingly'. Wassily Kandinsky was an influential Russian painter of abstract art.

Watson

English, meaning 'son' or 'son of Walter'. The right-hand man of the famous fictional detective Sherlock Holmes.

Waverley

(alt. Waverly)

English, meaning 'meadow of aspens'. A common name for towns and cities in the USA.

Waylon

English, meaning 'land by the road'. American Waylon Jennings has been a popular country singer for decades.

Wayne

English, meaning 'a cartwright'. Famous Waynes include footballer Wayne Rooney, comedian Wayne Brady and rapper Lil Wayne.

Webster

English, meaning 'weaver'.

Weldon

English, meaning 'from the hill of well' or 'hill with a well'.

Wendell

(alt. Wendel)

German, meaning 'a wend'. American novelist and poet Wendell Berry has penned dozens of works throughout his career.

Werner

German, meaning 'army guard'.

Werther

German, meaning 'a soldier in the army'.

Weston

English, meaning 'from the west town'.

Wheeler

English, meaning 'wheel maker'.

Whitley

English, meaning 'white wood'.

Whitman

Old English, meaning 'white man'.

Whitney

Old English, meaning 'white island'. Can be used as a boys' or girls' name.

Wilber

(alt. Wilbur)

Old German, meaning 'bright will'. As one of the Wright brothers, Wilbur helped to invent the first powered aeroplanes.

Wildon

English, meaning 'wooded hill'.

Wiley

Old English, meaning 'beguiling' or 'enchanting'. The stage name of English rapper and songwriter Richard Kylea Cowie.

Wilford

Old English, meaning 'the ford by the willows'.

Wilfred

(alt. Wilfredo, Wilfrid; abbrev. Wilf)

English, meaning 'to will peace'.

Wilhelm

German, meaning 'strong-willed warrior'.

Wilkes

(alt. Wilkie)

Old English, meaning 'strong-willed protector' or 'strong and resolute protector'.

Willem

Dutch, meaning 'strong-willed warrior'.

William

(abbrev. Wil, Will, Willie, Willy, Bill, Billy)

Old German, meaning 'strong-willed warrior'. Famous Williams include Prince William, playwright William Shakespeare and rapper Will.i.am.

Willis

English, meaning 'server of William'.

Willoughby

Old Norse and Old English, meaning 'from the farm by the trees'.

Wilmer

English (Teutonic), meaning 'famously resolute'. Wilmer Eduardo Valderrama is an American actor. Wilmer Allison was a tennis champion in the 1930s.

Wilmot

English, meaning 'resolute mind'.

Wilson

English, meaning 'son of William'. Wilson Pickett was an American R&B, soul and rock 'n' roll singer-songwriter.

Wilton

Old Norse and English, meaning 'from the farm by the brook' or 'from the farm by the streams'. A town in Wiltshire with a history dating back to the eighth century.

Windell

German, meaning 'wanderer' or 'seeker'. Windell Middlebrooks is an American actor.

Windsor

Old English, meaning 'river bank' or 'landing place'.

Winfield

English, meaning 'from the field of Wina'.

Winslow

Old English, meaning 'victory on the hill'.

Winter

Old English, meaning 'to be born in the winter'.

Winthrop

Old English, meaning 'village of friends'.

Winton

Old English, meaning 'a friend's farm'.

Wirrin

Aboriginal, meaning 'a tea tree'.

Wistan

Old English, meaning 'battle stone' or 'mark of the battle'. St Wistan was martyred in AD 840 and has his feast day on 1 June.

Wittan

Old English, meaning 'farm in the woods' or 'farm by the woods'. The Witan were a group of advisers to the king that operated from the seventh to eleventh centuries.

Wolf

(alt. Wolfe)

English, meaning 'strong as a wolf'.

Wolfgang

Teutonic, meaning 'the path of wolves'. Wolfgang Amadeus Mozart was one of the most important composers of the classical period.

Wolfrom

Teutonic, meaning 'raven wolf'.

Wolter

Dutch, a form of Walter, meaning 'ruler of the army'. Wolter Kroes is a Dutch singer.

Woodburn

Old English, meaning 'a stream in the woods'.

Woodrow
(abbrev. Woody)

English, meaning 'from the row of houses by the wood'. Woodrow Wilson was the 28th president of the USA. Woody Guthrie, named after the president, was an influential American folk singer. Woody is also the well-known cowboy in *Toy Story*.

Woodward

English, meaning 'guardian of the forest'.

Worcester

Old English, meaning 'from a Roman site'.

Worth

American, meaning 'worth much' or 'wealthy place' or 'wealth and riches'.

Wren

Old English, meaning 'tiny bird'. Often associated with the species of small birds found throughout the world.

Wright

Old English, meaning 'to be a craftsman' or 'from a carpenter'.

Wyatt

Teutonic, meaning 'from wood' or 'from the wide water'. Famous Wyatts include wild-west sheriff Wyatt Earp and comedian Wyatt Cenac.

Wyclef
(alt. Wycleff, Wycliff, Wycliffe)

English, meaning 'inhabitant of the white cliff'. Wyclef Jeanelle Jean is an American-Haitian rapper best known for his role in the Fugees.

Wynn
(alt. Wyn)

Welsh, meaning 'very blessed' or 'the fair blessed one'. Also used in old English to mean 'friend'.

Popular song names

Alfie ('Alfie' – Lily Allen)

Carmen ('Carmen' – Lana Del Ray)

Diana ('Diana' – One Direction)

George ('Oh George' – Foo Fighters)

Maddie ('Alone With You (Maddie's Song)' – Ne Yo)

Mary ('Blind Mary' – Gnarls Barkley)

Simone ('Simone' – Goldfrapp)

Stephen ('Hey Stephen' – Taylor Swift)

Wyatt ('Lullaby for Wyatt' – Sheryl Crow)

Boys' names

Xadrian

American, a combination of X and Adrian, meaning 'from Hadria'.

Xander

Greek, meaning 'defender of the people'. A short form of Alexander.

Xannon

American, meaning 'descendant of an ancient family'.

Xanthus

Greek, meaning 'golden-haired'. One of the horses belonging to Achilles.

Xavier

(alt. Xzaviar)

Spanish, meaning 'the new house'. A name originating from the Catholic saint, Francis Xavier.

Xenon

Greek, meaning 'the guest'. Also one of the noble gases.

Xerxes

Persian, meaning 'ruler of the people' or 'respected king'. A king who attempted to invade the Greek mainland, but failed.

Xeven

Slavic, meaning 'lively'.

Xylander

Greek, meaning 'man of the forest'.

Boys' names

Yaal
Hebrew, meaning 'ascending' or 'one to ascend'.

Yadid
Hebrew, meaning 'the beloved one'.

Yadon
Hebrew, meaning 'against judgment'. Name of one of the many Pokemon characters.

Yahir
Spanish, meaning 'handsome one'. A Mexican singer.

Yaholo
Native American, meaning 'yells'.

Yair
Hebrew, meaning 'the enlightening one' or 'illuminating'.

Yakiya
Hebrew, meaning 'pure' or 'bright'.

Yanis
(alt. Yannis)
Greek, a form of John, meaning 'gift of God'.

Yarden
Hebrew, meaning 'to flow downward'. The Hebrew name Jordan comes from Yarden.

Ye
Chinese, meaning 'bright one' or 'light'.

Yehuda
(alt. Yehudi)
Hebrew, meaning 'to praise and exalt'. Often translated to mean Judah. Judah was a son of Jacob in the Bible.

Yered
Hebrew, a form of Jared, meaning 'descending'.

Yerik
Russian, meaning 'God-appointed one'.

Yerodin
Swahili, meaning 'studious'.

Yervant
Armenian, meaning 'king of people'.

Yitzak
(alt. Yitzaak)
Hebrew, meaning 'laughter' or 'one who laughs'.

Ynyr
Welsh, meaning 'to honour'.

Yobachi
Swahili, meaning 'one who prays to God' or 'prayed to God'.

Yogi
Sanskrit, meaning 'master of oneself'. Popularised by the American cartoon character, Yogi Bear.

Yoloti
Aztec, meaning 'heart'.

Yona
Native American, meaning 'bear'; and also Hebrew, meaning 'dove'. A name used to refer to ancient people who spoke Greek.

York
Celtic, meaning 'yew tree' or 'from the farm of the yew tree'. Used as a surname by people originating from the city of York.

Yosef
Hebrew form of Joseph, meaning 'Jehovah increases'.

Yuri
Aboriginal, meaning 'to hear'; Japanese, meaning 'one to listen'; Russian, a form of George, meaning 'farmer'. Name of a South Korean pop singer.

Yuuta
Japanese, meaning 'excellent'.

Yves
French, meaning 'miniature archer' or 'small archer'. Yves Saint Laurent was a famous French fashion designer.

Z

Boys' names

Zachariah
(alt. Zachary, Zecheriah; abbrev. Zac, Zach)
Hebrew, meaning 'remembered by the Lord' or 'God has remembered'.

Zad
Persian, meaning 'my son'.

Zada
(alt. Zadan, Zadin, Zadun)
Dutch, meaning 'a man who sowed seeds'.

Zadok
Hebrew, meaning 'righteous one'. The priest who anointed Solomon, made famous in Handel's anthem.

Zador
Hungarian, meaning 'violent demeanour'.

Long names
Alexander
Bartholomew
Christopher
Demetrius
Giovanni
Montgomery
Obadiah
Roberto
Salvatore
Zachariah

Zafar
Arabic, meaning 'triumphant'. Zafar Younis is a character from the BBC drama *Spooks*.

Zaid
Swahili, meaning 'increase the growth' or 'growth'.

Zaide

Yiddish, meaning 'the elder ones'. An unfinished opera by Mozart.

Zain
(alt. Zane)

Arabic, meaning 'the handsome son'.

Zaire

Swahili, meaning 'river'. Formerly the name of a country in Africa, now known as Democratic Republic of the Congo.

Zander

Greek, meaning 'defender of my people'.

Zarek

Persian, meaning 'God protect our king'. A Marvel comic book character created by Stan Lee and Gene Colan.

Zoltan
(alt. Zoltin)

Hungarian, meaning 'life'. Zoltan Karpathy is a character from the musical My Fair Lady.

Zuma

Arabic, meaning 'peace'.

Part three

Girls' names
A–Z

Baby names vary widely in spelling and pronunciation. To simplify
things, this book usually lists each name only once: under the most
common initial and spelling. If a name has an alternative spelling
with a different initial, it may be listed under that letter also.

Girls' names

Abigail
(alt. Abagail, Abbiegayle, Abbigail, Abigale, Abigayle; abbrev. Abbey, Abbi, Abi, Abie)

Hebrew, meaning 'my father's joy'. Found in the Bible. Abbey Clancy is a model and TV presenter. Abi Morgan is a screenwriter of films including *The Iron Lady*.

Abilene
(alt. Abilee)

Latin and Spanish for 'hazelnut'. Also from the Greek meaning 'plain' or 'meadow', it is the name of an ancient area of Syria.

Abina
(alt. Abena)

Akan, meaning 'born on Tuesday'.

Abra
Sanskrit, meaning 'clouds'. Female variation of Abraham.

Abril
Spanish for the month of April.

Acacia
Greek, meaning 'point' or 'thorn'. Also a type of flowering tree and shrub.

Acadia
Variation of the Greek word arcadia meaning 'paradise'. Originally a French colony in Canada.

Ada
(alt. Adair)

Hebrew, meaning 'adornment'. The mathematician Ada Lovelace is generally considered to be the world's first computer programmer, in the nineteenth century.

Adalee
Derived from German, meaning 'noble'. Sometimes used as a contraction of Ada and Lee.

Adalia

Hebrew, meaning 'God is my refuge'. Also the name of a type of ladybird.

Addison

(alt. Addisyn, Addyson; abbrev. Addie)

English, meaning 'son of Adam'. Used equally for girls and boys. Historically, more popular for boys in the nineteenth century.

Adelaide

(alt. Adelaida; abbrev. Addie)

German, meaning 'noble'. Popular after the rule of William IV and Queen Adelaide of England in the nineteenth century. Also an Australian city and name of Australian actor Adelaide Kane.

Adele

(alt. Adela, Adelia, Adell, Adella, Adelle; abbrev. Addie)

German, meaning 'noble'. Award winning singer-songwriter Adele Laurie Blue Adkins is better known as simply 'Adele'.

Adeline

(alt. Adalyn, Adalynn, Adelina, Adelyn)

Variant of Adelaide, meaning 'noble'.

Adeola

(alt. Adeolah, Adeolla)

Nigerian, meaning 'weaver of a crown of honour'.

Aderyn

Welsh, meaning 'bird'. Also the name of several places in Wales.

Adesina

Swahili, meaning 'she paves the way'. Often given to a firstborn daughter in Nigerian communities.

Adia

Variant of Ada, meaning 'adornment'. Usually associated with the song 'Adia'.

Adina

(alt. Adena)

Hebrew, meaning 'high hopes' or 'precious'. Found in the Bible.

Adira

Hebrew, meaning 'noble' or 'powerful'.

Adrian

Latin, meaning 'from Hadria'. Used more commonly for boys than girls, although it did enjoy a spell of popularity for girls in the USA.

Adrienne

(alt. Adriana, Adriane, Adrianna, Adrianne)

A feminine form of Adrian.

Aegle

Greek, meaning 'brightness' or 'splendour'. Also the name of several characters in ancient Greek mythology.

Aerin

Name of a character in J.R.R. Tolkien's *Lord of the Rings* trilogy.

Aerith

American, from a character in the computer game *Final Fantasy VII*.

Aero
(alt. Aeron)

Greek, meaning 'flight'.

Aerolynn

Combination of the Greek Aero, meaning 'flight', and the English Lynn, meaning 'waterfall'.

Afia
(alt. Aafia, Aff, Affi)

Arabic, meaning 'a child born on Friday'. The name's profile rose while Afia Masoon was a character in *EastEnders*.

Africa

Celtic, meaning 'pleasant', as well as the name of the continent.

Afsaneh

Persian, meaning 'a fairy tale'.

Afsha

Persian, meaning 'one who sprinkles light'. Actor Afsha Azad is known for her role as Padma Patil in the 'Harry Potter' film series.

Afton

Originally the name of a river in Ayrshire, Scotland, or a town on the Isle of Wight.

Agatha
(abbrev. Aggie)

Greek and Latin, meaning 'good'. St Agatha was a third-century Christian saint, patron saint of fire, earthquakes and bells, amongst other things. Crime writer Agatha Christie is the world's best-selling novelist.

Aglaia
(alt. Aglaya, Aglaja)

Greek, meaning 'brilliance'. In Greek mythology, one of the Three Graces. Also the name of a kind of mahogany tree, an opera, an eighteenth-century British ship and a saint.

Agnes

Greek, meaning 'virginal' or 'pure'. St Agnes of Rome is the patron saint of chastity and girls, amongst other things.

Agrippina

Latin, meaning 'born feet first'. The name of several influential women of ancient Rome.

Aida

Arabic, meaning 'reward' or 'present'. Also the name of an opera by Giuseppe Verdi.

Aidanne
(alt. Aden, Aidan, Aidanne, Aiden, Aidenne)

Gaelic, meaning 'fire'. A feminine variation of Aidan. Aidan is used most commonly for boys but also for girls.

A

Ailbhe

Irish, meaning 'noble' or 'bright'. Has also been used as a boys' name.

Aileen
(alt. Aelinn, Aleen, Aline, Alline, Eileen)

Gaelic variant of Helen, meaning 'light'. Aileen Cust was the first female veterinarian in Great Britain.

Ailith
(alt. Ailish)

Old English, meaning 'seasoned warrior'. Rare since the Middle Ages.

Ailsa

Scottish, meaning 'pledge from God'. Also the name of a Scottish island, Ailsa Craig.

Aimee
(alt. Aimie, Amie)

French form of Amy, meaning 'beloved'. Famous Aimees include actor Aimee Garcia, singer Aimee Mann, and Aimee Osbourne of the Osbourne family.

Aina

Scandinavian, meaning 'forever'.

Aine
(alt. Aino)

Celtic, meaning 'happiness'. Aine was a Celtic goddess of summer and prosperity.

Ainsley
(alt. Ansley)

Old English, meaning 'meadow' or 'clearing'. Also variant of an old Scottish last name used as a first name. Ainsley is used as both a girls' and a boys' name. Ainsley Hayes was a leading character in TV hit *The West Wing*.

Aisha
(alt. Aeysha, Aysha)

Arabic, meaning 'woman'; also Swahili, meaning 'life'. Aisha was one of the prophet Muhammad's wives.

Aishwarya

Variant of the Arabic Aisha, meaning 'woman'. Actor Aishwarya Rai Bachchan is one of the most recognisable Bollywood stars.

Aislinn
(alt. Aislin, Aisling, Aislyn, Alene, Allene)

Irish Gaelic, meaning 'dream'.

Aiyanna
(alt. Aiyana)

Native American, meaning 'forever flowering'.

Aja

Hindi, meaning 'goat'. Also Scandinavian.

Aka
(alt. Akah, Akkah)

Maori, meaning 'loving one' or 'affectionate'.

Akela
(alt. Akilah)

Hawaiian, meaning 'noble'. Usually associated with the character of Akela in Rudyard Kipling's *The Jungle Book*.

Akilina

Greek or Russian, meaning 'eagle'.

Akiva

Hebrew, meaning 'protect and shelter'.

Alaina
(alt. Alane, Alani, Alayna, Aleena)

Feminine of Alan, from the Gaelic for 'rock'. Also used as a spelling alternative to Eleanor.

Alana
(alt. Alanna, Alannah)

Gaelic, meaning 'beauty'. In Hawaiian it means 'beautiful offering', and in Old German it means 'precious'.

Alanis
(alt. Alarice)

Variant of Alaina, meaning 'rock'. Canadian-American Alanis Morissette is a multi-award-winning singer.

Alba

Latin, meaning 'white'. Also the Gaelic word for Scotland. Name of the central character in the novel *The Time Traveller's Wife*.

Alberta
(alt. Albertha, Albertine)

Feminine of Albert, from the Old German for 'noble, bright, famous'. Also the name of a province in Canada.

Albina

Latin, meaning 'white' or 'fair'. Also the name of an Etruscan goddess of the dawn.

Alda

German, meaning 'old' or 'prosperous'. St Alda was an Italian mystic in the eleventh century, who took care of the sick.

Aldis

English, meaning 'battle-seasoned'. Used most commonly for boys but also for girls.

Aleah

Arabic, meaning 'high'; also Persian, meaning 'one of God's beings'. Often used as a spelling alternative for Aliyah.

Alesha
(alt. Alisha, Alysha)

Variant of Alice, meaning 'nobility'. Alesha Dixon is a British singer, dancer, model and TV presenter.

Aleta
(alt. Aletha)

Greek, meaning 'footloose'. Usually associated with the character of Queen Aleta Ellis in the comic strip *The Legend of Prince Valiant*.

Alethea
(alt. Aletheia)

Greek, meaning 'truth'. The first use of this name was in the seventeenth century.

Alexandra

(alt. Alejandra, Alejhandra, Aleksandra, Alessandra, Alexandria; abbrev. Alex, Alexa, Alexi, Alexia, Alexina)

Feminine of Alexander, meaning 'defender of mankind'. Also one of the names of the ancient Greek goddess Hera.

Alexis

(alt. Alexus, Alexys)

Greek, meaning 'helper'. Alexis was also an ancient Greek comic poet and an ancient Greek sculptor.

Aleydis

Variant of Alice, meaning 'noble' or 'nobility'. Also an alternative name for St Alice of Scharbeek, patron saint of the blind and paralysed.

Alfreda

(alt. Alfre)

Old English, meaning 'elf' or 'magical counsel'. The female version of Alfred. Alfreda Benge is a lyricist and illustrator and Alfreda Hodgson is a singer.

Ali

(alt. Allie, Ally)

Shortened version of Alexandra, Aliyah, Alison or Alice, as well as a name in its own right.

Alibeth

Variant of Elizabeth, meaning 'consecrated to God'. More commonly used in the Middle Ages.

Alice

(alt. Alicia, Alize, Alyce, Alys, Alyse)

English, meaning 'noble' or 'nobility'. Usually associated with *Alice in Wonderland* by Lewis Carroll. Famous Alicias include singer Alicia Keys and actor Alicia Silverstone. Also the birth name of actor Jodie Foster.

Alida

(alt. Aleida)

Latin, meaning 'small winged one'. More commonly used in Dutch-speaking communities.

Alienor

(alt. Aliana)

Variant of Eleanor, from the Greek for 'light'. Also a spelling variation used by Queen Eleanor of Aquitaine in the twelfth century.

Aliki

(alt. Alika)

Variant of Alice, meaning 'noble' or 'nobility'. Actor Aliki Vougiouklaki was considered to be one of Greece's greatest actors of the twentieth century.

Alima

Arabic, meaning 'cultured'.

Alina

(alt. Alena)

Variation of Helen, meaning 'light'. More commonly used in Brazil, France, Italy, and Spain.

Alison
(alt. Allison, Allisyn, Allyson, Alyson)

Variant of Alice, meaning 'noble' or 'nobility'. Originally the name was Alis in the Middle Ages, with the suffix 'on', which means 'little'.

Alivia

Variant of Olivia, meaning 'olive tree'. More commonly used in the USA.

Aliya
(alt. Aaliyah, Aleah, Alia, Aliah, Aliyah)

Arabic, meaning 'exalted' or 'sublime'.

Alla

Variant of Ella or Alexandra.

Allegra

Italian, meaning 'joyous'. Allegra Byron was the lovechild of the poet Lord Byron. Allegra Versace is the heiress to the Versace fashion empire.

Allura

French, from the word for entice, meaning 'the power of attraction'.

Allyn

Feminine of Alan, meaning 'rock'.

Alma

Three possible origins: Latin for 'giving nurture', Italian for 'soul' and Arabic for 'learned'.

Almeda
(alt. Almeta)

Latin, meaning 'ambitious'. Also the name of a district in Barcelona, Spain.

Almera
(alt. Almira)

Feminine of Elmer, from the Arabic for 'aristocratic' and the Old English meaning 'noble'.

Alohi

Variant of the Hawaiian greeting Aloha, meaning 'love and affection'. More commonly used in the USA.

Alona
(alt. Alora)

Hebrew, meaning 'oak tree'. Alona is the first name of a Ukrainian tennis player and of an Israeli actor.

Alpha

The first letter of the Greek alphabet, usually given to a first-born daughter.

Alta

Latin, meaning 'elevated'. Also the name of many towns throughout Europe and the USA.

Altagracia

Spanish, meaning 'grace'. Alta Gracia is also the name of a city in Argentina.

Althaea
(alt. Altea, Altha, Althea)

Greek, meaning 'healing power'. Althaea was a prominent character in Greek mythology.

Alva

Spanish, meaning 'blonde' or 'fair skinned'. In Norway and Sweden it is considered the female version of Alf, which means 'elf'.

Alvena
(alt. Alvina)

Old English, meaning 'elf friend'. In Old German, it is considered the female version of Adelwin, which means 'noble friend'.

Alvia
(alt. Alyvia)

Variant of Olivia, meaning 'olive tree'; or Elvira, from the ancient Spanish city.

Alyssa
(alt. Alisa, Alissa, Allyssa, Alysa)

Greek, meaning 'rational'. Usually associated with the flower alyssum.

Amabel

Variant of Annabel, meaning 'grace and beauty'.

Amadea

Feminine of Amadeus, meaning 'love God'. More commonly used in German-speaking communities.

Amal

Arabic, meaning 'hope and aspiration'.

Amalia

Hebrew, meaning 'labour of love'. Also German, meaning 'work'.

Amana

Hebrew, meaning 'loyal and true'. Also the name of a type of tulip.

Amanda
(alt. Amandine)

Latin, meaning 'much loved'. Famous Amandas include presenter and actor Amanda Holden, and actors Amanda Bynes and Amanda Seyfried.

Amara
(alt. Amani)

Greek, meaning 'lovely forever'. Actor Amara Miller is known for her role in *The Descendants*.

Amarantha

Contraction of Amanda and Samantha, meaning 'much loved listener'. Also associated with the amaranth plant.

Amari
(alt. Amaris, Amasa, Amata, Amaya)

Hebrew, meaning 'pledged by God'. Also the name of a province in Greece.

Amaryllis
(alt. Ameris)

Greek, meaning 'fresh'. Usually associated with the flowering plant.

Amber

French, from the word for the semi-precious stone of the same name. Famous Ambers include actors Amber Heard and Amber Benson.

Amberly

Contraction of Amber and Leigh, meaning 'stone' and 'meadow'.

Amboree
(alt. Amber, Ambree)
American, meaning 'precocious'. More commonly used in the USA.

Amelia
(alt. Aemilia, Amalie, Amelie)
Greek, meaning 'industrious'. Famous Amelias include flying legend Amelia Earhart, and two Princess Amelias of Great Britain during the eighteenth century.

America
From the country of the same name. Actor America Ferrera is known for her roles in *Ugly Betty* and *How to Train Your Dragon*.

Amethyst
Greek, from the word for the purple precious stone of the same name.

Amina
(alt. Aamina)
Arabic, meaning 'honest and trustworthy'. Also the name of an influential Nigerian princess in the seventeenth century. Aamina Sheik is a Pakistani–American actor and model.

Amira
(alt. Amiya, Amiyah)
Arabic, meaning 'a high-born girl'. In Hebrew, the name also means 'rich princess'.

Amity
Latin, meaning 'friendship and harmony'. Also a name of a faction in the novel *Divergent*.

Amory
Variant of the Spanish name Amor, meaning 'love'. Also used as a boys' (more commonly) and girls' name in America during late 1800s to early 1900s, probably then derived from the French Ameury.

Amy
(alt. Aimee, Amee, Ami, Amie, Ammie, Amya)
Latin, meaning 'beloved'. Famous Amys include actor Amy Adams, Winter Olympic skeleton gold medallist Amy Williams and singer Amy Winehouse.

Anafa
Hebrew, meaning 'heron'.

Anaïs
Persian, meaning 'love'.

Ananda
Hindi, meaning 'bliss'. Also the name of one of the Buddha's disciples.

Anastasia
(alt. Athanasia)
Greek, meaning 'resurrection'. Usually associated with the Grand Duchess Anastasia of Russia, who was a member of the Russian royal family at the time of the Revolution of 1917.

Anat
Jewish, meaning 'water spring'. Name of a Semitic goddess.

Anatolia

Greek, meaning 'east sunrise'. The name of a large area within Turkey. Also a Christian saint.

Andrea

(alt. Andreia, Andria, Andrina)

Feminine of Andrew, from the Greek term for 'a man's woman'. Famous Andreas include singer Andrea Corr and writers Andrea Levy and Andrea Dworkin. Andrina is a Disney character who first appeared in *The Little Mermaid*. Andrina Carroll is a British actor.

Andromeda

Greek, meaning 'leader of men'. From the heroine of an ancient Greek legend.

Anemone

Greek, meaning 'breath'. Also the name of a type of flowering plant.

Angela

(alt. Angel, Angeles, Angelia, Angelle; abbrev. Angie)

Greek, meaning 'messenger from God' or 'angel'. Famous Angelas include actor Angela Lansbury and German Chancellor Angela Merkel.

Angelica

(alt. Angelina, Angeline, Angelique, Angelise, Angelita, Anjelica, Anjelina)

Latin, meaning 'angelic'. Famous Angelicas include actor Anjelica Huston and *Rugrats* cartoon character Angelica Pickle.

Angelina

(alt. Anjelina)

Derived from Angela, meaning 'messenger from God' or 'angel'. Famous Angelinas include actor Angelina Jolie and book and TV mouse Angelina Ballerina.

Anise

(alt. Anisa, Anissa)

French, from the liquorice-flavoured plant of the same name. Female form of Anis, a boys' name common in Tunisia and Morocco.

Anita

(alt. Anitra)

Variant of Ann, meaning 'grace'. Famous Anitas include actor Anita Dobson, *Body Shop* founder Anita Roddick and singer Anita Baker.

Anna

(alt. Ana, Anne)

Derived from Hannah, meaning 'grace'. Taken from the name of Anna the prophetess in the Bible. Anna Maxwell Martin is a BAFTA award-winning English actor.

Annabel

(alt. Anabel, Anabelle, Annabell, Annabella, Annabelle)

Contraction of Anna and Belle, meaning 'grace' and 'beauty'. Annabel Croft is known for her careers as a tennis pro and TV presenter.

Annalise
(alt. Annalee, Annaliese, Annalisa, Anneli, Annelie, Annelies, Annelise)

Combination of Anna and Lise, meaning 'grace' and 'pledged to God'. More commonly used in the USA and parts of Scandinavia.

Anne
(alt. Ann, Annie)

Derived from Hannah, meaning 'grace'. Famous Annes include actors Anne Hathaway and wives of Henry VIII Anne Boleyn and Anne of Cleeves.

Annemarie
(alt. Annamae, Annamarie, Annelle, Annmarie, Anne-Marie)

Combination of Anne and Mary, meaning 'grace' and 'star of the sea'. Actor Anne-Marie Duff is known for her roles in *Shameless* and *The Virgin Queen*.

Annette
(alt. Annetta)

Derived from Hannah, Hebrew, meaning 'grace'. Famous Annettes include actors Annette Bening, Annette Crosby and Annette Funicello.

Annis

Greek, meaning 'finished or completed'. May also be a variant of Agnes. In English mythology the Black Annis is a blue-faced witch who eats children.

Annora

Latin, meaning 'honour'. More commonly used in Eastern European communities.

Anoushka
(alt. Anousha, Anushka)

Variant of Anne, meaning 'grace'. Most popular in Russia, Greece and India.

Anthea
(alt. Anthi)

Greek, meaning 'flowerlike'. Famous Antheas include presenters Anthea Turner and Anthea Redfern, and director Anthea Benton.

Antigone

In ancient Greek mythology, Antigone was the daughter of Oedipus.

Antoinette
(alt. Antonetta, Antonette, Antonietta)

Both a variation of Ann and the feminine of Anthony, meaning 'invaluable grace'. Usually associated with eighteenth-century French queen consort Marie Antoinette. Often shortened to Toni.

Antonia
(alt. Antonella, Antonina)

Latin, meaning 'invaluable'. Also the name of dozens of influential ancient Roman women.

Anwen

Welsh, meaning 'very fair'. Usually associated with the character of Anwen Williams in *Torchwood*.

Anya
(alt. Aanya, Aniya, Aniyah, Aniylah, Anja)

Russian, meaning 'favour' or 'grace'; or Sanskrit, meaning 'the inexhaustible'. Anya Hindmarch is known for her designs of fashion accessories.

Aoife
Gaelic, meaning 'beautiful joy'. Usually associated with the goddess Esuvia.

Apollonia
Feminine of Apollo, the Greek god of the sun. St Apollonia was a virgin martyr in the third century and is the patron saint of dentistry.

Apple
From the name of the fruit. Famous Apples include the technology company Apple Inc, and the name of Gwyneth Paltrow's daughter.

April
(alt. Avril)

Latin, meaning 'opening up'. Also the name of the month, which has associations with the goddess Venus.

Aquilina
(alt. Aqua, Aquila)

Spanish, meaning 'like an eagle'. St Aquilina was a child martyr in the third century.

Ara
Arabic, meaning 'brings rain'. Also the name of a star constellation. Used as both a girls' and a boys' name.

Arabella
Latin, meaning 'answered prayer'. Also the name of an opera by Richard Strauss.

Araceli
(alt. Aracely)

Spanish, meaning 'altar of Heaven'.

Araminta
(abbrev. Minnie, Minty)

Hebrew, meaning 'lofty'.

Araylia
(alt. Araelea)

Latin, meaning 'golden'. Associated with aralia, a genus of trees and shrubs.

Arcadia
Greek, meaning 'paradise'. Also the name of a daughter of the ancient Roman Emperor Arcadius.

Ardelle
(alt. Ardell, Ardella)

Latin, meaning 'burning with enthusiasm'. Ardelle Kloss was an early leading American ice skater.

Arden
(alt. Ardis, Ardith)

Latin, meaning 'burning with enthusiasm'.

Arella
(alt. Areli, Arely)

Hebrew, meaning 'angel'. More commonly used in the USA.

Aretha

Greek, meaning 'woman of virtue'. Aretha Franklin is a soul singer.

Aria

(alt. Ariah)

Hebrew, meaning 'lioness', and Italian, meaning 'melody'.

Ariadne

Greek and Latin, meaning 'the very holy one'. In ancient Greek mythology, Ariadne was the daughter of King Minos.

Ariana

(alt. Aaryanna, Ariane, Arianna, Arianne, Arienne)

Derived from Welsh word for 'silver'. Also the name of a large geographical area in ancient Greek times, covering most of modern-day Afghanistan. Ariana Grande is a popular singer and actor.

Ariel

(alt. Ariela, Ariella, Arielle)

Hebrew, meaning 'lioness of God'. Character in Disney's *The Little Mermaid*.

Arlene

(alt. Arleen, Arlie, Arline, Arly)

Gaelic, meaning 'pledge'. Arlene Phillips is known for her appearances on *Strictly Come Dancing* and *So You Think You Can Dance*, as well as her work as a choreographer.

Armida

Latin, meaning 'little armed one'. Taken from the character of Armida in the epic poem *La Gerusalemme liberata*.

Artemisia

(alt. Artemis; abbrev. Artie, Arti)

Greek and Spanish, meaning 'perfect'. Also the name of a legendary female naval commander in Persia during the fifth century.

Arwen

Welsh, meaning 'fair' or 'fine'. Also an Elven character in J.R.R. Tolkien's *Lord of the Rings* trilogy.

Arya

Fictional brave tomboy character from George R. R. Martin's 'A Song of Ice and Fire' series.

Ashanti

From the geographical area in Ghana, Africa. Singer Ashanti Shequoiya Douglas is better known as just 'Ashanti'.

Ashby

English, meaning 'ash tree farm'.

Ashley

(alt. Ashely, Ashlee, Ashleigh, Ashli, Ashlie, Ashly)

English, meaning 'ash tree meadow'. Also a boys' name. Famous female Ashleys include actors Ashley Jensen and Ashley Judd, and singer Ashley Roberts.

Ashlynn
(alt. Ashlyn)

Irish Gaelic, meaning 'dream'. Also a spelling variation for Aislinn.

Ashton
(alt. Ashtyn)

Old English, meaning 'ash tree town'. Used as a girls' and boys' name, but most commonly for boys.

Asia

From the name of the continent. Also a name for an Oceanid in ancient Greek mythology.

Asma
(alt. Aasmah, Asmara)

Arabic, meaning 'high-standing'. Aasmah Mir is a BBC TV presenter and radio journalist. Asmara is the capital city of Eritrea.

Aspen
(alt. Aspynn)

From the name of the tree. Also name of a city in the US state of Colorado.

Assumpta
(alt. Asumpta, Assunta)

Irish, meaning 'assumption', and Italian, meaning 'raised up'. Assumpta Serna is a Spanish actor, and several Irish actors have this given name.

Asta
(alt. Asteria, Astor, Astoria)

Greek or Latin, meaning 'star-like'. Also the name of a type of moth.

Astrid

Old Norse, meaning 'beautiful like a God'. Author Astrid Lundgren is known for her children's novels such as *Pippi Longstocking*.

Atara

Hebrew, meaning 'diadem' or 'crown'. Also the name of a type of butterfly.

Athena
(alt. Athenais)

Greek, meaning 'wise'. From the ancient Greek goddess of wisdom, mathematics and arts and crafts.

Aubrey
(alt. Aubree, Aubriana, Aubrie)

French, meaning 'elf ruler'. Originally a name for boys, although it is now far more common for girls.

Audrey
(alt. Audra, Audrie, Audry, Autry, Audrina)

English, meaning 'noble strength'. St Etheldreda was known as St Audrey, and was an English princess in the seventh century. Famous Audreys include actors Audrey Hepburn and Audrey Tautou.

Augusta
(alt. August, Augustine)

Latin, meaning 'venerated'. The female version of the ancient Roman name Augustus.

Aura
(alt. Aurea)

Greek or Latin, meaning either 'soft breeze' or 'gold'.

Aurelia
(alt. Aurelie)

Latin, meaning 'gold'. The name of various ancient Roman women, including Julius Caesar's mother.

Aurora
(alt. Aurore)

Latin, meaning 'dawn'. In ancient Roman mythology, Aurora was the goddess of sunrise.

Austine
(alt. Austen, Austin)

Latin, meaning 'venerated'. Feminine version of Austin.

Autumn

Latin, from the name of the harvest season. Canadian-born Autumn Phillips is granddaughter-in-law to Queen Elizabeth II.

Ava
(alt. Avah, Avia, Avie)

Latin, meaning 'like a bird'. Ava Gardner was an iconic American actor during the 1950s–1970s.

Avalon
(alt. Avalyn, Aveline)

Celtic, meaning 'island of apples'. The name comes from a mythological island in the legend of King Arthur.

Axelle

Greek, meaning 'father of peace'. More commonly used in French- and Flemish-speaking communities.

Aya
(alt. Ayah)

Hebrew, meaning 'bird'.

Ayanna
(alt. Ayana)

Swahili, meaning 'beautiful flower'.

Azalea
(alt. Azalia)

Latin, meaning 'dry earth'. Also the name of a type of flowering shrub. Often associated with Australian singer Iggy Azalea.

Aziza

Hebrew, meaning 'mighty', or Arabic, meaning 'precious'.

Azure
(alt. Azaria)

French, meaning 'sky-blue'.

B Girls' names

Babette

French version of Barbara, from the Greek word meaning 'foreign'. Babette Cole is an author of children's books.

Badia

(alt. Badiyn, Badea)

Arabic, meaning 'elegant'.

Bailey

(alt. Baeli, Bailee)

English, meaning 'law enforcer'. Used as a girls' and boys' name, much more commonly for boys in recent years.

Bambi

Shortened version of the Italian Bambina, meaning 'child'. Usually associated with the cartoon Disney character.

Barbara

(alt. Barbra; abbrev. Barb, Barbie)

Greek, meaning 'foreign'. Famous Barbaras include actor Barbara Windsor, singer Barbra Streisand and Barbara McClintock, who won a Nobel Prize for genetics.

Basma

Arabic, meaning 'smile'.

Bathsheba

Hebrew, meaning 'daughter of the oath'. Usually associated with the story of Bathsheba and King David in the Bible. Also a character in the novel *Far From the Madding Crowd*.

Bay

(alt. Baya, Bae)

From the bay tree, with edible leaves used in cooking, or the indentation in a coastline (e.g. Byron Bay). Used as a boys' name most commonly, but also for girls.

Beata

Latin, meaning 'blessed'. Can be used as a shortened form of Beatrice or as a name in its own right.

Beatrice

(alt. Beatrix, Beatriz, Bellatrix, Betrys)

Latin, meaning 'blessed' or 'voyager'. A recent rapid riser in names for girls in the UK. Famous Beatrices include children's book author Beatrix Potter and Princess Beatrice, granddaughter of Queen Elizabeth II.

Becky

(alt. Becca, Beccie, Beccy, Beckie)

Shortened form of Rebecca, meaning 'joined', used as a name in its own right.

Belinda

(alt. Belen, Belina)

Contraction of Belle and Linda, meaning 'beautiful'. Famous Belindas include singer Belinda Carlisle and actor Belinda Stewart-Wilson.

Bell

Shortened form of Isabel, meaning 'pledged to God'.

Bella

(alt. Belle)

Latin, meaning 'beautiful'. Usually associated with the character of Isabella (Bella) Swan from the *Twilight* series or Belle from Disney's film *Beauty and the Beast*.

Movie inspirations

Bella (*Twilight*)
Elsa (*Frozen*)
Fiona (*Shrek*)
Holly (*Breakfast at Tiffany's*)
Lara (*Tomb Raider*)
Maria (*The Sound of Music*)
Marla (*Fight Club*)
Mary (*Mary Poppins*)
Nina (*Black Swan*)
Pandora (*Avatar*)
Trinity (*The Matrix*)

Belva

Latin, meaning 'beautiful view'. The inspiration for one of the characters in the musical *Chicago* was real-life murderer Belva Gaertner.

Bénédicta

(abbrev. Bennie, Benny)

Latin, the feminine of Benedict, meaning 'blessed'. Benedicta Henrietta of the Palatinate is a common ancestor of many present-day monarchs.

Benita

(alt. Bernita)

Spanish, meaning 'blessed'.

Berit

(alt. Beret)

Scandinavian, meaning 'splendid' or 'gorgeous'.

Bernadette
(alt. Bernadine; abbrev. Bernie)
French, meaning 'courageous'. St Bernadette was known for her visions of the Virgin Mary.

Bernice
(alt. Berenice, Berniece, Burnice)
Greek, meaning 'she who brings victory'. The name of Herod's daughter in the Bible.

Bertha
(alt. Berta, Berthe, Bertie)
German, meaning 'bright'. There are four saints called Bertha, all from the early Middle Ages.

Beryl
Greek, meaning 'pale green gemstone'. Beryl Reid was a classic British actor and Beryl Cook an English artist.

Bess
(alt. Bessie)
Shortened form of Elizabeth, meaning 'consecrated to God'. Queen Elizabeth I has the nickname Good Queen Bess. Bessie Smith was a blues singer.

Beth
Hebrew, meaning 'house'. Also shortened form of Elizabeth, meaning 'consecrated to God', used in its own right.

Bethany
(alt. Bethan)
Hebrew, referring to a geographical location found in the Bible. The name has seen a return to popularity in recent years.

Bethel
Hebrew, meaning 'house of God'. Also the name of a city in the Bible.

Bettina
Spanish or German version of Elizabeth, meaning 'consecrated to God'.

Betty
(alt. Betsy, Bette, Bettie, Bettye)
Shortened version of Elizabeth, meaning 'consecrated to God', also used in its own right. Famous Bettys include cartoon character Betty Boop and actor Betty White and Betty Grable.

Beulah
Hebrew, meaning 'married'. Also the name for a place that exists between Earth and Heaven.

Beverly
(alt. Beverlee, Beverley)
English, meaning 'beaver stream'. Beverley Knight is a British soul singer, actor and TV personality.

Bevin
Celtic, meaning 'fair lady'.

Beyoncé

Modern American, from the singer. Beyoncé's name was created by her parents as a tribute to her mother's maiden name, which was Beyince. However, some sources say the name is Swahili, meaning 'beyond others'.

Bianca
(alt. Blanca)

Italian, meaning 'white'. Famous Biancas include activist Bianca Jagger, model Bianca Gascoigne, the character of Bianca from Shakespeare's *Othello* and the long-running *EastEnders* character of that name.

Bibiana

Greek, meaning 'alive'. St Bibiana was a Roman virgin and martyr during the fourth century.

Bijou

French, meaning 'jewel'.

Billie
(alt. Bill, Billy, Billye)

Shortened version of Wilhelmina, meaning 'determined' as well as a name in its own right. Billie Holiday was an iconic jazz singer. Billie Piper is a singer turned actor.

Bina

Hebrew, meaning 'knowledge'.

Birgit
(alt. Birgitta)

German, meaning 'power and strength'. Used as a variation of Bridget.

Blaer

Icelandic, meaning 'light breeze'.

Blair

Scottish Gaelic, meaning 'flat, plain area'. Blair Waldorf is the main character in *Gossip Girl*, the novel series, TV series and film.

Blaise

French, meaning 'lisp' or 'stutter'. Also common as a boys' name.

Blake
(alt. Blakely, Blakelyn)

Old English, meaning 'dark, black'. Used as a girls' and a boys' name, but most commonly male.Blake

Blanche
(alt. Blanch)

French, meaning 'white or pale'. Extremely common in the Middle Ages, Blanche saw an increase in popularity before World War II, but hasn't been widely used since then.

Blodwen

Welsh, meaning 'white flower'.

Blossom

English, meaning 'flowerlike'.

Blythe
(alt. Blithe, Bly)

English, meaning 'happy and carefree'. Actor Blythe Danner is known for her roles in *Will & Grace*, *Meet the Parents*, and for being the mother of Gwyneth Paltrow.

Bobbi
(alt. Bobbie, Bobby)

Shortened version of Roberta, meaning 'bright fame', as well as a name in its own right. Usually associated with the cosmetics brand Bobbi Brown.

Bonamy
(alt. Bomani, Bonamia, Bonamea)

Derived from French, meaning 'close friend'.

Bonita

Spanish, meaning 'pretty'. Often associated with the song 'La Isla Bonita' by Madonna.

Bonnie
(alt. Bonny)

Scottish, meaning 'fair of face'. Actor Bonnie Langford was a child star who grew up to appear in West End musicals and *Dr Who*.

Brandy
(alt. Brandee, Brandi, Brandie)

From the name of the liquor created by distilling wine. Singer Brandy is known for her various pop songs as well as her role in *Moesha*.

Branwen

Welsh, meaning 'a white crow'.

Brea
(alt. Bree, Bria)

Shortened form of Brianna, meaning 'strong', but used in its own right. Also the name of a god in ancient Irish mythology.

Brenda

Old Norse, meaning 'sword'. Can also be used as a female variation of Brendan.

Brianna
(alt. Breana, Breanna, Breanne)

Irish Gaelic, meaning 'strong'. More commonly used in the USA.

Bridget
(alt. Bridgett, Bridgette, Brigette, Brigid, Brigitta, Brigitte)

Irish Gaelic, meaning 'strength and power'. Famous Bridgets include actor Bridget Fonda, Brigitte Bardot, Brigitte Nielsen and the protagonist in the novel *Bridget Jones's Diary* by Helen Fielding.

Brier
(alt. Briar)

French, meaning 'heather'.

Brit
(alt. Britt, Britta)

Celtic, meaning 'spotted' or 'freckled'. Usually a shortened form of Brittany, though it can be used in its own right. Actors Britt Ekland and Britt Robertson are both Brittanys.

Britannia

Latin, meaning 'Britain'. Britannia is the female personification of Great Britain.

Brittany

(alt. Britany, Britney, Britni, Brittani, Brittanie, Brittney, Brittni, Brittny)

Latin, meaning 'from England', though the name also refers to a region of France. Famous Brittanys include actor Brittany Murphy and singer Britney Spears.

Brontë

Greek, meaning 'the sound of thunder'.

Bronwen

(alt. Bronwyn)

Welsh, meaning 'fair breast'. In Wales it is more common to give the spelling Bronwen to girls and Bronwyn to boys, although the rest of the world doesn't follow the same pattern.

Brooke

(alt. Brook)

English, meaning 'small stream'. Brooke Shields is an American actor and model and Brooke Vincent a British TV actor.

Brooklyn

(alt. Brooklynn)

From the name of a New York borough. Used as a girls' name rarely, more commonly a boys' name.

Brunhilda

(alt. Brunhilde, Brynhildr)

German, meaning 'armour-wearing fighting maid'. Brynhildr, from which Brunhilda and Brunhilde orginated, was an important character in Old German mythology.

Bryn

(alt. Brynn)

Welsh, meaning 'mount' or 'hill'. Used as a boys' name and, less commonly, a girls' name.

Bryony

(alt. Briony)

English, from the name of bryonia, a European vine. Bryony Hannah is an Olivier-nominated British actor and star of *Call the Midwife*.

Buffy

A shortened form of Elizabeth, meaning 'consecrated to God'. Usually associated with the protagonist of the sci-fi series *Buffy the Vampire Slayer*.

Girls' names

Cadence

Latin, meaning 'with rhythm'. Used as feminine form of Caden.

Cadew

Derived from French, meaning 'gift'. English, meaning 'coarse woollen fabric'.

Cai

Vietnamese, meaning 'feminine'.

Caitlin

(alt. Cadyn, Caitlann, Caitlyn, Caitlynn, Katelin, Katelyn, Katelynn, Katlin, Katlyn)

Greek, meaning 'pure'. Caitlin Moran is a British broadcaster, newspaper columnist and author.

Calandra

Greek, meaning 'lark'. The calandra lark is a small bird found in Mediterranean countries. It is also the name of an asteroid belt.

Calantha

(alt. Calanthe)

Greek, meaning 'lovely flower'. Also refers to dozens of flowering shrubs.

Caledonia

Latin, meaning 'from Scotland'. Also an old name for Scotland.

Calia

American, meaning 'renowned beauty'. Also refers to several species of shrubs and trees.

Calista

(alt. Callista, Callisto, Kallista)

Greek, meaning 'most beautiful'. Actor Calista Flockhart is known for her roles in *Ally McBeal* and *Brothers and Sisters*.

Calla

Greek, meaning 'beautiful'. Also refers to a type of white-flowered plant.

Callie
(alt. Caleigh, Cali, Calleigh, Cally)
Greek, meaning 'beauty'. Screen-writer Callie Khouri is known for *Thelma & Louise* and *Nashville*.

Calliope
Greek, meaning 'beautiful voice'. From the muse of epic poetry in ancient Greek mythology.

Camas
Native American, from the root and bulb of the same name.

Cambria
Welsh, from the alternative name for Wales.

Camden
(alt. Camdin, Camdyn)
English, meaning 'winding valley'. More popular as a boys' name.

Cameo
Italian, meaning 'skin'. A cameo in the acting world usually refers to a small part played by a big star.

Cameron
(alt. Camryn)
Scottish Gaelic, meaning 'bent nose'. Used as a boys' name but also for girls, as with actor Cameron Diaz.

Camilla
(alt. Camille, Camelia, Camellia, Camila, Camillia)
Latin, meaning 'spiritual serving girl'. Camilla, Duchess of Cornwall, is married to Prince Charles. The French form, Camille, is often also used for boys.

Candace
(alt. Candice, Candis, Kandice; abbrev. Candy, Candi, Kandy, Kandi)
Latin, meaning 'brilliant white'. In the African ancient kingdom of Kush, Candace was the title given to queens and queen mothers.

Candida
Latin, meaning 'white', associated with purity and salvation. Unfortunately, also the name of a fungal infection.

Candra
Latin, meaning 'glowing'. The Candra family dynasty ruled eastern Bengal in the tenth century. Also the name of an immmortal villainess in Marvel comics.

Canei
Greek, meaning 'pure'. Also refers to a type of shrub.

Caoimhe
Celtic, meaning 'gentle' or 'precious'. Can be pronounced as 'kyva' or 'keeva', depending on where in Ireland it is used.

Caprice
Italian, meaning 'ruled by whim'. Caprice Bourret is a model best known simply as 'Caprice'.

Cara
Latin, meaning 'darling'. Cara Delevingne is a top model.

Caren
(alt. Carin, Caron, Caryn)

Greek, meaning 'pure'. Comedian Whoopi Goldberg's real name is Caryn Elaine Johnson.

Carey
(alt. Cari, Carie, Carrey, Carri, Carrie, Cary)

Gaelic, meaning 'love'. Carey Mulligan is an English actor. Can also be used for boys.

Carina
(alt. Corina)

Italian, meaning 'dearest little one'. Also the name of a star constellation.

Carissa
(alt. Carisa)

Greek, meaning 'grace'. Also the name of a type of shrub.

Carla
(alt. Charla)

Feminine of the Old Norse Carl, meaning 'free man'. Singer Carla Bruni Sarkozy is married to the former president of France Nicolas Sarkozy.

Carlin
(alt. Carleen, Carlene)

Gaelic, meaning 'little champion'.

Carlotta
(alt. Carlota)

Italian form of Charlotte, meaning 'little and feminine'. Also the name of a character in *The Phantom of the Opera*.

Carly
(alt. Carlee, Carley, Carli, Carlie)

Feminine of the German Charles, meaning 'free man'. Famous Carlys include singers Carly Simon and Carly Rae Jepson, and model Karlie Kloss.

Carmel
(alt. Carmela, Carmelita, Carmella)

Hebrew, meaning 'God's vineyard'. Mount Carmel is a place mentioned in the Bible.

Carmen
(alt. Carma, Carmina)

Latin, meaning 'song'. Usually associated with the opera *Carmen* by Georges Bizet.

Carol
(alt. Carole, Carrol, Carroll, Caryl)

Shortened form of Caroline, commonly used in its own right. Famous Carols include actor Carol Burnett, poet laureate Carol Ann Duffy and TV personality Carol Vorderman.

Caroline
(alt. Carolann, Carolina, Carolyn, Carolynn)

German, meaning 'man'. Famous Carolines include writer, actor and comedian Caroline Aherne and Caroline Herschel, the astronomer.

Carrington

English, meaning 'Charles's town'.

Carys
(alt. Cerys)

Welsh, meaning 'love'. Singer Cerys Matthews was a founder member of the band Catatonia.

Casey
(alt. Kacey, Kaci, Kacie, Kacy, Kasey, Kasie, Kassie)

Irish Gaelic, meaning 'watchful'. Used especially in the USA and for both girls and boys.

Cassandra
(alt. Casandra, Cassandre, Kassandra)

Greek, meaning 'one who prophesies doom' or 'entangler of men'. Usually associated with the seer in ancient Greek mythology and sister of Helen of Troy. Cassandra Clare is the pen name of bestselling author Judith Rumelt.

Cassia
(alt. Casia, Casie, Cassie)

Greek, meaning 'cinnamon'. Cassia Leo is an American author.

Cassidy

Irish, meaning 'clever' or 'curly-haired'. Cassidy Wolf is an American teen beauty queen.

Cassiopeia
(alt. Cassiopia, Cassiopea)

Greek, from the constellation and the ancient Greek myth about a vain queen.

Catalina
(alt. Catarina, Caterina)

Spanish version of Catherine, meaning 'pure'.

Catherine
(alt. Catharine, Cathrine, Cathryn)

Greek, meaning 'pure'. Famous Catherines include Catherine, Duchess of Cambridge, actor Catherine Zeta Jones and two wives of King Henry VIII.

Cathleen

Irish version of Catherine, meaning 'pure'. Actor Cathleen Nesbitt was known for her roles in dozens of West End and Broadway productions.

Cathy
(alt. Caitie, Cathey, Cathi, Cathie, Caty, Cato, Caitia, Kathie, Kathy)

Shortened form of Catherine, meaning 'pure'. Can be used in its own right. Author Cathy Cassidy is known for her young adult fiction.

Catrina
(alt. Caitrina, Caitriona)

Greek, meaning 'pure'.

Cayley
(alt. Cayla, Caylee, Caylen)

American, meaning 'pure'.

Cecilia
(alt. Cecile, Cecelia, Cecily, Cicely, Cicily)

Latin, meaning 'blind one'. Associated with the song 'Cecilia' by Simon and Garfunkel.

Celena

Greek, meaning 'goddess of the moon'. A spelling alternative to the Spanish name Selena.

Celeste
(alt. Celestina, Celestine)

Latin, meaning 'heavenly'. American Celeste Holm was an Oscar-winning actor in films and on Broadway.

Celine
(alt. Celia, Celina)

French version of Celeste, meaning 'heavenly'. Canadian Celine Dion is one of the most enduringly successful singers in pop music history.

Cerise

French, meaning 'cherry'. The colour cerise is a deep, pinky red.

Chanah
(alt. Chana)

Hebrew, meaning 'grace'. Usually used as a spelling alternative to Hannah.

Chandler
(alt. Chandell)

English, meaning 'candle maker'. Most commonly used as a boys' name.

Chandra
(alt. Chanda, Chandry)

Sanskrit, meaning 'like the moon'. Chandra is a god of the moon in Hinduism.

Chanel
(alt. Chanelle)

French, meaning 'pipe'. Usually associated with the designer and fashion brand Coco Chanel.

Chantal
(alt. Chantel, Chantelle, Chantilly)

French, meaning 'stony spot'. Chantelle Houghton was the first non-celebrity to win *Celebrity Big Brother* and is now a TV personality and columnist.

Chardonnay

French, from the wine variety of the same name.

Charis
(alt. Charissa, Charisse)

Greek, meaning 'grace'. Charis is one of the Graces in ancient Greek mythology.

Charity

Latin, meaning 'brotherly love'. Of the classic trio of names, Faith, Hope and Charity, this has been the least used, with a high point in the USA in the 1970s.

Charlene
(alt. Charleen, Charline)

German, meaning 'man'. Famous Charlenes include actor Charlene McKenna and the character Charlene in Aussie soap *Neighbours*, played by Kylie Minogue.

Charlotte
(alt. Charnette, Charolette, Charlize; abbrev. Charlie, Charly)

French, meaning 'little and feminine'. Famous Charlottes include author Charlotte Brontë, singer Charlotte Church and Princess Charlotte, born May 2015.

Charmaine

Latin, meaning 'clan'. The name possibly comes from Charmian, who was a favourite servant of Cleopatra.

Charnelle
(alt. Charnell, Charnel, Charnele)

American, meaning 'sparkles'. The spelling Charnel refers to a building that houses human remains, often located near a church.

Chastity

Latin, meaning 'purity'.

Chava
(alt. Chaya)

Hebrew, meaning 'beloved'.

Chelsea
(alt. Chelsee, Chelsey, Chelsi, Chelsie, Chelsy)

English, meaning 'port or landing place'. Chelsy Davy is a Zimbawean former girlfriend of Prince Harry.

Cher

French, meaning 'beloved'. Cher is an American singer and actor, originally part of the duo Sonny and Cher (with husband Sonny Bono) and later a hugely successful solo artist.

Cherie
(alt. Cheri, Cherise)

French, meaning 'dear'. Cherie Blair is a barrister and wife of former British prime minister Tony Blair.

Cherish
(alt. Cherith)

English, meaning 'to treasure'.

Chermona

Hebrew, meaning 'sacred mountain'. Sometimes used as a female spelling alternative for Sherman.

Cherry
(alt. Cherri)

English, meaning 'cherry fruit'.

Cheryl
(alt. Cheryle)

English, meaning 'little and womanly'. Singer Cheryl found fame with girl group Girls Aloud and has been a judge on *The X Factor*.

Chesney

English, meaning 'place to camp'. Used as both a girls' and a boys' name.

Cheyenne
(alt. Cheyanne)

Native American, from the tribe of the same name from the state of Wyoming in the USA.

Chiara
(alt. Ceara, Chiarina)

Italian, meaning 'light'. Usually used as a spelling alternative to Ciara.

China

From the Asian country of the same name.

Chiquita
Spanish, meaning 'little one'.

Chloe
(alt. Cloe)
Greek, meaning 'pale green shoot'. Sometimes spelled with an accent on the 'e'. Famous Chloes include the fashion house Chloé, actors Chloë Moretz and Chloë Sevigny and author Toni Morrison – whose birth name was Chloe Wofford.

Chloris
Greek, meaning 'pale'. Chloris was a nymph in ancient Greek mythology.

Christabel
Latin and French, meaning 'fair Christian'. The title of a poem by Samuel Taylor Coleridge.

Christina
(alt. Christine, Christiana, Cristina; abbrev. Chris, Chrissy, Christa, Christie, Christy, Crissy, Cristy)
Greek, meaning 'anointed Christian'. The female version of Christian, the name was originally constructed as a tribute to Jesus Christ. Christina Aguilera is a world famous pop singer.

Chuma
Aramaic, meaning 'warmth'.

Ciara
Irish, meaning 'dark beauty'. Ciara Princess Harris, known simply as Ciara, is an American singer, dancer, actor and model.

Cierra
(alt. Ciera)
Irish, meaning 'black'. Usually used as a spelling alternative to Sierra.

Cinderella
French, meaning 'little ash-girl'. Most often associated with the fairy tale.

Cinnamon
Greek, from the exotic spice of the same name.

Citlali
(alt. Citlalli)
Nahuatl, meaning 'star'. An ancient Aztec name.

Citrine
Latin, from the gemstone of the same name.

Claire
(alt. Clare, Clara, Claira)
Latin, meaning 'bright'. A very popular name, especially in 1960s and 1970s Britain. Famous Claires include actor Claire Danes, agony aunt Claire Rayner, and sports presenter Clare Balding.

Clarabelle
(alt. Clarabella, Claribel)
Contraction of Clara and Isobel, meaning 'bright' and 'consecrated to God'. Clarabelle is a Disney cow character and Clarabella is the title of a Beatles song.

Clarissa
(alt. Clarice, Clarisse)

Variation of Claire, meaning 'bright'. One of the longest novels in English is the eighteenth-century *Clarissa, or, The History of a Young Lady*, by Samuel Richardson.

Clarity

Latin, meaning 'lucid'.

Claudette

Latin, meaning 'lame'. The first female prime minister of Haiti was Claudette Werleigh. Claudette Colvin was a pioneer of the American civil rights movement.

Claudia
(alt. Claudie, Claudine)

Latin, meaning 'lame'. TV presenter and film critic Claudia Winkleman co-presents *Strictly Come Dancing* and German Claudia Schiffer is a supermodel.

Clematis

Greek, meaning 'vine'. Also the name of a type of flowering plant.

Clementine
(alt. Clemency, Clementina, Clemmie)

Latin, meaning 'mild and merciful'. Also the name of the sweet orange fruit.

Cleopatra
(alt. Cleo, Clio, Cliona)

Greek, meaning 'her father's renown'. Cleopatra was the last acting Pharaoh of ancient Egypt.

Clodagh

Irish, meaning 'river'.

Clotilda
(alt. Clothilda, Clothilde, Clotilde)

German, meaning 'renowned battle'. St Clotilde was known for her works of charity in the fifth century.

Clover

English, from the flower of the same name.

Coco

Spanish, meaning 'help'. Usually associated with the fashion designer Coco Chanel.

Cody

English, meaning 'pillow'. Used as a name for girls and, more commonly, boys.

Colleen
(alt. Coleen)

Irish Gaelic, meaning 'girl'. Colleen Nolan is the youngest of the singing sisters The Nolans, now a TV presenter.

Collette
(alt. Colette)

Greek and French, meaning 'people of victory'. Author Sidonie-Gabrielle Colette is known for her novel *Gigi*.

Connie
(alt. Konnie)

Latin, meaning 'steadfast'. Also used as a shortened version of Constance. Kanak Asha Huq, known as Konnie, is a former *Blue Peter* presenter.

Constance
(alt. Constanza)

Latin, meaning 'steadfast'. Oscar Wilde's wife was called Constance Lloyd.

Consuelo
(alt. Consuela)

Spanish, meaning 'comfort'. The name originated from a Spanish name for the Virgin Mary, Our Lady of Consolation.

Cora

Greek, meaning 'maiden'.

Coral
(alt. Coralie, Coraline, Corelia, Corene)

Latin, from the marine life of the same name.

Corazon

Spanish, meaning 'heart'. Also a slang term in Spanish meaning 'darling'.

Cordelia
(alt. Cordia, Cordie)

Latin, meaning 'heart'. Also the name of a tragic character in Shakespeare's play *King Lear*.

Corey
(alt. Cori, Corrie, Cory)

Irish Gaelic, meaning 'the hollow'. Used for girls and, more commonly, for boys.

Corinne
(alt. Corin, Corinna, Corrine)

French version of Cora, meaning 'maiden'. Famous Corinnes include Corinne Bailey Rae, the British singer-songwriter, and Corinne Day, the fashion photographer.

Corliss

English, meaning 'cheery'.

Cornelia

Latin, meaning 'like a horn'. Also the name of several important women in the ancient Roman empire.

Cosette

French, meaning 'people of victory'. Also the heroine in *Les Misérables*.

Cosima
(alt. Cosmina)

Greek, meaning 'order'. Cosima is the feminine version of Cosmo, who is one of the patron saints of medical doctors. Cosima Lawson is the daughter of celebrity chef Nigella Lawson.

Courtney
(alt. Cortney)

English, meaning 'court-dweller'. Actor Courtney Cox is known for her roles in *Friends* and *Cougar Town*.

Creola

French, meaning 'American-born, English descent'. Usually associated with the Creole people and language.

Crescent

French, meaning 'increasing'. Usually associated with the shape of the same name.

Cressida

From the Trojan heroine in Greek mythology.

Crystal

(alt. Christal, Chrystal, Cristal, Kristal, Kristel)

Greek, meaning 'ice'. Can also be spelled using a K in all forms. Very popular in the USA for many years, only recently dropping off in popularity.

Csilla

Hungarian, meaning 'defences'. More commonly used in Eastern European countries.

Cyd

Shortened form of Sidney, meaning 'wide island'. Dancer and actor Cyd Charisse was known for her roles in *Singin' in the Rain*, *The Band Wagon* and *Silk Stockings*.

Cynara

Greek, meaning 'thistly plant'. Also the name of a type of thistle plant.

Cynthia

(abbrev. Cinda, Cindi, Cyndi, Cindy)

Greek, meaning 'goddess from the mountain'. Also the name of an ancient Greek goddess of the moon. Lady Cynthia Mosley was a British politican and Cynthia Nixon the American actor who played Miranda in *Sex in the City*. Famous Cindys include Cindy Crawford, one of the original supermodels, and Cyndi Lauper the singer, songwriter and actor.

Cyra

Persian, meaning 'sun'. Also the name of a type of ladybird.

Cyrilla

Latin, meaning 'lordly'. Also the name of a type of flowering plant.

Girls' names

Dacey
Irish Gaelic, meaning 'from the south'.

Dada
Swahili, meaning 'curly haired'.

Daelan
English, meaning 'aware'. Used most commonly as a boys' name but can also be used for girls.

Dagmar
German, meaning 'day's glory'. Dagmar was the stage name of the first real television star, Virginia Egnor.

Dagny
Nordic, meaning 'new day'.

Dahlia
Scandinavian, from the flowering plant of the same name.

Dai
Welsh, meaning 'darling'. Also Japanese for 'large, great'. Used in Wales for boys as a shortened form of Daffyd (David). Used rarely for girls.

Daisy
(alt. Dasia)
English, meaning 'eye of the day'. Also the common flower. Daisy has seen a rise in popularity in recent years.

Flower names
Acacia	Lily
Daisy	Petunia
Flora	Poppy
Hyacinth	Primrose
Lilac	Rose

Dakota
Native American, meaning 'allies'. There are two American states named after the Dakota people. Actor Dakota Johnson stars in the film version of 50 Shades of Grey.

Dalia
(alt. Dalila)

Hebrew, meaning 'delicate branch'. Also the name of a goddess of property in ancient Lithuanian mythology.

Dallas

Scottish Gaelic, from the village of the same name. Also the name of a city in Texas, USA.

Damaris

Greek, meaning 'calf'. Found in the Bible.

Damica
(alt. Damika)

French, meaning 'friendly'. Often used as a spelling alternative to Danica.

Damita

Spanish, meaning 'little noblewoman'.

Dana
(alt. Dania, Danna, Dayna)

English, meaning 'from Denmark'. In Persian, the name also means 'a perfect and valuable pearl'. Actor Dana Delany played one of the *Desperate Housewives*.

Danae

Greek, from the ancient Greek mythological heroine of the same name.

Danica
(alt. Danika)

Latin, meaning 'from Denmark'. Danica Patrick made waves as the most successful female racing driver in history.

Danielle
(alt. Danelle, Daniela, Daniella, Danila, Danyelle; abbrev. Dani, Danii)

The feminine form of the Hebrew Daniel, meaning 'God is my judge'. Model Danielle O'Hara is known for her glamour modelling and *Big Brother* career.

Danita

English, meaning 'God will judge'. More commonly used in the USA.

Daphne
(alt. Dafne, Daphna)

Greek, meaning 'laurel tree'. Daphne was a water nymph in ancient Greek mythology.

Dara

Hebrew and Persian, meaning 'wisdom'. Found in the Bible. Used for both girls and boys.

Darby
(alt. Darbi, Darbie)

Irish, meaning 'a park with deer'.

Darcy
(alt. Darcey, Darci, Darcie)

Irish Gaelic, meaning 'dark'. Ballerina Darcey Bussell is one of the reasons behind the recent rise in popularity of the name in the UK.

Daria

Greek, meaning 'rich'. Usually associated with the teenage cartoon character Daria.

Darla

English, meaning 'darling'. Actor Darla Hood was known for her roles as a child star in the 1930s and 1940s.

Darlene
(alt. Darleen, Darline)

American, meaning 'darling'. Actor Darlene Gillespie was one of the original *Mickey Mouse Club* members.

Darva

Slavic, meaning 'honeybee'. Also the name of several locations in Iran.

Daryl
(alt. Darrell, Darryl)

English, originally used as a surname. Famous Daryls include actor Daryl Hannah. Darrell Rivers was the central character in Enid Blyton's classic *Malory Towers* books.

Dascha
(alt. Dasha)

Russian, meaning 'of the sea'. Actor Dascha Polanco is known for her role in the US television series *Orange is the New Black*.

Davina

Hebrew, meaning 'loved one'. English TV presenter Davina McCall is the best-known owner of the name.

Dawn
(alt. Dawna)

English, meaning 'to become day'. Dawn French is one of the most successful comedy actors and writers of recent decades.

Daya

Hebrew, meaning 'bird of prey'. Also the term used for a form of teaching in the Sikh religion.

Deanna
(alt. Dayana, Deana, Deanna, Deanne)

English, meaning 'girl from the valley'. Singer and actor Deanna Durbin was a Hollywood star in the 1930s and 1940s. Deanna Troi was a central female character in *Star Trek*.

Deborah
(alt. Debbra, Debora, Debra, Debrah, Dvora; abbrev. Debbi, Debbie, Debby)

Hebrew, meaning 'bee'. Also the name of a prophetess in the Bible. Among the many famous Deborahs are actor Deborah Kerr and entrepreneur Deborah Meaden, star of *Dragons' Den*.

December

Latin, meaning 'tenth month'.

Decima
(alt. Decia)

Latin, meaning 'tenth'. Also the name of a goddess in ancient Roman mythology.

Dee

Welsh, meaning 'swarthy'.

Deidre
(alt. Deidra, Deirdre)
Irish, meaning 'raging woman'.
Deirdre Barlow was one of *Coronation Street*'s longest-running characters.

Deja
(alt. Dejah)
French, meaning 'already'. The commonly used French phrase *déjà vu* means 'already seen'.

Delaney
Irish Gaelic, meaning 'offspring of the challenger'.

Delia
Greek, meaning 'from Delos'. Delia Smith is one of the most enduringly successful stars of cookery TV programmes and books.

Delilah
(alt. Delina)
Hebrew, meaning 'seductive'. Famous Delilahs include the lover of Samson in the Bible, and the song 'Delilah' by Tom Jones.

Della
(alt. Dell)
Shortened form of Adele, meaning 'noble'. Used as a name in its own right. Donald Duck's twin sister is called Della Duck.

Delores
(alt. Deloris, Dolores, Doloris)
Spanish, meaning 'sorrows'. In Spanish, the shortened form of Delores is Lolita or Lola.

Delphine
(alt. Delpha, Delphia, Delphina, Delphinia)
Greek, meaning 'dolphin'. More commonly used in French-speaking communities.

Delta
Greek, meaning 'fourth child'. Also the name of the fourth letter of the Greek alphabet.

Demetria
(alt. Demetrice, Dimitria)
Greek, from the ancient Greek mythological heroine of the same name.

Demi
French, meaning 'half'. American actor Demi Moore is a star of Hollywood films across several decades.

Dena
(alt. Deena)
English, meaning 'from the valley'. Also the name of a mountain range in Iran.

Denise
(alt. Denice, Denisa, Denisse)
French, meaning 'devoted to Bacchus'. Denise is the French female form of Dionysius, the ancient Greek god of wine.

Derora
Hebrew, meaning 'stream'. Also the name of a clan in India.

Desdemona

Greek, meaning 'wretchedness'. A character in Shakespeare's play *Othello*.

Desiree
(alt. Desirae, Des'ree)

French, meaning 'much desired'. Singer Des'ree adapted her name from Desiree, her given name.

Desma

Greek, meaning 'blinding oath'. More commonly used as a shortened version of Desdemona.

Destiny
(alt. Destany, Destinee, Destiney, Destini)

French, meaning 'fate'.

Deva

Hindi, meaning 'God-like'. Deva is also a name for several Buddhist, Hindu and New Age spiritual entities or people.

Devin
(alt. Devinne)

Irish Gaelic, meaning 'poet'. Used for boys most commonly but can be used for girls, often using the feminine form Devinne.

Devon

English, from the southern English county of the same name.

Diamond

English, meaning 'brilliant'.

Diana
(alt. Dian, Diane, Dianna, Dianne)

Roman, meaning 'divine'. Famous Dianas include Princess Diana, singing legend Diana Ross and Diana the Roman goddess of hunting.

Diandra

Greek, meaning 'two males'.

Dilys

Welsh, meaning 'reliable'. Famous Dilyses include actor Dilys Watling and actor and screenwriter Dilys Laye.

Dimona

Hebrew, meaning 'south'. Also the name of a town in the Bible, now situated in modern Israel.

Dinah
(alt. Dina)

Hebrew, meaning 'justified'.

Dionne

Greek, from the mythological heroine of the same name. Famous Dionnes include singers Dionne Warwick and Dionne Bromfield.

Divine

Italian, meaning 'heavenly'.

Dixie

French, meaning 'tenth'. Usually used as a term for the South of the USA.

Dodie

Hebrew, meaning 'well-loved'. Author Dodie Smith is best known for her children's novel *101 Dalmations*.

Dolly
(alt. Dollie)

Shortened form of Dorothy, meaning 'gift of God'. Can be used in its own right. Dolly Parton is the world-famous country and western singer. Reality TV star Chantelle Houghton named her daughter Dolly, perhaps signifying a name revival.

Dominique
(alt. Domenica, Dominica, Domonique)

Latin, meaning 'Lord'. Usually associated with the song 'Dominique' by Soeur Sourire, a singing nun.

Donata
(alt. Donatella)

Latin, meaning 'given', also Italian for 'gift'. Donatella Versace is a leading Italian fashion designer and vice president of the Versace empire.

Donna
(alt. Dona, Donnie)

Italian, meaning 'lady'. Actor and presenter Donna Air started out as a child star in *Byker Grove*.

Dora

Greek, meaning 'gift'. Usually associated with the cartoon character Dora the Explorer.

Dorcas

Greek, meaning 'gazelle'. Also the name of a character in the Bible.

Doreen
(alt. Doren, Dorene, Dorine)

Greek, meaning 'gift'. In Irish Gaelic, the suffix 'een' indicates that a child has the same name as a parent.

Doria

Greek, meaning 'of the sea'. Also the name of an influential Genoese family in the twelfth century.

Doris
(alt. Dorris)

Greek, from the region of the same name. Actor and singer Doris Day was a big star in the 1940s and 1950s, and is also a leading animal rights campaigner.

Dorothy
(alt. Dorathy, Doretha, Dorotha, Dorothea, Dorthy; abbrev. Dot, Dottie, Dotty)

Greek, meaning 'gift of God'. Famous Dorothys include the central character in *The Wizard of Oz* and Dorothy Hodgkin, who won a Nobel Prize for chemistry.

Dorrit
(alt. Dorit)

Greek, meaning 'gift of God'. Usually associated with the novel *Little Dorrit* by Charles Dickens.

Dory
(alt. Dori)

French, meaning 'gilded'. Usually associated with the character from the Disney films *Finding Nemo* and *Finding Dory*.

Dove
(alt. Dovie)

English, from the bird of the same name. Often used as a symbol for peace.

Drew

Greek, meaning 'masculine'. Actor Drew Barrymore became a child star when she appeared in *E.T.*

Drusilla
(alt. Drucilla)

Latin, meaning 'of the Drusus clan'. Found in the Bible.

Dulcie
(alt. Dulce, Dulcia)

Latin, meaning 'sweet'. Actor Dulcie Gray was known for her roles on stage and screen in the mid-twentieth century.

Dusty
(alt. Dusti)

Old German, meaning 'brave warrior'. Singer Dusty Springfield was a 1960s star.

E

Girls' names

Eadlin
(alt. Eadlinn, Eadlyn, Eadlen, Edlin)
Anglo-Saxon, meaning 'royalty'. Can also be a nickname for Adeline.

Earla
English, meaning 'leader'. Also a variation of the German name Herlinde, meaning 'shield'.

Eartha
English, meaning 'earth'. Singer Eartha Kitt was best known for her hit 'Santa Baby'.

Easter
From the festival of the same name.

Ebba
English, meaning 'fortress of riches'. One of the Top 10 names for baby girls in Sweden.

Ebony
(alt. Eboni)
Latin, meaning 'deep black wood'.

Echo
Greek, meaning 'reflected sound'. From the mythological nymph of the same name.

Eda
(alt. Edda)
English, meaning 'wealthy and happy'. An ancient goddess of time and wealth.

Edelmira
Spanish, meaning 'admired for nobility'. Feminine form of Edelmiro.

Eden
Hebrew, meaning 'pleasure'. In the Bible, the Garden of Eden was humankind's first home on Earth.

Edina
Scottish, meaning 'from Edinburgh'. Jennifer Saunders's character in TV hit Absolutely Fabulous was named Edina Monsoon.

Edith
(alt. Edyth; abbrev. Edie)

English, meaning 'prosperity through battle'. Pulitzer Prize-winner Edith Wharton is the author of *The Age of Innocence*. Actor Edie Falco starred in *The Sopranos*.

Edna
Hebrew, meaning 'enjoyment'. Australian comedian Barry Humphries is best known for his alter ego Dame Edna Everage.

Edrea
English, meaning 'wealthy and powerful'. Edrea Vorsal was a soprano opera singer.

Edris
(alt. Edriss, Edrys)

Anglo-Saxon, meaning 'prosperous ruler'. Sometimes used as a female form of Idris.

Edwina
English, meaning 'wealthy friend'. Edwina Currie was a controversial British politician.

Effie
Greek, meaning 'pleasant speech'. Effie Trinket is a key character in the 'Hunger Games' trilogy, known for her outrageous fashion sense.

Eglantine
French, from the shrub of the same name covered in tiny roses.

Eibhlín
Irish Gaelic, meaning 'shining and brilliant'. Eibhlín Dubh Ní Chonaill was an Irish poet and noblewoman.

Eileen
Irish, meaning 'shining and brilliant'. English version of Eibhlín, and often associated with the song 'Come on Eileen' by Dexys Midnight Runners.

Ekaterina
(alt. Ekaterini)

Slavic, meaning 'pure'.

Elaine
(alt. Elaina, Elayne)

French, meaning 'bright, shining light'. Singer and performer Elaine Paige is a star of West End musical theatre.

Elba
Italian, from the island of the same name.

Elberta
English, meaning 'highborn'.

Eldora
Spanish, meaning 'covered with gold'. Eldora is also the name of a small 'ghost' town in Florida, USA, which has remained uninhabited for over 100 years.

Eldoris
(alt. Eldoriss, Eldorys)

Greek, meaning 'woman of the sea'. Usually found as a variation of Doris.

Eleanor

(alt. Elana, Elena, Elanor, Eleanora)

Greek, meaning 'light'. Queen Eleanor of Aquitaine was married to England's King Henry II, and one of the most influential, wealthy and powerful women of medieval times.

Electra

(alt. Elektra)

Greek, meaning 'shining'. Also a character from an ancient Greek myth. In psychology, Electra is the female counterpart of Oedipus.

Elfrida

(alt. Elfrieda)

English, meaning 'elf power'. Elfrida Andrée was a nineteenth-century composer and conductor, and the first female organist to be recognised in Sweden.

Eliana

(alt. Eliane)

Hebrew, meaning 'Jehovah is God'. Becoming increasingly popular in the UK and elsewhere, thanks to the growing trend for names for girls ending in -a.

Elise

(alt. Elisa, Elissa)

French, meaning 'my vow to God'. Commonly associated with Beethoven's 'Für Elise', a piano solo.

Elizabeth

(alt. Elisabet, Elisabeth, Elizabella, Elizabelle, Elsbeth, Elspeth, Elisha; abbrev. Beth, Eliza, Libby, Liz, Lizzie, Lizzy)

Hebrew, meaning 'consecrated to God'. Two queens of England have been named this: Queen Elizabeth I ruled England from 1558 to 1603, and Queen Elizabeth II has been on the throne since 1952. Enduringly popular, especially with its many variant and shortened forms including Beth, Lizzie and Libby.

Elke

German, meaning 'nobility'. A reasonably popular name in Germany.

Ella

German, meaning 'completely'. Now becoming a name in its own right, Ella is traditionally a shortened version of Eleanor, Elizabeth and Ellen.

Elle

French, meaning 'she'. Elle Macpherson was one of the original supermodels in the 1980s, and known as 'The Body'.

Ellema

(alt. Ellemah, Elema, Ellemma, Elemah)

Swahili, meaning 'dairy farmer' or 'milking a cow'.

Ellen

(alt. Elin, Eline, Ellyn)

Greek, meaning 'shining'. Ellen DeGeneres is a popular actor and TV host.

Ellice

(alt. Elyse)

Greek, meaning 'the Lord is God'.

Ellie
(alt. Elie)

Shortened form of Eleanor which can be used in its own right. A popular shortened form for many years. Singer and Brit Award winner Ellie Goulding is actually an Elena.

Elma
(alt. Elna)

Latin, meaning 'soul'. Elma Napier was the first woman to be elected to any Caribbean parliament, in 1940.

Elmira
(alt. Elmyra)

Arabic, meaning 'aristocratic lady'. Elmyra Duff is one of a host of characters on the cartoon *Tiny Toons*.

Elodie

French, meaning 'marsh flower'. Élodie Bouchez-Bangalter is a French actor.

Eloise
(alt. Elois, Eloisa, Elouise)

French, meaning 'renowned in battle'. Also a shortened version and English spelling of French name Héloïse.

Elsa
(alt. Else, Elsie)

Hebrew, meaning 'consecrated to God'. Elsa the Snow Queen is one of the lead characters in Disney's *Frozen*.

Elva

Irish, meaning 'noble'. Also the name of a British sports car manufacturer.

Elvina

English, meaning 'noble friend'. Also an ancient place name.

Elvira
(alt. Elvera)

Spanish, from the ancient city of the same name. Commonly associated with the 1980s film *Elvira, Mistress of the Dark*.

Ember
(alt. Embry)

English, meaning 'spark'. Sometimes used as a shortened version of, or instead of, the name September.

Emerald

English, meaning 'green gemstone'.

Emery
(alt. Emory)

German, meaning 'ruler of work'.

Emiko
(alt. Emuko)

Japanese, meaning 'pretty child'. Popular name for girls in Japan.

Emilia

Latin, meaning 'rival, eager'. British actor Emilia Clarke plays lead character Daenerys Targaryen in *Game of Thrones*.

Emily

(alt. Emalee, Emelie, Emely, Emilee, Emili, Emilie, Emlyn)

Latin, meaning 'rival, eager'. Emily Dickinson is one of the most well-known poets of the nineteenth century. A very popular name choice in recent years.

Emma

German, meaning 'embraces everything'. The title character of Jane Austen's novel. Acxtor Emma Watson starred as Hermione in the 'Harry Potter' films and has been linked with fair trade fashion.

Emmanuelle

Hebrew, meaning 'God is with us'. Female form of Emanuel.

Emmeline

(alt. Emmelina; abbrev. Emmy, Emmie, Emi)

German, meaning 'embraces everything' or 'industrious'. Emmeline Pankhurst was the leader of the Suffragettes, a political activist group in the UK that campaigned in the early twentieth century for women's right to vote.

Ena

Shortened form of Georgina, meaning 'farmer'. Ena Sharples was one of the original cast of characters on *Coronation Street*.

Enid

(alt. Eneida)

Welsh, meaning 'life spirit'. Enid Blyton was a hugely popular children's author, known for the *Noddy*, *Famous Five* and *Malory Towers* series, among others.

Enola

Native American, meaning 'solitary'.

Enya

Irish Gaelic, meaning 'fire'. Enya is an Irish singer and songwriter.

Eowyn

Fictional character from J.R.R. Tolkien's *Lord of the Rings* trilogy. Eowyn was a noblewoman who disguised herself as a man in order to fight in a major battle.

Eranthe

Greek, meaning 'delicate like the spring'.

Erica

(alt. Ericka, Erika)

Scandinavian, meaning 'ruler forever'. Also a flowering plant similar to heather.

Erin

(alt. Eryn)

Irish Gaelic, meaning 'from the isle to the west'. Used to be a romanticised name for Ireland. Erin Brockovich is an American housewife turned environmental activist, played by Julia Roberts in the film of the same name.

Eris

Greek, from the mythological goddess. Eris is responsible for chaos, strife and discord.

Erlinda

Hebrew, meaning 'spirited'. Erlinda Cortes was a popular actor after World War II.

Erma

German, meaning 'universal'. Erma Franklin, the sister of soul legend Aretha Franklin, was an American gospel singer.

Ermine

French, meaning 'weasel'. The white winter fur of a stoat is known as ermine.

Erna

English, meaning 'sincere'. Erna was a character in Norse mythology.

Ernestine
(alt. Ernestina)

English, meaning 'sincere'. Ernestine Gilbreth Carey was the co-author of *Cheaper by the Dozen*, the novel upon which the popular films of the same name were based.

Esme

French, meaning 'esteemed'. Esme Cullen is a key character in the *Twilight* series.

Esmeralda

Spanish, meaning 'emerald'. Esmeralda is the female protagonist in *The Hunchback of Notre Dame*.

Esperanza

Spanish, meaning 'hope'. Popular name for girls in Spain.

Estelle
(alt. Estela, Estell, Estella)

French, meaning 'star'. British R&B singer Estelle is known by her first name only.

Esther
(alt. Esta, Ester, Etha, Ethna, Ethne)

Persian, meaning 'star'. Esther is a Jewish and Persian queen mentioned in the Bible.

Eternity

Latin, meaning 'forever'.

Ethel
(alt. Ethyl)

English, meaning 'noble'. Ethel Merman was an enormously popular American actor and singer, a star of musical theatre.

Etinia
(alt. Eteniah, Etene, Eteniya)

Native American, meaning 'prosperous'.

Etta
(alt. Etter, Ettie)

Shortened form of Henrietta, meaning 'ruler of the house'. Etta James was a singer-songwriter known for her blues and soul records.

Eudora

Greek, meaning 'generous gift'.

Eugenia
(alt. *Eugenie*)

Greek, meaning 'well born'. Also a type of flowering plant. Princess Eugenie is a granddaughter of Queen Elizabeth II.

Eulalia
(alt. *Eula, Eulah, Eulalie*)

Greek, meaning 'sweet-speaking'. St Eulalia was a Spanish virgin who was martyred for her faith.

Eunice
Greek, meaning 'victorious'. Eunice Kennedy Shriver was John F. Kennedy's sister and the founder of the Special Olympics.

Euphemia
Greek, meaning 'favourable speech'. Great Martyr Euphemia was killed for her Christian faith.

Eva
Hebrew, meaning 'life'. Eva Perón, the First Lady of Argentina from 1946 to 1952, was the inspiration for the musical *Evita*.

Evadne
Greek, meaning 'pleasing one'. Found frequently in Greek mythology.

Evangeline
(alt. *Evangelina*)

Greek, meaning 'good news'. The very first 'musical comedy' was called *Evangeline*, and it premiered in 1874.

Evanthe
Greek, meaning 'good flower'. Occasionally used as an alternative to names Eve, Eva and Evelyn.

Eve
(alt. *Evie*)

Hebrew, meaning 'life'. Found in the Bible.

Evelina
(alt. *Evelia*)

German, meaning 'hazelnut'. Its popularity was at its peak in the late eighteenth century, after a novel called *Evelina* by Fanny Burney was published in 1778.

Evelyn
(alt. *Evalyn, Evelin, Eveline, Evelyne*)

German, meaning 'hazelnut'. Used as a name for girls and boys equally. Dame Evelyn Glennie is a multi-award winning Scottish virtuoso percussionist, despite being profoundly deaf.

Everly
(alt. *Everleigh, Everley*)

English, meaning 'grazing meadow'.

Evette
French, meaning 'yew wood'. Often used as a spelling variation of Yvette.

Evonne
(alt. *Evon*)

French, meaning 'yew wood'. Evonne Goolagong was a women's tennis legend in the 1970s.

Girls' names

Fabia
(alt. *Fabiana, Fabienne, Fabiola, Fabriana*)
Latin, meaning 'one who grows beans'. Originally an old Roman name.

Fabrizia
Italian, meaning 'works with her hands'. Also the name of an Italian town.

Fahari
Swahili, meaning 'splendour'. Can also mean 'magnificent'.

Faith
English, meaning 'loyalty'. Famous Faiths include singers Faith Hill and Faith Evans.

Faiza
Arabic, meaning 'victorious'. The first ever British Muslim superhero to be created by Marvel comics was Faiza Hussain, codenamed Excalibur.

Fallon
Irish Gaelic, meaning 'descended from a ruler'.

Fanny
(alt. *Fannie*)
Latin, meaning 'from France'. Extremely popular name in the eighteenth and nineteenth centuries. The protagonist of Jane Austen's *Mansfield Park* was Fanny Price.

Farica
German, meaning 'peaceful ruler'. A female form of Frederick.

Farrah
English, meaning 'fair haired', and Arabic, meaning 'joy'. American actor Farrah Fawcett was one of TV's original *Charlie's Angels*.

Fatima
Arabic, meaning 'baby's nurse'. Popular choice for girls in Muslim communities.

Faustine

Latin, meaning 'fortunate'. Female form of Faustinus.

Fawn

French, meaning 'young deer'.

Fay
(alt. Fae, Faye)

French, meaning 'fairy'. Bestselling author Fay Weldon has written more than 30 books.

Fayola
(alt. Fayolah, Fayeena)

Swahili, meaning 'walks with honour'. Can also mean 'lucky'.

Felicia
(alt. Felicity, Felecia, Felice, Felicita, Felisha)

Latin, meaning 'lucky and happy'. Actor Felicia Day starred in *Buffy the Vampire Slayer*. Felicity Kendall became a household name after her role in 1970s comedy series *The Good Life*.

Fenella

Irish Gaelic, meaning 'white shoulder'. Actor Fenella Fielding is known for her husky voice and sensual image.

Fenia

Scandinavian, from the mythological giantess of the same name.

Fennel

Latin, name of a herb. Also a boys' name.

Fern
(alt. Fearne, Ferne, Ferrin)

English, from the plant of the same name.

Fernanda

German, meaning 'peace and courage'. A popular name in Brazil and Mexico.

Ffion
(alt. Fion)

Irish Gaelic, meaning 'fair and pale'. Currently among the Top 25 names in Wales for baby girls.

Fia

Italian, meaning 'flame'. Also used as a nickname for Fiona.

Fifi

Hebrew, meaning 'Jehovah increases'. Famous Fifis include British children's TV character *Fifi and the Flowertots* and Fifi Trixibelle, eldest daughter of Bob Geldof and Paula Yates.

Filomena

Greek, meaning 'loved one'. Sometimes used as an alternative spelling to Philomena.

Finlay
(alt. Finley)

Irish Gaelic, meaning 'fair-haired courageous one'. More commonly used as a name for boys.

Finola
(alt. Fionnula)

Irish Gaelic, meaning 'white shoulder'. British actor Finola Hughes appears regularly on American TV, having featured in several soap operas.

Fiona

Scottish, meaning 'fair and pale'. The name was actually invented by poet James Macpherson in the eighteenth century. Famous Fionas include TV presenter Fiona Bruce and *Shrek* character Princess Fiona.

Fiora

Irish Gaelic, meaning 'fair and pale'. Sometimes used as an alternative to Fiona.

Fiorella

Italian, meaning 'little flower'. Feminine form of the Italian boys' name Fiorello.

Flanna
(alt. Flannery)

Irish Gaelic, meaning 'russet hair' or 'red hair'.

Flavia

Latin, meaning 'yellow hair'. Popular name in both ancient and modern literature, but rarely used for baby girls in the UK. Flavia Cacace was an Italian professional dancer on *Strictly Come Dancing*.

Names of poets

Amy (Lowell)

Anne (Sexton)

Carol Ann (Duffy)

Charlotte (Smith)

Emily (Dickinson)

Fleur (Adcock)

Gwyneth (Lewis)

Pam (Ayres)

Ruth (Padel)

Sylvia (Plath)

Wendy (Cope)

Fleur

French, meaning 'flower'. Fleur Delacour is a character in the 'Harry Potter' series.

Flora

Latin, meaning 'flower'. Flora was one of the fairy godmothers (the red one) in Disney's *Sleeping Beauty*.

Florence
(alt. Florencia, Florene, Florine; abbrev. Florrie, Flossie, Floy, Flo)

Latin, meaning 'in bloom'. Also an Italian city.

Florida

Latin, meaning 'flowery'. Also a state in the USA.

Fraisine

(alt. Fraise)

French, meaning 'strawberry'.

Frances

(alt. Francine, Francis; abbrev. Fran, Frankie, Frannie)

Latin, meaning 'from France'. Famous Franceses include actor Frances McDormand, author Frances Trollope and playwright Frances Hodgson Burnett.

Francesca

(alt. Franchesca, Francisca; abbrev. Fran, Frankie, Frannie)

Latin, meaning 'from France'. Francesca Simon is the author of the 'Horrid Henry' children's book series.

Freda

(alt. Freeda, Freida, Frida, Frieda)

German, meaning 'peaceful'. Frida Kahlo was a Mexican artist known for her self-portraits and heavy eyebrows.

Frederica

German, meaning 'peaceful ruler'. A popular name for European princesses, it has been used nearly 20 times since the seventeenth century.

Freya

Old Nordic, meaning 'lady'.

Fuchsia

German, from the flower of the same name. Fuchsia Dunlop is a renowned British chef who specialises in Chinese food.

Fumiko

Japanese, meaning 'little friend' or 'beautiful child'.

Girls' names

Gabrielle
(alt. Gabriel, Gabriela, Gabriella; abbrev. Gabby, Gabbi)
Hebrew, meaning 'heroine of God'. Gabriella Wilde is a rising star British actor. Gabby Logan is a high-profile female TV sports presenter.

Gadara
Armenian, meaning 'mountain's peak'. The ancient town of Gadara is situated in northern Jordan.

Gaia
(alt. Gaea)
Greek, meaning 'the earth'. In ancient Greece, Gaia was the Greek Mother Goddess and the most important.

Gail
(alt. Gale, Gayla, Gayle)
Hebrew, meaning 'my father rejoices'. Badminton player Gail Emms represented England at international level for many years.

Gala
French, meaning 'festive merrymaking'. Used more commonly in Spanish-speaking communities.

Galiena
German, meaning 'high one'.

Galina
Russian, meaning 'shining brightly'. Feminine form of Galen.

Garnet
(alt. Garnett)
English, meaning 'red gemstone'.

Gay
(alt. Gaye)
French, meaning 'glad and lighthearted'. Rarely used in recent years.

Gaynor
Welsh, meaning 'white and smooth'.

Gemini

Greek, meaning 'twins'. One of the signs of the zodiac.

Gemma

Italian, meaning 'precious stone'. Bond girl Gemma Arterton was born in the 1980s, when Gemma was at its most popular.

Gene

Greek, meaning 'well born'. More commonly used for boys.

Genesis

Greek, meaning 'beginning'.

Geneva
(alt. Genevra)

French, meaning 'juniper tree'. Also the name of the Swiss city.

Genevieve
(abbrev. Genie)

German, meaning 'white wave'. St Genevieve is said to have saved Paris.

Georgette

French, meaning 'farmer'. Georgette Heyer was an author of historical romance novels.

Georgia
(alt. Georgiana, Georgianna, Georgie)

Greek, meaning 'farmer'. Also the name of the European country and a state in the USA.

Georgina
(alt. Georgene, Georgine, Giorgina)

Greek, meaning 'farmer'. The name's popularity was at its peak during the 1980s. Georgina was the spirited character in Enid Blyton's Famous Five books, who insisted on being referred to as George.

Geraldine
(abbrev. Geri, Gerri, Gerry)

German, meaning 'spear ruler'. Spice Girls singer Geri Halliwell's full name is Geraldine.

Gerda

Nordic, meaning 'shelter'. Gerda is the female protagonist in Hans Christian Andersen's Snow Queen.

Germaine

French, meaning 'from Germany'. Germaine Greer is the Australian author and activist who lives mostly in the UK.

Gertrude
(abbrev. Gertie)

German, meaning 'strength of a spear'. Gertrude Stein was an influential nineteenth-century American author. One of the earliest animated cartoon films was called Gertie the Dinosaur, made in 1914.

Ghislaine

French, meaning 'pledge'. Believed to have derived from Giselle.

Gia
(alt. Ghia)

Italian, meaning 'God is gracious'. Often used by itself, or as a shortened form of Gianna.

Gianina
(alt. Giana)

Hebrew, meaning 'God's graciousness'. Sometimes associated with the town of Ioannina in Greece.

Gigi
(alt. Giget)

Shortened form of Georgina, meaning 'farmer'. Also the name of a successful 1958 musical film.

Gilda

English, meaning 'gilded'. The name of Rigoletto's daughter in Verdi's opera *Rigoletto*.

Gilia

Hebrew, meaning 'joy of the Lord'. Also the name of a genus of flowering plants.

Gillian
(abbrev. Gill, Gilly, Gillie)

Latin, meaning 'youthful'. Famous Gillians include actor Gillian Anderson and children's author Gillian Cross.

Gina
(alt. Geena, Gena)

Shortened form of Regina, meaning 'queen', often used in its own right. Bestselling author Gina Ford has published nine books on the subject of babies and bringing up children.

Ginger

Latin, from the spicy root of the same name. Ginger Rogers was an Oscar-winning American singer, dancer and actor, best known for dancing with Fred Astaire. Her real first name was Virginia.

Ginny

Shortened form of Virginia, meaning 'virgin'. Made popular by the character of Ginny Weasley in the 'Harry Potter' series.

Giovanna

Italian, meaning 'God is gracious'. The English equivalent is Joanna or Jane.

Giselle
(alt. Gisela, Gisele, Giselle, Gisselle)

German, meaning 'pledge'. *Giselle* is the name of a romantic ballet. Gisele Bündchen is a Brazilian supermodel and actor.

Gita
(alt. Geeta)

Sanskrit, meaning 'song'. The *Bhagavad Gita* is a 700-verse Hindu scripture.

Giulia
(alt. Giuliana)

Italian, meaning 'youthful'. The Italian form of the name Julia.

Gladys
(alt. Gladyce)

Welsh, meaning 'lame'. Singer Gladys Knight is known as the 'Empress of Soul'.

Glenda

Welsh, meaning 'fair and good'.
A variation of Glenna and Glynda.
Glenda Jackson is a British actor
turned politician.

Glenna
(alt. Glennie)

Irish Gaelic, meaning 'glen'. Feminine
form of Glenn.

Gloria
(alt. Glory)

Latin, meaning 'glory'. There have
been many famous Glorias including
singers Gloria Estefan and Gloria
Gaynor.

Less common three-syllable names

Cassandra	Jessamy
Dolores	Julia
Gloria	Marilyn
Harriet	Miranda
Imogen	Nigella

Glynda
(alt. Glinda)

Welsh, meaning 'fair'. The good
witch in the *Wizard of Oz*.

Glynis

Welsh, meaning 'small glen'. The
first Olympic gold medallist of the
heptathlon was Australian athlete
Glynis Nunn.

Golda
(alt. Goldia, Goldie)

English, meaning 'gold'. Golda Meir
was the prime minister of Israel from
1969 to 1974.

Grace
(alt. Graça, Gracie, Gracin, Grayce)

Latin, meaning 'grace'. Film actor
Grace Kelly became Princess Grace
of Monaco. Grace Darling was an
English lighthouse keeper's daughter,
famous for her part in the rescue of
survivors from a shipwreck.

Gráinne
(alt. Grania)

Irish Gaelic, meaning 'love'.

Gratia
(alt. Grasia)

Latin, meaning 'blessing'. Gratia was
the ancient Greek goddess of charm,
beauty and fertility, amongst other
things.

Greer
(alt. Grier)

Latin, meaning 'alert and watchful'.

Gregoria

Latin, meaning 'alert'. Empress
Gregoria was a key figure in the
Byzantine empire.

Greta
(alt. Gretel)

Greek, meaning 'pearl'. Gretel is
the name of the female protagonist
in the fairy tale Hansel and Gretel.
Greta also refers to a genus of
butterfly.

Gretchen

German, meaning 'pearl'. Actor Gretchen Mol is known for her role in *Boardwalk Empire*.

Griselda

(alt. Griselle)

German, meaning 'grey fighting maid'. Nicknames include Zelda and Selda.

Grytha

English, meaning 'fiery'. Denmark's Queen Grytha ruled during the fifth century.

Gudrun

Scandinavian, meaning 'battle'. Key recurring figure in Norse and Germanic literature.

Guinevere

Welsh, meaning 'white and smooth'. The queen in Arthurian legend.

Gwen

Shortened form of Gwenda or Gwendolyn, as well as a name in its own right. Gwen Stefani is a singer-songwriter and member of pop group No Doubt.

Gwenda

Welsh, meaning 'fair and good'. As well as being a name in its own right, Gwenda can also be a shortened form of Gwendolyn or Gwyneth.

Gwendolyn

(alt. Gwendolen, Gwenel)

Welsh, meaning 'fair bow'. Gwendolyn Brooks was a Pulitzer Prize-winning poet.

Gwyneth

(alt. Gwynneth, Gwynyth; abbrev. Gwyn, Gwynn)

Welsh, meaning 'happiness'. Actor and author Gwyneth Paltrow is mum to Apple and Moses.

Gypsy

English, meaning 'of the Roma tribe'.

Girls' names

Habibah
(alt. Habiba)

Arabic, meaning 'beloved'.

Hadassah

Hebrew, meaning 'myrtle tree'. Usually associated with the character of Esther in the Bible, whose Hebrew name is Hadassah.

Hadley

English, meaning 'heather meadow'. Hadley Freeman is an author and journalist.

Hadria

Latin, meaning 'from Hadria'. Also the name of two ancient cities in Italy.

Hala

Arabic, meaning 'halo'. Also the name of a female weather demon in Serbian and Bulgarian mythology.

Halima
(alt. Halimah, Halina)

Arabic, meaning 'gentle'. The prophet Mohammad's foster mother was called Halimah.

Hallie
(alt. Halle, Halley)

German, meaning 'ruler of the home or estate'. Oscar-winning actor Halle Berry was originally given the name Maria Halle.

Hannah
(alt. Haana, Hana, Hanna)

Hebrew, meaning 'grace'. Famous Hannahs include Hannah Cockroft, the wheelchair athlete and world record holder, and Hannah Montana, of the musical comedy series.

Harika

Turkish, meaning 'superior one'. In India, the name is associated with Parvati, the Hindu goddess of power and creation.

Harley
(alt. Harlene)

English, meaning 'the long field'.

Harlow

English, meaning 'army hill'.

Harmony

Latin, meaning 'harmony'.

Harper

English, meaning 'minstrel'. Harper Lee is the author of classic novel *To Kill a Mockingbird*. Harper Seven is the name of David and Victoria Beckham's fourth child.

Harriet

(alt. Harriett, Harriette; abbrev. Hattie)

German, meaning 'ruler of the home or estate'. Famous Harriets include activist Harriet Tubman, author Harriet Beecher Stowe, and politician Harriet Harman.

Haven

English, meaning 'a place of sanctuary'.

Hayden

(alt. Haydn)

Old English, meaning 'hedged valley'. Used as a boys' name as well as a girls' name.

Hayley

(alt. Haelee, Haely, Hailee, Hailey, Hailie, Haleigh, Haley, Hali, Halie, Haylee, Hayleigh, Haylie)

English, meaning 'hay meadow'. The name became popular in the 1980s after the success of child actor Hayley Mills, but is less common now.

Hazel

(alt. Hazle)

English, from the tree of the same name. Famous Hazels include children's author Hazel Hutchins, singer Hazel O'Connor and politician Hazel Blears.

Heather

English, from the flower of the same name. Famous Heathers include actors Heather Graham and Heather Locklear, and model Heather Mills.

Heaven

English, meaning 'everlasting bliss'.

Hedda

German, meaning 'warfare'. Also the name of the protagonist in the play *Hedda Gabler*, by Henrik Ibsen.

Hedwig

German, meaning 'warfare and strife'. Although the name stems from two different St Hedwigs, it is now most associated with Harry Potter's owl!

Heidi

(alt. Heidy)

German, meaning 'nobility'. One of the top-selling children's books of all time is the Swiss novel *Heidi*, by Johanna Spyri.

Helen

(alt. Halen, Helena, Helene, Hellen)

Greek, meaning 'light'. In ancient Greek mythology Helen of Troy was considered to be the most beautiful woman in the world.

Helga

German, meaning 'holy and sacred'. Extemely popular name in Germany and Norway.

Helia

Greek, meaning 'sun'.

Héloïse

French, meaning 'renowned in war'. Hélöise d'Argenteuil was a nun and writer known for having an affair with the theologian Peter Abelard in the twelfth century.

Henrietta
(alt. Henriette)

German, meaning 'ruler of the house'. Usually associated with Henrietta Maria of France, who was queen consort to Charles I.

Hephzibah
(alt. Hefzibah)

Hebrew, meaning 'my delight is in her'. Found in the Bible.

Hera

Greek, meaning 'queen'. Hera is the Queen of the Gods, and the goddess of marriage, women and birth in ancient Greek mythology.

Hermia
(alt. Hermina, Hermine, Herminia)

Greek, meaning 'messenger'. Also the name of a character in Shakespeare's play *A Midsummer Night's Dream*.

Hermione

Greek, meaning 'earthly'. Now inseparable from the main female character in the 'Harry Potter' series.

Hero

Greek, meaning 'brave one of the people'.

Hertha

English, meaning 'earth'. Also another name for Nerthus, the goddess of fertility in ancient German mythology.

Hesper
(alt. Hesperia)

Greek, meaning 'evening star'.

Hester
(alt. Hestia)

Greek, meaning 'star'. Also the name of the protagonist in *The Scarlet Letter* by Nathaniel Hawthorne.

Hettie

Shortened form of Hester or Henrietta, also used as a name in its own right.

Hilary
(alt. Hillary)

Greek, meaning 'cheerful and happy'. Also a boys' name. Famous Hilarys include US politician Hillary Rodham Clinton and actor Hilary Swank.

Hilda
(alt. Hildur)

German, meaning 'battle woman'. Famous Hildas include the first female pilot to hold a licence, Hilda Hewlett, the *Coronation Street* character Hilda Ogden and author Hilda Doolittle – known as H.D.

Hildegarde
(alt. Hildegard)
German, meaning 'battle stronghold'.

Hildred
German, meaning 'battle counsellor'. More commonly used as a name for boys.

Hilma
German variant of Wilhelmina, meaning 'helmet'. The female equivalent of Hilmar or Hilmer.

Hirkani
Sanskrit, meaning 'like a diamond'.

Hollis
English, meaning 'near the holly bushes'.

Holly
(alt. Holli, Hollie)
English, from the tree of the same name. Famous Hollys include TV presenter Holly Willoughby and actor Holly Hunter.

Honey
English, from the word 'honey'.

Honor
(alt. Honour, Honora, Honoria)
Latin, meaning 'woman of honour'. Actor Honor Blackman played the Bond girl Pussy Galore.

Hope
English, meaning 'desire and expectation'. One of three virtues in most religions: faith, hope and charity. Hope Powell represented England in football for many years before becoming the England Women's coach for more than a decade.

Hortense
(alt. Hortencia, Hortensia)
Latin, meaning 'of the garden'. Also the name of one of Napoleon Bonaparte's stepdaughters, and a character in Charles Dickens's novel *Bleak House*.

Hudson
English, meaning 'adventurous'.

Hulda
German, meaning 'loved one'. Also the name of a prophetess in the Bible.

Hyacinth
Greek, from the flower of the same name. Hyacinth was also a hero in ancient Greek mythology.

Girls' names

Ianthe
(alt. Iantha)

Greek, meaning 'purple flower'. Also the name of a character in ancient Greek mythology.

Ichigo

Japanese, meaning 'strawberry'.

Ida

English, meaning 'prosperous'. Also the name of several characters in both ancient Greek mythology and the Hindu religion.

Idella
(alt. Idell)

English, meaning 'prosperous'. Idella Purnell was an academic and author of children's books, best known in the 1930s and 1940s.

Idona

Nordic, meaning 'renewal'.

Ignacia
(alt. Iggy)

Latin, meaning 'ardent' or 'burning'. The female variation of Ignatius.

Ila

French, meaning 'island'. In Hindu mythology Ila is a character able to change sex at will.

Ilana

Hebrew, meaning 'tree'. Ilana Vered is a classical pianist known for her work with dozens of major international orchestras.

Ilaria

Italian, meaning 'cheerful'. Ilaria has featured as a Top 10 name for girls in Italy in recent years. The English equivalent is Hilary.

Ilene

American, meaning 'light'. Ilene Woods was a voice actor known for being the voice of Cinderella in Disney's film of the same name.

Iliana
(alt. Ileana)

Greek, meaning 'Trojan'. Actor Ileana D'Cruz is a star in Bollywood films.

Ilona

Hungarian, meaning 'light'. Also the name of the Queen of the Fairies in Magyar mythology.

Ilsa

German, meaning 'pledged to God'. Also the name of Ingrid Bergman's character in the film *Casablanca*.

Ima

German, meaning 'embraces everything'. Ima Hogg was an influential philanthropist in the early twentieth century.

Iman

Arabic, meaning 'faith'. The Somali supermodel known simply as Iman is also an entrepreneur and was married to David Bowie.

Imara

Hungarian, meaning 'great ruler'. Also the name of a genus of moths.

Imelda

German, meaning 'all-consuming fight'. Famous Imeldas include actor Imelda Staunton, politician Imelda Marcos and actor Anne Crawford, whose real name was Imelda.

Imogen
(alt. Imogene)

Latin, meaning 'last-born'. Famous Imogens include actors Imogen Stubbs and Imogen Hassall and singer-songwriter Imogen Heap.

Ina

Latin, meaning 'to make feminine'. Famous Inas include author and presenter Ina Garten and childbirth pioneer Ina May Gaskin.

Inaya

Arabic, meaning 'taking care'. Singer Inaya Day's voice features on many dancefloor house music classics.

India
(alt. Indie)

Hindi, from the country of the same name. India Knight is a British journalist and author.

Indiana

Latin, meaning 'from India'. Also the name of a state in the USA.

Indigo

Greek, meaning 'deep blue dye'. Also the name of one of the seven colours of the rainbow.

Indira
(alt. Inira)

Sanskrit, meaning 'beauty'. Indira Gandhi was the first and to date only female prime minister of India.

Inez
(alt. Ines)

Spanish, meaning 'pure'. Also a spelling variation of Agnes.

Inga
(alt. Inge, Ingeborg, Inger)
Scandinavian, meaning 'guarded by Ing'. Also the name of a type of tropical shrub and tree.

Ingrid
Scandinavian, meaning 'beautiful'. Actor Ingrid Bergman was known for her roles in *Casablanca*, *Notorious* and *Gaslight*.

Io
(alt. Eyo)
Greek, from the mythological priestess and heroine of the same name in ancient Greek mythology.

Ioanna
Greek, meaning 'grace'. Usually used as a spelling alternative to Joanna.

Iola
(alt. Iole)
Greek, meaning 'cloud of dawn'. The novel *Iola Leroy*, by Frances Harper, was one of the first novels published by a black female author.

Iolanthe
Greek, meaning 'violet flower'. Usually associated with the opera *Iolanthe* by Gilbert and Sullivan.

Iona
Greek, from the island of the same name. Also the name of a small island off the coast of Scotland.

Ione
Greek, meaning 'violet'. Also the name of a type of orchid.

Iorwen
Welsh, meaning 'fair'.

Iphigenia
Greek, meaning 'sacrifice'. Iphigenia was an ancient Greek victim of slaughter whose name became synonymous with strength and being the mother of strong children.

Ira
(alt. Iva)
Hebrew, meaning 'watchful'. More commonly used as a name for boys.

Irene
(alt. Irelyn, Irena, Irina, Irini)
Greek, meaning 'peace'.

Iris
Greek, meaning 'rainbow'. Also from the flower of the same name.

Irma
German, meaning 'universal'. Often associated with Irma Bunt, a Bond villainess.

Isabel
(alt. Isabela, Isabell, Isabella, Isabelle, Isabeth, Isobel, Izabella, Izabelle)
Spanish, meaning 'pledged to God'. Dozens of royals have been called Isabel or Isabella over the centuries, including Queen Isabella I of Spain, who financed Christopher Columbus' voyage to North America.

Isadora

Latin, meaning 'gift of Isis'. Isadora Duncan was a famed dancer at the turn of the twentieth century, whose life was made into the film *Isadora*.

Ishana

Sanskrit, meaning 'desire'. One of the names for Shiva in the Hindu faith.

Isis

From the ancient Egyptian goddess of motherhood, magic and fertility.

Isla
(alt. Isa, Isela, Isley)

Scottish Gaelic, meaning 'river'. Actor Isla Fischer was born in Oman to Scottish parents and was raised in Australia.

Isolde

Welsh, meaning 'fair lady'. Usually associated with the opera *Tristan und Isolde* by Richard Wagner.

Istas

Native American, meaning 'snow'. In Latin, istas also refers to the feminine form of 'that person'.

Ivana

Slavic, meaning 'Jehovah is gracious'. Model Ivana Trump is known for her former marriage to the 45th US President Donald Trump.

Ivette

Variation of Yvette, meaning 'yew wood'. This spelling is more commonly used in Spanish-speaking communities.

Ivonne

Variation of Yvonne, meaning 'yew wood'. This spelling is more commonly used in Spanish-speaking communities.

Ivory

Latin, meaning 'white as elephant tusks'.

Ivy

English, from the plant of the same name. Famous Ivys include elderly internet sensation Ivy Bean, the first British female lawyer, Ivy Williams, and children's author Ivy Wallace.

Ixia

Afrikaans, from the flower of the same name.

Girls' names

Jaamini
Hindi, meaning 'evening'.

Jacinda
(alt. Jacinta)
Spanish, meaning 'hyacinth'. Jacinda Ardern is the Prime Minister of New Zealand. Jacinda Barrett is an Australian-American model turned actor.

Jacqueline
(alt. Jacalyn, Jacklyn, Jaclyn, Jacquelin, Jacquelyn, Jacquline, Jaqlyn, Jaquelin, Jaqueline; abbrev. Jack, Jacky, Jackie, Jacque, Jacqui)
French, meaning 'he who supplants'. Famous Jacquelines include children's author Jacqueline Wilson, actor Jacqueline Bisset and cellist Jacqueline du Pré.

Jade
(alt. Jada, Jaida, Jayda, Jayde)
Spanish, meaning 'green stone'. Famous Jades include former reality TV star Jade Goody, athletes Jade Jones and Jade Johnson and designer Jade Jagger.

Jaden
(alt. Jadyn, Jaiden, Jaidyn, Jayden)
Hebrew, meaning 'Jehovah has heard'. More commonly used as a name for boys.

Jael
Hebrew, meaning 'mountain goat'. Also the name of a character in the Bible.

Jaime
(alt. Jaima, Jaimie, Jami, Jamie)
Spanish, meaning 'he who supplants'. Jamie is a common short form of James, more commonly used for boys.

Jamila

Arabic, meaning 'lovely'. Author Jamila Gavin is known for her children's books, most of which have an Indian influence.

Jan
(alt. Jana, Jann, Janna, Janae)

Hebrew, meaning 'the Lord is gracious'. In Arabic, the name Jan also means 'dear', and in Persian it means 'life'.

Jane
(alt. Jayne, Janie)

Feminine form of the Hebrew John, meaning 'the Lord is gracious'. A very popular name in the 1960s and 1970s but much less common now. Famous Janes include Tarzan's friend Jane and Henry VIII's third wife, Jane Seymour.

Janelle
(alt. Janel, Janell, Jenelle)

American, meaning 'the Lord is gracious'. A very popular name in the 1970s and 1980s in both America and Australia but less common now.

Janet
(alt. Janette)

Scottish, meaning 'the Lord is gracious'. Singer Janet Jackson is known for being part of the musical Jackson family, as well as a performer in her own right.

Janice
(alt. Janis)

American, meaning 'the Lord is gracious'. Famous Janices include rower Janice Meek, former supermodel Janice Dickinson and the character of Janice Battersby in *Coronation Street*.

Janine
(alt. Janeen)

English, meaning 'the Lord is gracious'. Famous Janines include the character of Janine Butcher in *EastEnders*, the character of Janine in *Friends* and actor Janine Turner.

Janoah
(alt. Janiya, Janiyah)

Hebrew, meaning 'quiet and calm'. Also used as a spelling alternative for Genoa.

January

Latin, meaning 'the first month'. Actor January Jones is known for her roles in *Mad Men*, *Unknown* and *X-Men: First Class*.

Jarita

Hindi-Sanskrit, meaning 'famous bird'. Usually associated with the bird character in the Hindu *Mahabharata*.

Jasmine
(alt. Jasmin, Jazim, Jazmine)

Persian, meaning 'jasmine flower'.

Jay

Latin, meaning 'jaybird'. Jays are colourful birds from the crow family, found throughout the world.

Jayna

Sanskrit, meaning 'bringer of victory'. More commonly used in Indian communitites.

Jean

(alt. Jeane, Jeanne)

Scottish, meaning 'the Lord is gracious'. Famous Jeans include actors Jean Harlow and Jean Marsh and author Jean Auel.

Jeana

(alt. Jeanna)

Latin, meaning 'queen'.

Jeanette

(alt. Jeannette, Janette; abbrev. Jeannie, Jeanie)

French, meaning 'the Lord is gracious'. Jeanette Winterson is a BAFTA-winning British author and journalist. The shortened form is commonly associated with the sitcom *I Dream of Jeannie*.

Jeanine

(alt. Jeannine)

Latin, meaning 'the Lord is gracious'. Jeanine Tesori is known for her musical theatre arrangements and compositions.

Jemima

Hebrew, meaning 'dove'. Jemima Khan is a writer and campaigner.

Jemma

English variant of Gemma, meaning 'precious stone'. Actor Jemma Redgrave is a fourth-generation member of the Redgrave acting dynasty.

Jena

Arabic, meaning 'little bird'. Actor Jena Malone starred in *Donnie Darko*, *Pride and Prejudice* and *The Hunger Games: Catching Fire*.

Jenna

Shortened form of Jennifer, meaning 'white and smooth'. The name was very popular in the 1980s, especially in the USA, and there are many actors of that era with the name.

Jennifer

(alt. Jenifer; abbrev. Jenny, Jennie, Jenni)

Cornish alternative to Guinevere, meaning 'white and smooth'. Famous Jennifers include actors Jennifer Lawrence and Jennifer Aniston and singer Jennifer Hudson.

Jerri

(alt. Jeri, Jerrie, Jerrie, Jerry)

German, meaning 'spear ruler'. Famous Jerries include actor Jerri Manthey, model Jerry Hall and pioneering South Pole physician Dr Jerri Nielsen.

Jerusha

Hebrew, meaning 'married'. Jerusha Hess and husband Jared Hess are filmmakers whose films include *Napoleon Dynamite*.

Jeryl

English, meaning 'spear ruler'. Jeryl Prescott is an American actor.

Jessa

Shortened form of Jessica, meaning 'He sees'. Jessa Gamble is an English-Canadian author and scientific researcher and Jessa Johansson is a leading character in *Girls*.

Jessamy

(alt. Jessame, Jessamine, Jessamyn)

Persian, meaning 'jasmine flower'. Usually associated with the children's book *Jessamy* by Barbara Sleigh.

Jessica

(alt. Jesica, Jesika, Jessika; abbrev. Jess, Jessi, Jessie, Jessye)

Hebrew, meaning 'He sees'. A popular name over several decades. Famous Jessicas include actors Jessica Alba and Jessica Lange and athlete Jessica Ennis. Famous Jessies include singer Jessie J.

Jesusa

Spanish, meaning 'mother of the Lord'. Also a shortened form of Jerusalem.

Jethetha

Hebrew, meaning 'princess'.

Jette

(alt. Jetta, Jettie)

Danish, meaning 'black as coal'. Also the name of a town in Belgium.

Jewel

(alt. Jewell)

French, meaning 'delight'. Singer-songwriter, producer and actor Jewel is professionally known just by her first name.

Jezebel

(alt. Jezabel, Jezabelle)

Hebrew, meaning 'pure and virginal'. Conversely, widely used as a term for 'bad women' after the misbehaving wife of a king in the Bible.

Jill

Latin, meaning 'youthful'. Famous Jills include actor Jill Clayburgh, presenter Jill Dando and children's author Jill Murphy.

Jillian

Latin, meaning 'youthful'. Often used as a spelling alternative to Gillian.

Jimena

Spanish, meaning 'heard'. Jimena Diaz was the ruler of Valencia in the twelfth century.

Jo

Shortened form of Joanna, meaning 'the Lord is gracious'. Famous Jos include supernanny Jo Frost, presenter Jo Coburn and athlete Jo Ankier.

Joan

Hebrew, meaning 'the Lord is gracious'. Famous Joans include St Joan of Arc, actor Joan Collins and comedian Joan Rivers.

Joanna

(alt. Joana, Joanie, Joann, Joanne, Johanna, Joni)

Hebrew, meaning 'the Lord is gracious'. Famous Joannas include author J.K. Rowling (real name Joanne) and actors Joanna Lumley and Joanna Page.

Jocasta

Italian, meaning 'lighthearted'. Jocasta was an influential character in ancient Greek mythology.

Jocelyn

(alt. Jauslyn, Jocelyne, Joscelin, Joslyn)
German, meaning 'cheerful'.

Jody

(alt. Jodee, Jodi, Jodie)
Shortened form of Judith, meaning 'Jewish'. Famous Jodys include actors Jodie Foster and Jody Lawrance and singer Jody Watley.

Joelle

(alt. Joela)
Hebrew, meaning 'Jehovah is the Lord'. Famous Joelles include teen singer Joelle and actor Joelle Carter.

Joie

French, meaning 'joy'.

Jolene

Contraction of Joanna and Darlene, meaning 'gracious darling'. Usually associated with the song 'Jolene' by Dolly Parton.

Jolie

(alt. Joely)
French, meaning 'pretty'.

Jordan

(alt. Jordana, Jordin, Jordyn)
Hebrew, meaning 'down-flowing'. Model and reality television star Katie Price is known by her professional name Jordan. Also used for boys.

Josephine

(alt. Josefina, Josephina; abbrev. Jo, Joss, Josie)
Hebrew, meaning 'Jehovah increases'. Famous Josephines include the first Empress of France, wife of Napoleon, pioneering actor Josephine Baker and mystery author Josephine Bell.

Jovita

(alt. Jovie)
Latin, meaning 'made glad'. St Jovita was a Christian martyr with her brother St Faustinus during the second century.

Joy

Latin, meaning 'joy'. Famous Joys include comedian Joy Behar, actor Joy Lauren and poet Joy Harjo.

Joyce

Latin, meaning 'joyous'. Famous Joyces include author Joyce Carol Oates and actors Joyce Blair and Joyce DeWitt.

Juanita

(alt. Juana)
Spanish, meaning 'the Lord is gracious'.

Jubilee

Hebrew, meaning 'horn of a ram'. Usually associated with the celebration of an anniversary, such as the Queen's Diamond Jubilee.

Judith
(alt. Judit; abbrev. Judi, Judie, Judy)

Hebrew, meaning 'Jewish'. Found in the Bible. Very popular in the 1940s and 1950s. Actor Judy Garland was the star of *The Wizard of Oz*.

Jules

French, meaning 'Jove's child'. Sometimes used as a variant of Julie or Julia but more commonly used as a name for boys.

Julia
(alt. Julie, Juli)

Latin, meaning 'youthful'. Famous Julias include actors Julia Roberts and Julia Sawalha and TV chef Julia Child, while famous Julies include three Golden Globe and BAFTA-winning actors: Julie Andrews, Julie Christie and Julie Walters.

Julianne
(alt. Juliana, Juliann, Julianne)

Latin, meaning 'youthful'. Oscar-nominated British-American actor Julianne Moore has starred in a string of blockbuster films and is also a children's author.

Juliet
(alt. Joliet, Juliette)

Latin, meaning 'youthful'. Usually associated with the heroine of Shakespeare's play *Romeo and Juliet*.

June
(alt. Juna)

Latin, after the month of the same name. Famous Junes include actor June Bland, singer June Carter Cash and presenter June Sarpong.

Juniper

Dutch, from the shrub of the same name, used for distilling the spirit gin.

Juno
(alt. Juneau)

Latin, meaning 'queen of heaven'. Juno was an ancient Roman Queen of the Gods, and the goddess of marriage and Rome.

Justice

English, meaning 'to deliver what is just'.

Justine
(alt. Justina)

Latin, meaning 'fair and righteous'. Famous Justines include singer Justine Frischmann and actors Justine Bateman and Justine Waddell.

Jørgina

Dutch, meaning 'farmer'. More commonly used as a spelling alternative for Georgina.

Girls' names

Kadenza
(alt. Kadence)
Latin, meaning 'with rhythm'.
More commonly used as a spelling
alternative for Cadenza.

Kadisha
Hebrew, meaning 'religious one'.

Kaitlin
(alt. Kaitlyn)
Greek, meaning 'pure'. Variant of
Caitlin that became popular, especially
in the USA, after the 1970s. Kaitlin
Doubleday is a Hollywood actor.

Kala
(alt. Kaela, Kaiala, Kaila)
Sanskrit, meaning 'black one'. Also
known for being the great ape that
saved Tarzan as a baby.

Kali
*(alt. Kailee, Kailey, Kaleigh, Kaley,
Kalie, Kalli, Kally, Kaylee, Kayleigh)*
Sanskrit, meaning 'black one'. Also
known in Hinduism as the Goddess
of Time and Change.

Kalila
Arabic, meaning 'beloved'.

Kalina
Slavic, meaning 'flower'.

Kalliope
(alt. Calliope)
Greek, meaning 'beautiful voice'.
From the muse of the same
name.

Kama
Sanskrit, meaning 'love'. Known in
Hinduism as one of the four goals
of life, kama refers to intellectual
fulfilment.

Kami
Japanese, meaning 'lord'.

Kamilla
(alt. Kamilah)
Slavic, meaning 'serving girl'. A
spelling alternative for Camilla.

Kana

Hawaiian, from the demi-god of the same name. In Hawaiian mythology Kana could take the form of a rope that could stretch from the island of Molokai to Hawaii.

Kanika

Swahili, meaning 'black cloth'. The stage name of Indian actor Divya Venkatasubramaniam.

Kara

Latin, meaning 'dear one'.

Karen

(alt. Karan, Karalyn, Karin, Karina, Karon, Karren; abbrev. Kari, Karrie)

Greek, meaning 'pure'. Very popular during the 1960s and 1970s in England. Famous Karens include comedian Karen Taylor, actor Karen Walker and musician Karen Carpenter. Kari is one of Saturn's moons.

Karimah

Arabic, meaning 'giving'. A spelling variation of Karima.

Karishma

(alt. Karisma)

Sanskrit, meaning 'miracle'. Both Karisma and Karishma are popular names in India, reflected in the number of Indian actors with the name.

Karla

German, meaning 'man'. A spelling variation for Carla.

Karly

(alt. Karlee, Karley, Karli)

German, meaning 'free man'. Has become popular in Scotland especially, including Karly Robertson the ice skater and Karly Ashworth from Big Brother.

Karlyn

German, meaning 'man'. Also a spelling variation of Carlin.

Karma

Hindi, meaning 'destiny'. Known as a principle of Buddhism where good deeds lead to a positive influence on a person's future and bad deeds lead to a bad influence.

Karol

(alt. Karolina, Karolyn)

Slavic, meaning 'little and womanly'. A spelling variation of Carol.

Kasumi

Japanese, meaning 'of the mist'.

Katarina

(alt. Katarine, Katerina, Katharina)

Greek, meaning 'pure'. Katarina was one of the first companions of Doctor Who.

Kate

(alt. Kat, Katie, Kathi, Kathie, Kathy, Kati, Katy)

Shortened form of Katherine, meaning 'pure'. Famous Kates include actor Kate Winslet, actor Kate Hudson and the current Duchess of Cambridge.

Katherine
(alt. Katharine, Katheryn, Kathrine, Kathryn; abbrev. Kathie, Kathy)
Greek, meaning 'pure'. A spelling variation for Catherine that became very popular earlier than some of the other K-variation spelling names.

Kathleen
(alt. Kathlyn)
Greek, meaning 'pure'. Very popular in the 1960s and so shared by many actors, politicans and scientists.

Katrina
(alt. Katina)
Greek, meaning 'pure'. More commonly used as a shortened version of Katherine.

Kaveri
Sanskrit, meaning 'sacred river'. Known for the large river that flows across India.

Kay
(alt. Kaye)
Shortened form of Katherine, meaning 'pure'. A popular name in both Kay and Kaye forms, in North America, Australia and England.

Kaya
Sanskrit, meaning 'nature', or Turkish, meaning 'rock'. Kaya also refers to a sweet coconut jam popular in Asia.

Kayla
(alt. Kaylah)
Greek, meaning 'pure'. Kayla Harrison won a gold medal in judo at the 2012 London Olympics.

Kayley
(alt. Kayley, Kayli)
American, meaning 'pure'. Also known as one of the main characters in *The Magic Sword: Quest for Camelot*.

Kaylin
American, meaning 'pure'. A spelling variation for Caylin.

Keary
Gaelic, meaning 'black-haired'. Also a boys' name.

Keeley
(alt. Keely)
Irish, meaning 'battle maid'. Actor Keeley Hawes is a popular star of British TV drama.

Keila
Hebrew, meaning 'citadel'.

Keira
Irish Gaelic, meaning 'dark'. A rise in popularity of the name followed the success of actor Keira Knightley.

Keisha
(alt. Keesha)
Arabic, meaning 'woman'. Keisha Castle-Hughes is an Australian actor.

Kelis
American, meaning 'beautiful'. Award-winning singer Kelis is known widely by her first name only.

Kelly
(alt. Keli, Kelley, Kelli, Kellie)

Irish Gaelic, meaning 'battle maid'. Famous Kellys include singer Kelly Clarkson, TV personality Kelly Osbourne and Olympic winning athlete Kelly Holmes.

Kelsey
(alt. Kelcee, Kelcie, Kelsea, Kelsi, Kelsie)

Old English, meaning 'victorious ship'. More popular in the USA, where it is the name of several cities and is used for both girls and boys.

Kendall
(alt. Kendal)

English, meaning 'the valley of the River Kent'. Also a place in Cumbria.

Kendra

English, meaning 'knowing'. Name of a character in *Buffy The Vampire Slayer*. Kendra Wilkinson is an American TV personality.

Kenna

Irish Gaelic, meaning 'handsome'.

Kennedy
(alt. Kenadee, Kennedi)

Irish Gaelic, meaning 'helmet head'. Also used as a boys' name.

Kenzie

Shortened form of Mackenzie, meaning 'son of the wise ruler'. Mackenzie is also commonly used as a boys' name.

Kerensa

Cornish, meaning 'love'. Also a variation on the name Karen.

Kerrigan

Irish, meaning 'black haired'.

Kerry
(alt. Keri, Kerri, Kerrie)

Irish, from the county of the same name. Used for both girls and boys.

Khadijah
(alt. Khadejah)

Arabic, meaning 'premature baby'. Khadija bint Khuwaylid was the first wife of Muhammad and is known as the 'Mother of Islam'.

Kiana
(alt. Kia, Kiana)

American, meaning 'fibre'. Kiana is an American TV personality known for her physical fitness and physical training videos.

Kiara

It is possible that the name could come from two sources – Irish 'ciar' meaning 'dark' or 'dark haired', or the Latin 'chiara', meaning 'light'.

Kiki

Spanish, meaning 'home ruler'. Also an American slang term for a party centred around gossip and laughter.

Kimana

Native American, meaning 'butterfly'.

Kimberly
(alt. Kimberleigh, Kimberley; abbrev. Kim)

Old English, meaning 'royal forest'. Famous Kimberlys include singers Kimberly Wyatt and Kimberley Walsh and rapper Kimberly 'Lil' Kim' Denise Jones. Famous Kims include TV personality Kim Kardashian, actor Kim Basinger and singer Kim Wilde.

Kingsley
(alt. Kinsley)

English, meaning 'king's meadow'. More commonly used as a boys' name.

Kinsey

English, meaning 'king's victory'.

Kira

Greek, meaning 'lady'.

Kiri

Maori, meaning 'tree bark'. Dame Kiri Te Kanawa is known for her opera singing career spanning over 40 years.

Kirsten
(alt. Kirstin; abbrev. Kirstie, Kirsty)

Scandinavian, meaning 'Christian'. Kirsten Dunst is a German-American actor, singer and model. Famous Kirsties include TV presenters Kirsty Young and Kirstie Allsopp and American actor Kirstie Alley.

Kitty
(alt. Kittie)

Shortened form of Katherine, meaning 'pure'. Can be used in its own right.

TV personality names

Alesha (Dixon)

Alex (Jones)

Caroline (Flack)

Cherry (Healey)

Christine (Bleakley)

Davina (McCall)

Emma (Willis)

Fearne (Cotton)

Holly (Willoughby)

Kirstie (Allsopp)

Lauren (Laverne)

Tess (Daly)

Kizzy

Hebrew, meaning the plant 'cassia'. Singer Kizzy Crawford sings in both English and Welsh.

Klara

Hungarian, meaning 'bright'. Commonly used in German-speaking communities.

Komal

Hindi, meaning 'soft and tender'. Most commonly used as a name for Indian boys.

Konstantina

Latin, meaning 'steadfast'. The female version of the male name Constantine.

Kora
(alt. Kori)

Greek, meaning 'maiden'. A spelling variation for Cora.

Kristen
(alt. Kristan, Kristin, Kristine, Krysten; abbrev. Kris, Krista, Kristi, Kristie, Kristy)

Greek, meaning 'Christian'. Actor Kristen Stewart is known for her roles in the *Twilight* films.

Kwanza
(alt. Kwanzaa)

Swahili, meaning 'beginning'. Also known for the week-long celebration of African–American culture near Christmas time.

Kyla
(alt. Kya, Kylah, Kyle)

Scottish, meaning 'narrow spit of land'.

Kylie
(alt. Kiley, Kylee)

Irish Gaelic, meaning 'graceful'. The rise in popularity of this name is likely to be linked to the career of Kylie Minogue, developing from Australian soap star to international queen of pop.

Kyoko

Japanese, meaning 'girl who sees her own true image'.

Kyra

Greek, meaning 'lady'. Also known as a village in Cyprus.

Kyrie

Greek, meaning 'the Lord'. Also a prayer sung at the beginning of the Christian mass.

Girls' names

Lacey
(alt. Laci, Lacie, Lacy)

French, from a nobleman's surname. Most popular in North America, but English Lacey Turner is an actor and *EastEnders* star.

Ladonna
Italian, meaning 'lady'. Usually used as a spelling alternative to Madonna.

Lady
English, meaning 'bread kneader' and an aristocratic title for a woman. Usually associated with the character of Lady from Disney's *Lady and the Tramp*.

Laidh
Scottish meaning 'a ship's course'. Also a spelling alternative to Lady.

Laila
(alt. Laelia, Layla, Leila, Lejla, Lela, Lelah, Lelia)

Arabic, meaning 'night'. Famous Lailas include boxer Laila Ali and the song 'Layla' by Eric Clapton. Has become popular in recent years.

Lainey
(alt. Laine, Laney, Lany)

French, meaning 'bright light'. In Poland, the most common spelling is Lany, whereas in other countries it can be Lainey or Laney.

Lakeisha
(alt. Lakeshia)

American, meaning 'woman'. Its origins seem to be a combination of La and Keisha.

Lakshmi
(alt. Laxmi)

Sanskrit, meaning 'good omen'. Also the Hindu goddess of wealth.

Lana

Greek, meaning 'light'. Famous Lanas include singer Lana Del Rey, actor Lana Turner and the language-communication chimpanzee Lana.

Lani
(alt. Lanie)

Hawaiian, meaning 'heaven and sky'.

Lara

Latin, meaning 'famous'. Famous Laras include actor Lara Flynn Boyle, *Tomb Raider* protagonist Lara Croft and the ancient Roman nymph of the same name.

Larissa
(alt. Larisa)

Greek, meaning 'lighthearted'. Larissa was a nymph in ancient Greek mythology.

Lark
(alt. Larkin)

English, meaning 'playful songbird'.

Larsen
(alt. Larsen)

Scandinavian, meaning 'son of Lars'.

Latifa
(alt. Latifah)

Arabic, meaning 'gentle and pleasant'. Queen Latifah is the stage name of the singer and pioneer of female hip hop.

Latika
(alt. Lotika)

Hindi, meaning 'a plant'. Usually associated with the character of Latika from *Slumdog Millionaire*.

Latisha

Latin, meaning 'happiness'. More commonly used in the USA.

Latona
(alt. Latonia)

Roman, from the ancient Roman mythological heroine of the same name who had twin sons with the god Zeus.

Latoya

Spanish, meaning 'victorious one'. Singer LaToya Jackson is known for being a member of the musical Jackson family.

Latrice
(alt. Latricia)

Latin, meaning 'noble'. More commonly used in the USA.

Laura
(alt. Lora)

Latin, meaning 'laurel'. Famous Lauras include designer Laura Ashley, author Laura Ingalls Wilder and actor Laura Dern.

Laurel

Latin, meaning 'laurel tree'. A Laurel is also a term used for young women in the Mormon Church.

Lauren
(alt. Lauran, Loren)

Latin, meaning 'laurel'. Famous Laurens include actors Lauren Bacall and Lauren Crace and DJ Lauren Laverne.

Laveda
(alt. Lavada)

Latin, meaning 'cleansed'.

Lavender

Latin, from the flowering plant of the same name.

Laverne
(alt. Lavern, Laverna)

Latin, from the goddess of the same name. Famous Lavernes include the Andrews Sisters member Laverne Andrews, and US sitcom *Laverne & Shirley*.

Lavinia
(alt. Lavina)

Latin, meaning 'woman of Rome'. Lavinia was an ancient Roman character whose hair caught fire during sacrifices to the gods.

Lavita

American, meaning 'charming'. The original 'la vita' means 'life' in Latin.

Lavonne
(alt. Lavon)

French, meaning 'yew wood'. More commonly used in the USA.

Leah
(alt. Lea, Leia)

Hebrew, meaning 'weary'.

Leandra

Greek, meaning 'lion man'. In the novel *Don Quixote* by Miguel de Cervantes, Leandra is a beautiful woman whose many suitors withdraw to the mountains to write about how beautiful she is.

Leanne
(alt. Leann, Leanna, Leeann, Lee Ann)

Contraction of Lee and Ann, meaning 'meadow grace'. Famous Leannes include singers LeAnn Rimes and Lee Ann Womack and actor Leanne Wilson.

Leda

Greek, meaning 'gladness'. Leda was an ancient Greek character who was seduced by the god Zeus in the form of a white swan, and whose children included Helen of Troy.

Lee
(alt. Leigh)

English, meaning 'pasture' or 'meadow'. Used equally for girls and boys.

Leilani

Hawaiian, meaning 'flower from heaven'. Actor Leilani Jones is known for her roles in *Little Shop of Horrors* and various voice acting roles.

Leith

Scottish Gaelic, meaning 'broad river'.

Lena
(alt. Leena, Lina)

Latin, meaning 'light'. Famous Lenas include actors Lena Dunham, Lena Headey and Lena Ashwell.

Lenna
(alt. Lennie)

German, meaning 'lion's strength'.

Lenore
(alt. Lenora, Leonora, Leonor, Leonore)

Greek, meaning 'light'. Usually associated with the poem *Lenore* by Edgar Allan Poe.

Léonie
(alt. Leona, Leone)

Latin, meaning 'lioness'. Poet Leonie Adams wrote during the mid-twentieth century.

Leora
(alt. Liora)

Hebrew, meaning 'light'. The male version of Leora is Leor.

Lerola

Latin, meaning 'like a blackbird'.

Lesley
(alt. Leslee, Lesli)

Scottish Gaelic, from the name of the prominent clan. Also meaning 'holly garden'. The boys' variation is usually spelt Leslie.

Leta

Latin, meaning 'glad and joyful'. Leta Hollingworth was an influential child psychologist in the twentieth century.

Letha

Greek, meaning 'forgetfulness'. Also the name of a type of butterfly.

Letitia
(alt. Leticia, Lettice, Lettie)

Latin, meaning 'joy and gladness'. St Leticia was a Spanish virgin martyr.

Lexia
(alt. Lexi, Lexie)

Greek, meaning 'defender of mankind'. Also the name of a type of butterfly.

Lia

Italian, meaning 'bringer of the gospel'. Actor Lia Williams is known for her roles in both theatre and film.

Liana

French, meaning 'to twine around'. Also the name of a type of vine.

Libby
(alt. Libbie)

Shortened form of Elizabeth, meaning 'consecrated to God'. Famous Libbys include journalist Libby Purves, *EastEnders* character Libby Fox and singer Libby Holman.

Liberty

English, meaning 'freedom'.

Lida

Slavic, meaning 'loved by the people'.

Liese
(alt. Liesel, Liesl)

German, meaning 'pledged to God'. Also used as a shortened form of Elizabeth.

Lila
(alt. Lilah)

Arabic, meaning 'night'. In the Hindu faith, Lila refers to playtime or pastimes.

Lilac

Latin, from the flower of the same name. Also associated with the pale purple colour.

Lilia
(alt. Lilias)

Scottish, meaning 'lily'. More commonly used in Russian and Ukrainian communities.

Lilith

Arabic, meaning 'ghost'. Also the name of a female demon in Hebrew mythology.

Lillian
(alt. Lilian, Liliana, Lilla, Lillianna)

Latin, meaning 'lily'. Famous Lillians include actor Lillian Gish, playwright Lillian Hellman and pioneering nurse Lillian Wald.

Lily
(alt. Lili, Lillie, Lilly)

Latin, from the flower of the same name. Famous Lilys include singer Lily Allen, actor Lily Collins and model Lily Cole.

Linda
(alt. Lynda)

Spanish, meaning 'pretty'. Famous Lindas include presenter Linda Barker, actor Linda Blair and singer Linda Ronstadt.

Linden
(alt. Lindie, Lindy)

From the tree of the same name. Used more commonly for boys.

Lindsay
(alt. Lindsey, Linsey)

English, meaning 'island of linden trees'. Famous Lindsays include actors Lindsay Lohan, Lindsay Sloane and Lindsay Wagner.

Linette

Welsh, meaning 'idol'.

Linnea
(alt. Linnae, Linny)

Scandinavian, meaning 'lime or linden tree'.

Lirit

Hebrew, meaning 'musically talented'.

Lisa
(alt. Leesa, Lise, Liza)

Hebrew, meaning 'pledged to God'. Famous Lisas include singer Lisa Bonet, *Friends* actor Lisa Kudrow and *The Simpsons* character Lisa Simpson.

Lissa

Greek, meaning 'bee'. Also used as a shortened form of Melissa.

Lissandra

(alt. Lisandra)

Greek, meaning 'man's defender'.

Liv

Nordic, meaning 'defence'. Actor Liv Tyler appeared in the Lord of the Rings trilogy.

Livia

Latin, meaning 'olive'. Livia Drusilla was a prominent ancient Roman woman, wife of the Emperor Augustus.

Liz

(alt. Lizzie, Lizzy)

Shortened form of Elizabeth, meaning 'consecrated to God'. Many Elizabeths go by Liz, including actor Liz Taylor.

Logan

Irish Gaelic, meaning 'small hollow'. More commonly used as a name for boys.

Lois

German, meaning 'renowned in battle'. Usually associated with the character of Lois Lane from the Superman comic series.

Lola

Spanish, meaning 'sorrows'. Also used as a shortened form of Delores.

Lolita

(alt. Lollie)

Spanish, meaning 'sorrows'. Usually associated with the character of Lolita in Vladimir Nabokov's novel Lolita.

Lona

Latin, meaning 'lion'. Lona is a moon deity in Hawaiian mythology.

Lora

Latin, meaning 'laurel'. Sometimes used as a spelling alternative to Laura.

Lorelei

(alt. Loralai, Loralie)

German, meaning 'dangerous rock'. Ancient German mythology tells of a maiden who lives on the Lorelei Rock in the river Rhine and lures sailors to their deaths.

Lorenza

Latin, meaning 'from Laurentium'.

Loretta

(alt. Loreto)

Latin, meaning 'laurel'. Mostly used in the USA, where actors with this name include Loretta Devine and Loretta Swit.

Lori

(alt. Laurie, Lorie, Lorri)

Latin, meaning 'laurel'. Actor Lori Petty is known for her roles in Point Break, A League of Their Own and Tank Girl.

Lorna

Scottish, from the town of Lorne. Usually associated with the protagonist in R.D. Blackmore's novel Lorna Doone.

Lorraine
(alt. Laraine, Loraine)
French, meaning 'from Lorraine'. TV presenter Lorraine Kelly is best known for breakfast TV and chat show work.

Lottie
(alt. Lotta, Lotte)
French, meaning 'little and womanly'. Usually used as a shortened form of Charlotte.

Lotus
Greek, meaning 'lotus flower'.

Louise
(alt. Louisa, Luisa; abbrev. Lou, Louie)
German, meaning 'renowned in battle'. Very popular as a name in 1970s England in particular.

Lourdes
French, from the town of the same name. Madonna famously chose this name for her daughter in 1996.

Love
English, from the word 'love'.

Lowri
Welsh, meaning 'crowned with laurels'. Lowri Turner is a TV presenter.

Luanne
(alt. Luann, Luanna)
German, meaning 'renowned in battle'. In Hawaiian, the name also means 'enjoyment'.

Luba
Hebrew, meaning 'dearly loved'.

Lucia
(alt. Luciana)
Italian, meaning 'light'. The female version of the ancient Roman name Lucius.

Lucille
(alt. Lucile, Lucilla)
French, meaning 'light'. American Lucille Ball was the star of *I Love Lucy*.

Lucinda
English, meaning 'light'. Lucinda Green (Lucinda Prior-Palmer) was a world champion equestrian who won Badminton six times.

Lucretia
(alt. Lucrece)
Spanish, meaning 'light'. Also an important character in ancient Roman mythology.

Lucy
(alt. Lucie)
Latin, meaning 'light'. St Lucy was a martyr in the fourth century.

Ludmilla
Slavic, meaning 'beloved of the people'.

Luella
(alt. Lue)
English, meaning 'renowned in battle'. Designer Luella Bartley is known for her fashion brands and journalism for various fashion magazines.

Lulu
(alt. Lula)

German, meaning 'renowned in battle'. Singer Lulu became a star of the 1960s and is a successful model still today.

Luna

Latin, meaning 'moon'. Luna was the personification of the moon in ancient Roman mythology.

Lupita

Spanish, short form of Guadelupe. Actor Lupita Nyong'o is known for her role in *12 Years a Slave*.

Luz

Spanish, meaning 'light'. Also the name of an ancient city in the Bible.

Lydia
(alt. Lidia)

Greek, meaning 'from Lydia'. Famous Lydias include activist Lydia Becker, ballerina Lydia Lopokova and the character of Lydia Bennet in *Pride and Prejudice*.

Lynn
(alt. Lyn, Lynne)

Spanish, meaning 'pretty'; English, meaning 'waterfall'. Actor Lynn Redgrave is part of the Redgrave acting dynasty.

Lynton

English, meaning 'town of lime trees'. Also the name of a town in Devon. Most commonly used for boys.

Lyra

Latin, meaning 'lyre'. The central character in Philip Pullman's 'His Dark Materials' trilogy.

Girls' names

Mab

Irish Gaelic, meaning 'joy'. Queen Mab is a character in Shakespeare's play *Romeo and Juliet*.

Mabel
(alt. Mabelle, Mable)

Latin, meaning 'loveable'. Although the name Mabel is very old and dates from the fifth century, it did not become popular until the nineteenth century, when the novel *The Heir of Redclyffe* was published.

Macaria

Spanish, meaning 'blessed'.

Machiko

Japanese, meaning 'knowledgeable child'. Machiko Kawana is a Japanese voice artist.

Macy
(alt. Macey, Maci, Macie)

French, meaning 'weapon'. Macy Gray is the stage name of the award winning R&B singer-songwriter and actor Natalie McIntyre.

Mada

English, meaning 'from Magdala'. In Hindu mythology, Mada also refers to an enormous monster who is able to swallow the entire universe.

Madaio

Hawaiian, meaning 'gift from God'.

Madden
(alt. Maddyn)

Irish, meaning 'little dog'.

Madeline
(alt. Madaline, Madalyn, Madeleine, Madelyn, Madelynn, Madilyn; abbrev. Maddy, Maddi, Maddie, Madie)

Greek, meaning 'from Magdala'. Madeleine Albright was the first female Secretary of State in the US. Maddy Prior is one of the best-known English folk singers.

Madge

Greek, meaning 'pearl'. Also a shortened form of several names including Margaret, Madeline and Marjorie. Madge was especially common around 1880–1900, being the name of several actors of that time. More recently, it's the nickname of pop icon Madonna.

Madhuri

Hindi, meaning 'sweet girl'. Madhuri Dixit is one of Bollywood's most well-known and popular actors, appearing in dozens of Hindi films.

Madison

(alt. Maddison, Madisen, Madisyn, Madyson)

English, meaning 'son of the mighty warrior'. The sudden increase in the popularity of Madison can be traced back to the mermaid character of Madison in the film *Splash*, played by Daryl Hannah.

Madonna

Latin, meaning 'my lady'. Usually associated with the pop singer legend Madonna, or as one of the Virgin Mary's many names.

Maeve

Irish Gaelic, meaning 'intoxicating'. Famous Maeves include Queen Maeve from Irish mythology, author Maeve Binchy and writer Maeve Brennan.

Mafalda

Spanish, meaning 'battle-mighty'. Mafalda is a popular Argentine comic strip.

Magali

Greek, meaning 'pearl'. More commonly used in French- or Portuguese-speaking communities.

Magdalene

(alt. Magdalen, Magdalena)

Greek, meaning 'from Magdala'. Mary Magdalene was one of Jesus's disciples in the Bible.

Magnolia

Latin, from the flowering plant of the same name.

Mahala

(alt. Mahalia)

Hebrew, meaning 'tender affection'.

Maia

(alt. Maja, Maya)

Greek, meaning 'mother'. Also an important character in ancient Greek mythology.

Maida

English, meaning 'maiden'.

Maisie

(alt. Maisey, Maisy, Maizie, Masie, Mazie)

Greek, meaning 'pearl'. Famous Maisies include children's book character Maisey Mouse and Maisie Williams, child star of *Game of Thrones*.

Malin

Hebrew and English, meaning 'of Magdala'. Malin is most common in Sweden.

Maliya
(alt. Malia, Maliyah)

Hawaiian, meaning 'beloved'. Malia Obama is the daughter of the 44th President of the USA, Barack Obama.

Malka

Hebrew, meaning 'queen'.

Mallory
(alt. Malorie)

French, meaning 'unhappy'. Author Malorie Blackman is known for her children's literature.

Malvina

Gaelic, meaning 'smooth brow'. The name was invented by poet James Macpherson in the eighteenth century.

Mamie
(alt. Maimie, Mammie)

Shortened form of Margaret, meaning 'pearl'. Famous Mamies include former US first lady Mamie Eisenhower, wife of President Dwight Eisenhower.

Mandy
(alt. Mandie)

Shortened form of Amanda, meaning 'much loved'. Famous Mandys include actor Mandy Moore and the song *Mandy* by Barry Manilow.

Manisha

Sanskrit, meaning 'desire'. Manisha is the goddess of wisdom in the Hindu faith.

Mansi

Hopi, meaning 'plucked flower'. Also the name of an indigenous group of people in Russia.

Manuela

Spanish, meaning 'the Lord is among us'. More commonly used in German-speaking communities.

Mara

Hebrew, meaning 'bitter'. Famous Maras include actor Mara Wilson and children's author Mara Bergman.

Marcela
(alt. Marceline, Marcella, Marcelle)

Latin, meaning 'war-like'.

Marcia
(alt. Marcy, Marci, Marcie)

Latin, meaning 'war-like'. Famous Marcias include legendary British leader Queen Marcia, actor Marcia Cross and voice actor Marcia Wallace.

Margaret
(alt. Margarete, Margaretta, Margarette, Margret; abbrev. Maggie)

Greek, meaning 'pearl'. Famous Margarets include former prime minister Margaret Thatcher, author Margaret Atwood and actor Margaret Rutherford. Famous Maggies include actors Maggie Gyllenhaal and Maggie Grace, and the song 'Maggie May' by Rod Stewart.

Margery
(alt. Marge, Margie, Margit, Margy, Marjorie)

French, meaning 'pearl'. Author Margery Kempe wrote the first English-language autobiography, *The Book of Margery Kempe*, in the fifteenth century. Marjorie Bruce was daughter of Robert the Bruce of Scotland.

Margot
(alt. Margo)

French, meaning 'pearl'. Famous Margots include ballerina Margot Fonteyn, actor Margot Kidder and the sister of Anne Frank, Margot Frank.

Marguerite
(alt. Margarita)

French, meaning 'pearl'. Marguerite de Valois was Queen of France during the sixteenth century.

Maria
(alt. Mariah)

Latin, meaning 'bitter'. Famous Marias include tennis pro Maria Sharapova, performer Maria von Trapp and the character of Maria from the musical *West Side Story*.

Marian
(alt. Mariam, Mariana, Mariann, Marianne, Maryann, Maryanne, Marion)

French, meaning 'bitter grace'. Usually associated with the character of Maid Marian from the legend of Robin Hood. Marianne Faithfull is an English singer and songwriter who began her career in the 1960s in 'swinging London'.

Maribel
Hebrew, meaning 'bitter'. Also used as a contraction of Maria and Isabel.

Marie
French, meaning 'bitter'. Famous Maries include French Queen Marie Antoinette, physicist Marie Curie, and singer Marie Osmond.

Mariel
(alt. Mariela, Mariella)

Dutch, meaning 'bitter'. Also the name of a city in Cuba.

Marietta
(alt. Marieta)

French, meaning 'bitter'. Activist Marietta Stow was an influential campaigner for women's suffrage during the nineteenth century.

Marigold
English, from the flowering plant of the same name.

Marika
Dutch, meaning 'bitter'. More commonly used in Greek-speaking communities.

Marilyn
(alt. Marilee, Marilene, Marilynn)

English, meaning 'bitter'. Marilyn Monroe starred in films such as *Gentlemen Prefer Blondes*, *The Seven Year Itch* and *Some Like It Hot*.

Marina
(alt. Marine)

Latin, meaning 'from the sea'. Marina is a truly global name, with famous Marinas of many nationalities and backgrounds. Marina Hyde is one of few Brits with the name – she's a journalist and newspaper columnist for the *Guardian*.

Mariposa
Spanish, meaning 'butterfly'. Also the name of a group of lilies.

Marisa
(alt. Maris, Marissa)

Latin, meaning 'of the sea'. Famous Marisas include actor Marisa Tomei and the notorious Yahoo! business executive Marissa Mayer.

Marisol

Spanish, meaning 'bitter sun'. Also a contraction of Maria de la Soledad, which is another title for the Virgin Mary in Spain.

Marjolaine

French, meaning 'marjoram'.

Marlene
(alt. Marlen, Marlena; abbrev. Marla)

Hebrew, meaning 'bitter'. Actor Marlene Dietrich was German born but became an American in 1939 and was a front-line entertainer for the troops during World War II. The character of Marla Singer in the film *Fight Club*, was played by Helena Bonham Carter.

Marley
(alt. Marlee)

American, meaning 'bitter'.

Marlo
(alt. Marlowe)

American, meaning 'bitter'. More commonly used as a name for boys.

Marnie
(alt. Marney)

Scottish, meaning 'from the sea'. Famous Marnies include the character of Marnie from *Girls* and the film *Marnie* by Alfred Hitchcock. It was also the birth name of ballerina Darcey Bussell.

Marseille

French, from the city of the same name in France.

Marsha

English, meaning 'war-like'. Famous Marshas include actor Marsha Thomason, singer Marsha Hunt and playwright Marsha Norman.

Martha
(alt. Marta)

Aramaic, meaning 'lady'. Found in the Bible. Martha Lane Fox was a leading dotcom entrepreneur in the 2000s, later becoming the youngest female member of the House of Lords.

Martina

Latin, meaning 'war-like'. Famous Martinas include tennis pros Martina Hingis and Martina Navratilova and Martina, Empress of the Byzantine empire.

Marvel

French, meaning 'something to marvel at'. Usually associated with the comic book brand.

Mary

Hebrew, meaning 'bitter'. Famous Marys include the Virgin Mary from the Bible, author Mary Shelley and morality campaigner Mary Whitehouse.

Masada

Hebrew, meaning 'foundation'. Also the name of an ancient Jewish fortification in Israel.

Matilda
(alt. Mathilda, Mathilde, Matilde)

German, meaning 'battle-mighty'. Famous Matildas include the lead character from the novel *Matilda* by Roald Dahl, Queen consort of England Matilda of Flanders, and twelfth-century Queen Matilda of England.

Mattea

Hebrew, meaning 'gift of God'.

Maude
(alt. Maud)

German, meaning 'battle-mighty'. Usually associated with the character of Maude Flanders from *The Simpsons* or the film *Harold and Maude*.

Maura

Irish, meaning 'bitter'. Also the name of a French saint of the fourth century.

Maureen
(alt. Maurine)

Irish, meaning 'bitter'. Famous Maureens include actors Maureen Lipman, Maureen McCormick and Maureen O'Hara.

Mavis

French, meaning 'thrush'. The name originated in the nineteenth century after the publication of the novel *The Sorrows of Satan*.

Maxine
(alt. Maxie)

Latin, meaning 'greatest'. Famous Maxines include the Andrews Sisters member Maxine Andrews, actor Maxine Audley and the character of Maxine Peacock from *Coronation Street*.

May
(alt. Mae, Maye)

Hebrew, meaning 'gift of God'. Also the name of the fifth month.

Maya
(alt. Mya, Myah)

Greek, meaning 'mother'. Famous Mayas include author Maya Angelou, comedian Maya Rudolph and the Mayan people of Central America.

Mckenna
(alt. Mackenna)

Irish Gaelic, meaning 'son of the handsome one'.

Mckenzie
(alt. Mackenzie, Mckenzy, Mikenzi)

Irish Gaelic, meaning 'son of the wise ruler'. More commonly used as a boys' name.

Meara

Gaelic, meaning 'filled with happiness'.

Medea
(alt. Meda)

Greek, meaning 'ruling'. Also the name of a prominent figure in ancient Greek mythology.

Meg

Shortened form of Margaret, meaning 'pearl'. Famous Megs include actor Meg Ryan and the character of Meg from Disney's *Hercules*.

Megan
(alt. Meagan, Meghan, Meghann)

Welsh, meaning 'pearl'. Famous Megans include actors Megan Fox and Megan Mullally and tennis pro Meghann Shaughnessy.

Mehri

Persian, meaning 'kind'. Also the name of a group of people and a language spoken in southern Arabia.

Meiwei

Chinese, meaning 'forever enchanting'.

Melanie
(alt. Melania, Melany, Melonie; abbrev. Mel)

Greek, meaning 'dark-skinned'. Famous Melanies include singers Melanie Brown and Melanie Chisholm of the Spice Girls and actor Melanie Griffith.

Melba

Australian, meaning 'from Melbourne'.

Melia
(alt. Meliah)

German, meaning 'industrious'.

Melina

Greek, meaning 'honey'. Actor Melina Kanakaredes has appeared in several US-based crime dramas, including *CSI:NY*.

Melinda

Latin, meaning 'honey'. Famous Melindas include TV presenter and model Melinda Messenger, philanthropist Melinda Gates and actor Melinda Clarke.

Melisande

French, meaning 'bee'. Melisandre is a character from George R.R. Martin's 'A Song of Ice and Fire' series.

Melissa
(alt. Melisa, Mellissa)

Greek, meaning 'bee'. Famous Melissas include singer Melissa Etheridge and actors Melissa Joan Hart and Melissa George.

Melody
(alt. Melodie)

Greek, meaning 'song'. Aptly, there are a number of Melodys who have gone on to be singers as well as actors. Melody is also a character in Disney's *The Little Mermaid*.

Melvina

Celtic, meaning 'chieftain'.

Menora
(alt. Menorah)
Hebrew, meaning 'candlestick'.

Mercedes
Spanish, meaning 'mercies'. Usually associated with the luxury car manufacturer Mercedes-Benz.

Mercy
English, meaning 'mercy'.

Meredith
(alt. Meridith)
Welsh, meaning 'great ruler'. Not common outside of Wales, the name is used equally for girls and boys.

Merle
French, meaning 'blackbird'. Used equally for girls and boys, though not a common name anywhere.

Merritt
English, from the word 'merit'. Can be used for both boys and girls.

Merry
English, meaning 'light-hearted'.

Meryl
(alt. Merrill)
Irish Gaelic, meaning 'sea-bright'. Actor Meryl Streep has made a string of top film appearances including *Kramer vs. Kramer*, *Sophie's Choice* and *The Iron Lady*.

Meta
German, meaning 'pearl'. Also a Greek term for 'after or beyond'.

Mia
Italian, meaning 'mine'. Famous Mias include actors Mia Wasikowska and Mia Farrow and singer M.I.A.

Michaela
(alt. Makaela, Makaila, Micaela, Mikaila, Mikayla)
Hebrew, meaning 'resembles God'. Famous Michaelas include presenter Michaela Strachan, actor Michaela Conlin, and gymnast McKayla Maroney.

Michelle
(alt. Machelle, Mechelle, Michaele, Michal, Michele, Michen; abbrev. Mickey, Mickie)
French, meaning 'resembles God'. Famous Michelles include singers Michelle Gayle and Michelle McManus, actor Michelle Rodriguez and the first African-American First Lady of the USA, Michelle Obama.

Mieko
(alt. Meiko)
Japanese, meaning 'born into wealth'.

Migdalia
Greek, meaning 'from Magdala'.

Mignon
French, meaning 'sweet'.

Mika
(alt. Micah)
Hebrew, meaning 'resembles God'.

Milada
Czech, meaning 'my love'. More commonly used in Slavic and Czech communities.

Milagros

Spanish, meaning 'miracles'. Also a term used for folk charms with healing properties in Mexico.

Milan

Italian, from the city of the same name in Italy.

Mildred

English, meaning 'gentle strength'. Famous Mildreds include the character of Mildred Hubble from the *Worst Witch* series, author Mildred B. Davies and actor Mildred Dunnock.

Milena

Czech, meaning 'love and warmth'.

Miley

American, meaning 'smiley'. Made popular by singer and actor Miley Cyrus.

Millicent

(alt. Milicent; abbrev. Millie, Milly)

German, meaning 'high-born power'. Famous Millicents include suffragist Millicent Fawcett and British spy Milicent Bagot.

Mimi

Italian, meaning 'bitter'. Also the name of the female protagonist in the opera *La bohème*, by Giacomo Puccini.

Mina

(alt. Mena)

German, meaning 'love'. In Persian, the name also means 'coloured glass'.

Mindy

(alt. Mindi)

Latin, meaning 'honey'. Used as a shortened form of Melinda as well as a name in its own right. Mindy Kaling is an American-Indian actor and comedian.

Minerva

Latin, from the goddess of the same name. Minerva was the goddess of wisdom, the arts and defence, in ancient Roman mythology.

Ming

Chinese, meaning 'bright'. Usually associated with the Ming Dynasty, which ruled China from the fourteenth to the seventeenth century.

Minnie

(alt. Minna)

German, meaning 'helmet'. Usually associated with the Disney character Minnie Mouse and actor Minnie Driver.

Mira

(alt. Meera)

Latin, meaning 'admirable'. Also the name of a giant red star.

Mirabel

(alt. Mirabella, Mirabelle)

Latin, meaning 'wonderful'. Also the name of a type of plum.

Miranda

(alt. Meranda; abbrev. Randi, Randy)

Latin, meaning 'admirable'. Famous Mirandas include actors Miranda Richardson and Miranda Hart and model Miranda Kerr.

Mirella
(alt. Mireille, Mirela)

Latin, meaning 'admirable'. Opera singer Mirella Freni is known in Italy as being one of the finest in her art.

Miriam

Hebrew, meaning 'bitter'. Also the name of a prophetess in the Bible. Miriam Margolyes is a popular British BAFTA-winning character actor.

Mirta

Spanish, meaning 'crown of thorns'.

Missy

Shortened form of Melissa, meaning 'bee'. Famous Missys include musician Missy Elliot, singer Missy Higgins, and performer Missy Malone.

Misty
(alt. Misti)

English, meaning 'mist'. Misty Copeland was the first black ballerina to become a principal dancer with a national ballet company.

Mitzi

German, meaning 'bitter'. Actor Mitzi Gaynor appeared in *South Pacific*.

Miu

Japanese, meaning 'beautiful feather'. Also the name of an endangered language spoken in Papua New Guinea.

Moana

Maori, meaning 'ocean'. Made famous by the Disney animation of the same name.

Moira
(alt. Maira)

Irish, meaning 'bitter'. Famous Moiras include actor Moira Brooker, ballet dancer Moira Shearer and news presenter Moira Stuart.

Molly
(alt. Mollie)

American, meaning 'bitter'. Famous Mollys include actors Molly Ringwald and Molly Sims.

Mona

Irish Gaelic, meaning 'aristocratic'. A character from the children's television programme *Mona the Vampire*.

Monica
(alt. Monika, Monique)

Latin, meaning 'adviser'. Famous Monicas include singer Monica, infamous White House intern Monica Lewinsky and tennis pro Monica Seles.

Monroe

Gaelic, meaning 'mouth of the river Rotha'. Usually associated with Marilyn Monroe.

Montserrat
(alt. Monserrate)

Spanish, from the town of the same name. Opera singer Montserrat Caballe is known for her work in the bel canto technique, and for the song 'Barcelona' with Freddie Mercury.

Morag

Scottish, meaning 'star of the sea'. Also the pet name of a monster that supposedly inhabits Loch Morar in Scotland.

Morgan
(alt. Morgann)

Welsh, meaning 'great and bright'. Used for both girls and, more commonly, boys.

Moriah

Hebrew, meaning 'the Lord is my teacher'. Also the name of a mountain mentioned in the Bible.

Morwenna
(alt. Modwenna)

Welsh, meaning 'maiden'. Morwenna Banks is a British comedy actor, writer and producer. She is known to toddlers everywhere as the voice of Mummy Pig in *Peppa Pig*.

Moselle
(alt. Mozell, Mozella, Mozelle)

Hebrew, meaning 'saviour'. Also the name of a river and a German wine.

Mulan

Chinese, meaning 'wood orchid'. Usually associated with the protagonist from the Disney film *Mulan*.

Munin

Scandinavian, meaning 'good memory'.

Muriel

Irish Gaelic, meaning 'sea-bright'. Author Muriel Spark was known for her novel *The Prime of Miss Jean Brodie*.

Myfanwy

Welsh, meaning 'my little lovely one'. The name originally appeared in a song called 'Myfanwy' by Joseph Parry.

Myra

Latin, meaning 'scented oil'. Famous Myras include pioneering lawyer Myra Bradwell and pianist Myra Hess, and also Moors murderer Myra Hindley.

Myrna
(alt. Mirna)

Irish Gaelic, meaning 'tender and beloved'. Actor Myrna Fahey appeared in Walt Disney's *Zorro*.

Myrtle

Irish, from the flowering shrub of the same name. Usually associated with the character of Myrtle Wilson from F. Scott Fitzgerald's novel *The Great Gatsby*.

Girls' names

Nadia
(alt. Nadya)

Russian, meaning 'hope'. Romanian Nadia Elena Comăneci was the first female Olympic gymnast to be awarded a perfect score of 10, and has three gold medals. Nadia Petrova is a tennis pro and Nadia Sawalha is a TV presenter and actor.

Nadine

French, meaning 'hope'. It is the title of a Chuck Berry song, released after he left prison. Nadine Gordimer is a South African writer and activist who won the Nobel Prize for literature.

Nahara

Aramaic, meaning 'light'.

Nahla
(alt. Nala, Nalo)

Arabic, meaning 'first drink of water', and Sanskrit meaning 'hollow reed'. Made popular by the character from Disney's *The Lion King*.

Naima

Arabic, meaning 'water nymph'. Naima Belkhiata is a singer with the group Honeyz.

Nakia

Egyptian, meaning 'pure'.

Nalani

Hawaiian, meaning 'serenity of the skies'.

Nan
(alt. Nanna, Nannie)

Hebrew, meaning 'grace'. A character in Louisa May Alcott's *Little Women*.

Nancy
(alt. Nanci, Nancie)

Hebrew, meaning 'grace'. Nancy Reagan was a former first lady of the USA and anti-drug advocate who began her career as a film actor.

Nanette
(alt. Nannette)

French, meaning 'grace'. *No, No Nanette* is a musical comedy from the 1920s. Nanette Lepor is an American fashion designer and Nanette Newman is a British actor.

Naomi
(alt. Naoma, Noemi)

Hebrew, meaning 'pleasant'. A character in the Bible. Naomi Campbell is one of the original five 'supermodels'.

Narcissa

Greek, meaning 'daffodil'. Narcissa Whitman, a missionary, became one of the most famous women of the early American West.

Nastasia

Greek, meaning 'resurrection'. Can also mean 'born on Christmas Day'.

Natalie
(alt. Natalee, Natalia, Natalya, Nathalie)

Latin, meaning 'birth day'. From the late Latin name Natalia, meaning 'Christmas Day'. Its popularity increased in the USA after the 1940s due to actor Natalie Wood, who was the daughter of Russian immigrants.

Natasha
(alt. Natasa)

Russian, meaning 'birth day'. A character in Leo Tolstoy's *War and Peace*. Used in the English-speaking world only since the twentieth century.

Natividad

Spanish, meaning 'Christmas'.

Neda

English, meaning 'wealthy'. Neda was also an Arcadian nymph who nursed the infant Zeus.

Nedra

English, meaning 'underground'.

Neema

Swahili, meaning 'born of prosperity'.

Neka

Native American, meaning 'goose'.

Nell
(alt. Nelda, Nell, Nella, Nellie, Nelly)

Shortened form of Eleanor, meaning 'light'. May have roots in old German *nelle*, meaning 'crown of the head', perhaps suggesting an obstinate person.

Nemi

Italian, from the lake of the same name.

Neoma

Greek, meaning 'new moon'.

Nereida

Spanish, meaning 'sea nymph'. A mermaid in Greek mythology.

Nerissa

Greek, meaning 'sea nymph'. The name of Portia's waiting woman in Shakespeare's *The Merchant of Venice*.

Nettie
(alt. Neta)
Shortened form of Henrietta, meaning 'ruler of the house'.

Neva
Spanish, meaning 'snowy'.

Nevaeh
American, meaning 'heaven'. The name Nevaeh is the word 'Heaven' spelled backwards. May also be linked with Spanish 'snowy'.

Nhung
Vietnamese, meaning 'velvet'.

Niamh
(alt. Neave, Neve)
Gaelic, meaning 'brightness'. In Irish mythology, Niamh was a goddess, the daughter of the god of the sea and a queen of the land of eternal youth. Now finding increasing popularity outside of Ireland.

Nicola
(alt. Nichola, Nichole, Nicole, Nicolette, Nicolle, Nikole; abbrev. Nicky, Nicki, Nikki)
Greek, meaning 'victory of the people'. Nicola is a boys' name in Italy, but became widely used in England and Germany as a girls' name, perhaps due to the -a ending of the name. As a girls' name in England it was especially popular around the 1960s–1970s. Nicole Kidman is an Oscar-winning Australian actor. Nicole Farhi is a French fashion designer and sculptor.

Nidia
Spanish, meaning 'graceful'.

Nigella
Irish Gaelic, meaning 'champion'. Nigella Lawson is a TV chef and author, famous for her sensual style of cookery.

Nikita
Greek, meaning 'unconquered'. Popular in Russia. Also the one-word title of a song by Elton John, a film and a recent US TV series.

Nila
Egyptian, meaning 'Nile'.

Nilda
German, meaning 'battle woman'.

Nimra
Arabic, meaning 'number'. Also a name of Punjabi origin, meaning 'humble'.

Nina
Spanish, meaning 'girl'. One of the three ships used by Christopher Columbus on his first voyage. Nina Conti is a comedian and ventriloquist and Nina Simone was a jazz singing legend and civil rights campaigner.

Nissa
Hebrew, meaning 'sign'.

Nita
Spanish, meaning 'gracious'.

Nixie

German, meaning 'water sprite'.

Noel
(alt. Noelle)

French, meaning 'Christmas'. Noel is used most commonly for boys. Noelle is a feminine variant.

Nola

Irish Gaelic, meaning 'white shoulder'. Also a city and area in Italy.

Nona

Latin, meaning 'ninth'.

Nora
(alt. Norah)

Shortened form of Eleanor, meaning 'light', used in its own right. Nora Roberts is an American author who has written over 200 romance novels, some under pseudonyms.

Noreen
(alt. Norine)

Irish, meaning 'light'. Professor Noreen Murray was a very highly regarded molecular geneticist who helped develop a vaccine against hepatitis B.

Norma

Latin, meaning 'pattern'. In Bellini's tragic opera of the same name, Norma is a druidess at the time of the Roman occupation of England.

Normandie
(alt. Normandy)

French, from the province of the same name.

Novia

Latin, meaning 'new'.

Nuala

Irish Gaelic, meaning 'white shoulder'. A popular name in Ireland, likely to follow the pattern of Irish names that have been emerging more in England.

Nydia

Latin, meaning 'nest'.

Nyimbo

Swahili, meaning 'song'.

Nyoko

Swahili, meaning 'snake'. Made popular by the 'Nyoka the Jungle Girl' comic book series.

Nysa
(alt. Nyssa)

Greek, meaning 'ambition'. A mountainous district in Greek mythology.

Girls' names

Oceana
(alt. Ocean, Océane, Ocie)
Greek, meaning 'ocean'.

Octavia
Latin, meaning 'eighth'. Sister
to Caesar and wife to Antony in
Shakespeare's Antony and
Cleopatra.

Oda
(alt. Odie)
Shortened form of Odessa, meaning
'long voyage'. Also Germanic,
meaning 'wealth' or 'inheritance'.

Odele
(alt. Odell)
English, meaning 'woad hill'. Woad is
a plant used as a natural blue dye.

Odelia
Hebrew, meaning 'I will praise
the Lord'. Also an eighth-century
French saint.

Odessa
Greek, meaning 'long voyage'. A
place in the Ukraine, known as the
pearl of the Black Sea.

Odette
(alt. Odetta)
French, meaning 'wealthy'. In the
famous ballet Swan Lake, Odette is
the good swan.

Odile
(alt. Odilia)
French, meaning 'prospers in battle'.
The evil black swan in the famous
ballet Swan Lake.

Odina
Feminine form of Odin, from the
Nordic god of the same name,
meaning 'creative inspiration'.

Odyssey
Greek, meaning 'long journey'.

Oksana

Russian, meaning 'praise to God'. Oksana Baiul is a Ukrainian Olympic figure-skating champion and Oksana Grigorieva is a Russian pianist and former wife of actor Mel Gibson.

Ola
(alt. Olie)

Greek, meaning 'man's defender'.

Olena
(alt. Olene)

Russian, meaning 'light'.

Olga

Russian, meaning 'holy'. The first Russian female ruler, later canonised as the first Russian saint of the Orthodox Church.

Oliana

American, meaning 'the Lord has answered'.

Olivia
(alt. Olive, Olivev, Oliviana, Olivié; abbrev. Ollie)

Latin, meaning 'olive'. Has featured in the Top 10 names for girls in England for several years now, including at number one.

Olwen

Welsh, meaning 'white footprint'. Olwen Hufton is a British historian of early modern Europe, women's history and social history.

Olympia
(alt. Olimpia)

Greek, meaning 'from Mount Olympus'. A sanctuary of ancient Greece, known as the site of the Olympic Games in classical times.

Oma
(alt. Omie)

Arabic, meaning 'leader'. In German, oma often refers to 'grandmother'.

Omyra

Latin, meaning 'scented oil'.

Ondine

French, meaning 'wave of water'. Also the name of a French play.

Oneida
(abbrev. Ona, Onnie)

Native American, meaning 'long awaited'. The Oneida Indians were believed to have emerged as a tribe in the fourteenth century.

Onyx

Latin, meaning 'veined gem'. A precious stone.

Oona
(alt. Oonagh)

Irish, meaning 'unity'.

Opal

Sanskrit, meaning 'gem'. A gemstone made of this mineral, noted for its rich iridescence.

Ophelia
(alt. Ofelia, Ophélie)

Greek, meaning 'help'. Lead character from Shakespeare's play *Hamlet*.

Oprah

Hebrew, meaning 'young deer'. Most often associated with Oprah Winfrey.

Ora

Latin, meaning 'prayer'.

Orabela

Latin, meaning 'prayer'.

Oralie
(alt. Oralia)

French, meaning 'golden'. Oralia Dominguez is a Mexican opera singer.

Orane

French, meaning 'rising'.

Orchid

Greek, from the flower of the same name.

Oriana
(alt. Oriane)

Latin, meaning 'dawning'. Oriana was the nickname for Queen Elizabeth I.

Orla
(alt. Orlaith, Orly)

Irish Gaelic, meaning 'golden lady'. Orla Kiely is an Irish fashion designer.

Orlean

French, meaning 'plum'. Orleans is a city in France.

Ornelia

Italian, meaning 'flowering ash tree'.

Orsa
(alt. Osia, Ossie)

Latin, meaning 'bear'.

Otthid

Greek, meaning 'prospers in battle'.

Ottilie
(alt. Ottie)

French, meaning 'prospers in battle'. Ottilie Metzger was a German opera singer well known in the early 1900s.

Ouida

French, meaning 'renowned in battle'. Pseudonym of the English novelist Maria Louise Ramé, known for her extravagant melodramatic romances.

Oyintsa

Native American, meaning 'white duck'.

Ozette

Native American, from the village of the same name.

Girls' names

Pacifica
(alt. Pacifika)

Spanish, meaning 'peaceful'. Pacifica Fernández was once Costa Rica's first lady; she also designed the Costa Rican flag.

Padma

Sanskrit, meaning 'lotus'. A major Buddhist symbol. Padma Lakshmi is an Indian-born American chef, cookbook author, model and TV presenter.

Paige
(alt. Page)

French, meaning 'serving boy'.

Paisley

Scottish, from the town of the same name.

Palma
(alt. Palmira)

Latin, meaning 'palm tree'.

Paloma

Spanish, meaning 'dove'. Paloma Picasso is the youngest daughter of artist Pablo Picasso. Singer Paloma Faith is known for her eccentric style.

Pamela
(alt. Pamala, Pamella, Pamla; abbrev. Pam)

Greek, meaning 'all honey'. Pamela Stephenson is an actor and comedian turned clinical psychologist and author. Pamela (P.L.) Travers is the author of *Mary Poppins*.

Pandora

Greek, meaning 'all gifted'. Also from the Greek myth, Pandora was given a box containing all the evils of the world, not to be opened. Now also commonly associated with the jewellery company.

Pangiota

Greek, meaning 'all is holy'. Comes from a Greek epithet widely used in reference to the Virgin Mary.

Paniz
Persian, meaning 'candy'.

Pansy
French, from the flower of the same name. Pansy Potter is a strong girl character in comic *The Beano* and Pansy Parkinson appears in the 'Harry Potter' series.

Paprika
English, meaning 'spice'.

Paradisa
(alt. Paradis)
Greek, meaning 'garden orchard'.

Paris
(alt. Parisa)
Greek, from the mythological hero of the same name. Also from the city. Paris Hilton is the hotel heiress and socialite.

Parker
English, meaning 'park keeper'.

Parthenia
Greek, meaning 'virginal'.

Parthenope
Greek, from the mythological Siren of the same name. Parthenope Nightingale was the elder sister of Florence Nightingale.

Parvati
Sanskrit, meaning 'daughter of the mountain'. The Hindu goddess of love and devotion.

Pascale
French, meaning 'Easter'.

Patience
French, meaning 'the state of being patient'. A Shakespearean name. Patience Wheatcroft was a respected journalist before joining the House of Lords.

Patricia
(alt. Patrice; abbrev. Pat, Patsy, Patti, Pattie, Patty)
Latin, meaning 'noble'. Patricia Routledge is an English character comedy actor and singer. Patricia Neal was an American actor whose birth name was Patsy Louise Neal.

Paula
Latin, meaning 'small'. Paula Radcliffe is a British long-distance runner, and current world record holder for the marathon.

Pauline
(alt. Paulette, Paulina)
Latin, meaning 'small'. The name of a British opera. A very popular name between the 1940s and the 1960s.

Paxton
Latin, meaning 'town of peace'.

Paz
Spanish, meaning 'peace'.

Pazia
Hebrew, meaning 'golden'.

Peace
English, meaning 'peace'.

Peaches

English, meaning 'peaches'. Rarely used. Peaches Geldof was the most famous bearer of the name.

Pearl
(alt. Pearle, Pearlie, Perla)

Latin, meaning 'pale gemstone'. Pearl Buck was an American author.

Peggy
(alt. Peggie)

Greek, meaning 'pearl'. Peggy Parish was the author of the children's story series Amelia Bedelia.

Pelia

Hebrew, meaning 'marvel of God'.

Penelope
(abbrev. Penny, Penni, Pennie)

Greek, meaning 'bobbin worker'. In Homer's *Odyssey*, Penelope is the faithful wife of Odysseus.

Peony

Greek, from the flower of the same name.

Perdita

Latin, meaning 'lost'. Perdita is one of the heroines of William Shakespeare's play *The Winter's Tale*.

Peri
(alt. Perri)

Hebrew, meaning 'outcome'. In Persian mythology, the Peri are spirits who have been denied paradise until they have done penance.

Perry

French, meaning 'pear tree'. Also an English alcoholic drink made from pears.

Persephone

Greek, meaning 'bringer of destruction'. In Greek mythology, Queen of the Underworld.

Petra
(alt. Petrina)

Greek, meaning 'rock'. City in Jordan dating back to the time of Jesus and the Apostles.

Petula

Latin, meaning 'to seek'. Petula Clark is an English singer, actor and composer.

Petunia

Greek, from the flower of the same name.

Phaedra

Greek, meaning 'bright'.

Philippa
(abbrev. Pippa, Pippie)

Greek, meaning 'lover of horses'. Philippa Foot was a twentieth-century philosopher and pioneer in the field of modern ethics. Philippa Gregory is an author of historical novels.

Philomena
(alt. Philoma)

Greek, meaning 'loved one'. Also a Catholic saint.

Phoebe

Greek, meaning 'shining and brilliant'. In Greek mythology, Phoebe was one of the original Titans and is associated with the moon.

Phoenix

Greek, meaning 'dark red'. In ancient Greek mythology, a phoenix is a bird that has the power to regenerate itself from its ashes.

Phyllida

Greek, meaning 'leafy bough'. Phyllida Lloyd is a British director, best known for her work in theatre and as the director of *Mamma Mia!* and *The Iron Lady*.

Phyllis

(alt. Phillia, Phylis)
Greek, meaning 'leafy bough'.

Pia

Latin, meaning 'pious'.

Piera

Italian, meaning 'rock'.

Pilar

Spanish, meaning 'pillar'. In Latin America, Nuestra Señora del Pilar (Our Lady of the Pillar), the name given to the Blessed Virgin Mary.

Piper

English, meaning 'pipe player'. Piper Laurie, an American actor, was born Rosetta Jacobs.

Plum

Latin, from the fruit of the same name.

Polly

Hebrew, meaning 'bitter'. A nickname for 'Mary'. Polly Dunbar is a British author-illustrator.

Pomona

Latin, meaning 'apple'. Pomona was a goddess of fruitful abundance in ancient Roman religion and myth.

Poppy

Latin, from the flower of the same name. Poppy Delevingne is a British socialite and model.

Portia

(alt. Porsha)
Latin, meaning 'from the Portia clan'. The heroine in Shakespeare's *The Merchant of Venice*.

Posy

English, meaning 'small flower'. Posy Hawthorne is a character in the 'Hunger Games' series.

Precious

Latin, meaning 'of great worth'.

Priela

Hebrew, meaning 'fruit of God'.

Primavera

Italian, meaning 'springtime'. Also the name of a painting by Botticelli.

Primrose

English, meaning 'first rose'.

Princess

English, meaning 'daughter of the monarch'.

Priscilla

(alt. Prisca, Priscila)

Latin, meaning 'ancient'. Priscilla Wakefield was an eighteenth-century Quaker educational writer and philanthropist.

Priya

Hindi, meaning 'loved one'.

Prudence

(abbrev. Pru, Prue, Prudie)

Latin, meaning 'caution'. Known as the mother of all virtues.

Prunella

Latin, meaning 'small plum'. Prunella Clough was a prominent British artist and Prunella Scales is an actor best known for playing Sybil in *Fawlty Towers*.

Psyche

Greek, meaning 'breath'. In Greek mythology, the wife of Eros. Also the name of an opera.

Girls' names

Qiana
(alt. Qianah, Qiania, Qyana, Qianne)
American, meaning 'gracious'. Qiana Chase is an American model.

Qiturah
Arabic, meaning 'incense'.

Queen
(alt. Queenie)
English, meaning 'queen'.

Quiana
American, meaning 'silky'. Quiana Grant is an American model.

Quincy
(alt. Quincey)
French, meaning 'estate of the fifth son'. Also used as a boys' name.

Quinn
Irish Gaelic, meaning 'counsel'. Quinn Fabray is a character from the American musical comedy-drama series *Glee*.

Quintessa
Latin, meaning 'creative'.

Girls' names

Rachel
(alt. Rachael, Rachelle)

Hebrew, meaning 'ewe'. Rachel is a figure in the Bible. A very popular name during the 1960s and 1970s, especially. Famous Rachels include actors Rachel Weisz and Rachel Bilson and the character of Rachel Green from *Friends*.

Radhika
(alt. Raadhika)

Sanskrit, meaning 'prosperous'. Raadhika Sarathkumar is one of Bollywood's most prolific actors and producers.

Rae
(alt. Ray)

Shortened form of Rachel, meaning 'ewe'. Rae Armantrout is known for her poetry and academic writing.

Rafferty

Irish, meaning 'abundance'. More commonly found as a surname.

Rahima

Arabic, meaning 'compassionate'.

Raina
(alt. Rain, Raine, Rainey, Rayne)

Latin, meaning 'queen'.

Raisa
(alt. Raissa)

Yiddish, meaning 'rose'. Extremely popular name in Russia, particularly as Mikhail Gorbachev's wife was called Raisa.

Raleigh
(alt. Rayleigh)

Old English, meaning 'deer's meadow'.

Rama
(alt. Ramey, Ramya)

Hebrew, meaning 'exalted'. Also one of the god Vishnu's avatars in the Hindu faith.

Ramona
(alt. Romona)

Spanish, meaning 'wise guardian'. Also the *Ramona* children's novels and the film *Ramona and Beezus*, by Beverly Cleary.

Ramsey
(alt. Ramsay)

Old English, meaning 'wild garlic island'. Can be used for girls and boys.

Rana
(alt. Rania, Rayna)

Arabic, meaning 'beautiful thing'.

Rani

Sanskrit, meaning 'queen'. Also a character from *Doctor Who*.

Raphaela
(alt. Rafaela, Raffaella)

Spanish, meaning 'God has healed'. A feminine form of Raphael, name of the painter and artist.

Raquel
(alt. Racquel)

Hebrew, meaning 'ewe'. Famous Raquels include actor Racquel Welch and the character in *Only Fools and Horses*.

Rashida

Turkish, meaning 'righteous'. Rashida Jones is an actor.

Raven
(alt. Ravyn)

English, from the black bird of the same name. Raven-Symoné is an actor often known as just Raven.

Razia

Arabic, meaning 'contented'. Razia Sultan was the only female ruler of the Sultanate Delhi and of the Mughal period of Indian history, during the thirteenth century.

Reagan
(alt. Reagen, Regan)

Irish Gaelic, meaning 'descendant of Riagán'.

Reba

Shortened form of Rebecca, meaning 'joined'. Reba McEntire is an American country singer.

Rebecca
(alt. Rebekah)

Hebrew, meaning 'joined'. Rebecca is a figure in the Bible. Also a classic novel by Daphne Du Maurier. A popular name through several decades, with many abbreviated forms including Reb, Becca, Becky, Bex, Becs and more.

Reese

Welsh, meaning 'fiery and zealous'. Actor Reese Witherspoon starred in *Legally Blonde* and *Walk the Line*.

Regina

Latin, meaning 'queen'. Famous Reginas include actors Regina King and Regina Hall and the character of Regina George in the film *Mean Girls*.

Reiko

Japanese, meaning 'thankful one'.

Reina
(alt. Rey, Reyna, Rheyna)
Spanish, meaning 'queen'.

Rena
(alt. Reena)
Hebrew, meaning 'serene'.

Renata
Latin, meaning 'reborn'. Renata Tebaldi was one of the best-loved post-war opera singers.

Rene
Greek, meaning 'peace'. Actor Rene Russo appeared in *Get Shorty*, *The Thomas Crown Affair* and the *Thor* series.

Renée
(alt. Renae, Renee)
French, meaning 'reborn'. Famous Renées include actors Renée Zellweger and Renee Roberts, and one half of the singing duo Renée and Renato.

Renira
A rare name with no clear agreed origin. Used, but rarely, in a range of countries including England and Scotland, the USA, Germany, Brazil and Hungary.

Renita
Latin, meaning 'resistant'. Most commonly used in the USA.

Reshma
(alt. Resha)
Sanskrit, meaning 'silk'.

Reta
(alt. Retha, Retta)
Shortened form of Margaret, meaning 'pearl'. In Portuguese the name also means 'straight'.

Rhea
Greek, meaning 'earth'. Also the name of the mother of the gods in ancient Greek mythology.

Rheta
Greek, meaning 'eloquent speaker'.

Rhiannon
(alt. Reanna, Reanne, Rhian, Rhianna)
Welsh, meaning 'witch'. Also the name of the mother of Pryderi, King of Dyfed, in Welsh mythology.

Rhoda
Greek, meaning 'rose'. Found in the Bible.

Rhona
Nordic, meaning 'rough island'. Popular in Scotland. Rhona Martin represented Britain in curling at the 2002 Salt Lake City Olympics. Rhona Cameron is a comedian.

Rhonda
(alt. Ronda)
Welsh, meaning 'noisy'.

Ría
(alt. Rie, Riya)
Shortened form of Victoria, meaning 'victor'.

Ricki
(alt. Rieko, Rika, Rikki)

Shortened form of Frederica, meaning 'peaceful ruler'. Actor and presenter Ricki Lake hosted a talk show bearing her name for a decade.

Riley

Irish Gaelic, meaning 'courageous'. Used as a boys' name and girls' name equally.

Rilla

German, meaning 'small brook'.

Rima

Arabic, meaning 'antelope'. Rima the Jungle Girl is the fictional heroine of novel *Green Mansions* and was briefly a comic book character also.

Riona

Irish Gaelic, meaning 'like a queen'. Sometimes used as a spelling alternative to Fiona.

Ripley

English, meaning 'shouting man's meadow'.

Risa

Latin, meaning 'laughter'. More commonly used in Japanese- and Spanish-speaking cultures.

Rita

Shortened form of Margaret, meaning 'pearl'. Famous Ritas include actors Rita Hayworth and Rita Moreno and singer Rita Coolidge.

River
(alt. Riviera)

English, from 'river'. Used as both a boys' and a girls' name, sometimes in the plural.

Roberta
(abbrev. Robbie, Robi, Roby, Bobby, Bobbie)

English, meaning 'bright fame'. Singer Roberta Flack won Grammy Record of the Year for two consecutive years in the 1970s with 'The First Time Ever I Saw Your Face' and 'Killing Me Softly with His Song'.

Robin
(alt. Robbin, Robyn)

English, meaning 'bright fame'. Used slightly more often for boys than for girls. Famous Robins include actor Robin Wright Penn and singer Robyn.

Rochelle
(alt. Richelle, Rochel)

French, meaning 'little rock'. Singer Rochelle Humes featured in S Club 8 and The Saturdays.

Rogue

French, meaning 'beggar'. A character from the *X-Men* comic series.

Rohina
(alt. Rohini)

Sanskrit, meaning 'sandalwood'.

Roisin

Irish Gaelic, meaning 'little rose'. Singer Roisin Murphy was one half of group Moloko before going solo.

Roja

Spanish, meaning 'red-haired lady'. The name also means 'rose' in Tamil.

Rolanda

German, meaning 'renowned land'.

Roma

Italian, meaning 'Rome'. Also the name of an ancient Roman deity, and of a group of nomadic European people.

Romaine
(alt. Romina)

French, meaning 'from Rome'.

Romola
(alt. Romilda, Romily)

Latin, meaning 'Roman woman'. Actor Romola Garai appeared in films including Atonement and Emma.

Romy

Shortened form of Rosemary, meaning 'dew of the sea', and often the German variation. Actor Romy Rosemont is known for her TV roles in Prison Break, Grey's Anatomy and Glee.

Rona
(alt. Ronia, Ronja, Ronna)

Nordic, meaning 'rough island'. Also the name of two Scottish islands, North Rona and South Rona.

Ronnie
(alt. Roni, Ronni)

English, meaning 'strong counsel'. Impressionist and actor Ronni Ancona has also appeared on TV panel shows.

Roro

Indonesian, meaning 'nobility'. Sometimes used as a nickname for Ro- names (Rosa, Rosalind, etc).

Rosa

Italian, meaning 'rose'. Activist Rosa Parks is credited with being the 'first lady of American civil rights' after she refused to give up her seat to a white passenger on a bus in 1955.

Rosabel
(alt. Rosabella)

Contraction of Rose and Belle, meaning 'beautiful rose'. Most commonly used in the USA.

Rosalie
(alt. Rosale, Rosalia, Rosalina)

French, meaning 'rose garden'. Actor Andie MacDowell's birth name is Rosalie.

Rosalind
(alt. Rosalinda)

Spanish, meaning 'pretty rose'. A character in Shakespeare's As You Like It.

Rosalyn
(alt. Rosaleen, Rosaline, Roselyn)

Contraction of Rose and Lynn, meaning 'pretty rose'. Also a song by the Pretty Things, which was later recorded by David Bowie.

Rosamund
(alt. Rosamond)

German, meaning 'renowned protector'. Famous Rosamunds include actor Rosamund Pike, author Rosamunde Pilcher and the long-time mistress of Henry II, Rosamund Clifford.

Rose

Latin, from the flower of the same name. Famous Roses include actors Rose Byrne and Rose McGowan and the character of Rose DeWitt Bukater from the film *Titanic*.

Roseanne
(alt. Rosana, Rosann, Rosanna, Rosanne, Roseann, Roseanna)

Combination of Rose and Anne, meaning 'graceful rose'. Actor and comedian Roseanne Barr is known for her stand-up work and sitcom *Roseanne*.

Rosemary
(alt. Rosemarie; abbrev. Ros, Rosy, Rosie, Romy)

Latin, meaning 'dew of the sea'. Rosemary has regularly been used over long periods. The name is also the title of several songs. Famous Rosies include actors Rosie O'Donnell and Rosie Perez and supermodel Rosie Huntington-Whiteley.

Rosita

Spanish, meaning 'rose'. A character in *Sesame Street*.

Rowena
(alt. Rowan)

Welsh, meaning 'slender and fair'. In ancient British mythology, Rowena was a powerful and beautiful seductress.

Roxanne
(alt. Roxana, Roxane, Roxanna; abbrev. Roxie, Roxey, Roxy)

Persian, meaning 'dawn'. A song by The Police. Famous Roxies include the character of Roxie Hart from the musical *Chicago*, inventor Roxey Ann Caplin, and the band Roxy Music.

Rubina
(alt. Rubena)

Hebrew, meaning 'behold, a son'. Also a tropical plant.

Ruby
(alt. Rubi, Rubie)

English, meaning 'red gemstone'. Associated with the comedian Ruby Wax, or the songs 'Ruby Tuesday' by The Rolling Stones and 'Ruby' by Kaiser Chiefs.

Rusty

American, meaning 'red-headed'. Used for girls and, more commonly, boys.

Ruth
(alt. Ruthe, Ruthie)

Hebrew, meaning 'friend and companion'. A prominent figure in the Bible.

S

Girls' names

Saba
(alt. Sabah)

Greek, meaning 'from Sheba'. Also the name of a small Caribbean island.

Sabina
(alt. Sabine)

Latin, meaning 'from the Sabine tribe'. Sabina was also the name given to certain women of political standing in ancient Rome.

Sabrina

Latin, meaning 'the River Severn'. Also a film starring Audrey Hepburn, and the title character of the sitcom *Sabrina, the Teenage Witch*.

Sadella

American, meaning 'fairytale princess'. More commonly used in the USA.

Sadie
(alt. Sade, Sadye)

Hebrew, meaning 'princess'. Famous Sadies include actor and businesswoman Sadie Frost, actor Sadie Miller and academic pioneer Sadie Tanner Mossell Alexander.

Saffron
(alt. Saffie)

English, from the reddish-yellow spice of the same name. Saffie is a character from *Absolutely Fabulous*, Edina's level-headed and long-suffering daughter.

Safiyya
(alt. Safiya)

Arabic, meaning 'sincere friend'. Also the name of one of Muhammad's wives.

Sage
(alt. Saga, Saige)

Latin, meaning 'wise and healthy'. Also the name of a herb.

Sahara
Arabic, meaning 'desert'.

Sakura
Japanese, meaning 'cherry blossom'.

Sally
(alt. Sallie)

Hebrew, meaning 'princess'. Famous Sallys include actors Sally Field and Sally Whittaker and athlete Sally Gunnell.

Salma
Arabic, meaning 'peaceful'. Also Persian, meaning 'sweetheart'. Actor Salma Hayek is a Mexican-American.

Salome
(alt. Salma)

Hebrew, meaning 'peace'. Also the name of an influential character in the Bible thought to be associated with seductive dance.

Samantha
(abbrev. Sam, Sammie, Sammy)

Hebrew, meaning 'told by God'. Famous Samanthas include actors Samantha Morton and Samantha Bond.

Samara
(alt. Samaria, Samira)

Hebrew, meaning 'under God's rule'. Also the name of several places in Russia.

Sanaa
Arabic, meaning 'brilliance'. Also the capital of Yemen.

Sandra
(alt. Saundra; abbrev. Sandi, Sandy)

Shortened form of Alexandra, meaning 'defender of mankind'. Famous Sandras include actor Sandra Bullock, and Sandy is the main female character in the film Grease.

Sangeetha
Hindi, meaning 'musical'. Actor Sangeetha Arvind Krish is known in Bollywood simply as Sangeetha.

Sanna
(alt. Saniya, Sanne, Sanni)

Hebrew, meaning 'lily'. Sometimes used as a shortened version of Susanna.

Santana
(alt. Santina)

Spanish, meaning 'holy'. Usually associated with the (male) guitar legend Carlos Santana.

Saoirse
Irish, meaning 'freedom'. Pronounced 'Ser-sha', Irish-American actor Saoirse Ronan has been nominated for numerous awards.

Sapphire
(alt. Saphira)

Hebrew, meaning 'blue gemstone'. Usually associated with the blue gem popular in jewellery.

Sarah
(alt. Sara, Sarai, Sariah)

Hebrew, meaning 'princess'. Also an important character in the Bible. A particularly popular name in the 1960s.

Sasha
(alt. Sacha, Sascha)

Russian, meaning 'defender of mankind'. Used for both girls and boys, and now spreading more widely outside of Russia. Sasha is one of Barack Obama's daughters.

Saskia
(alt. Saskie)

Dutch, meaning 'the Saxon people'. In Danish the name also means 'valley of light'.

Savannah
(alt. Savanah, Savanna, Savina)

Spanish, meaning 'treeless'. Also one of Queen Elizabeth II's great-grandchildren, Savannah Phillips.

Scarlett
(alt. Scarlet)

English, meaning 'scarlet'. Usually associated with the character of Scarlett O'Hara, from the novel and film *Gone with the Wind*, or actor Scarlett Johansson.

Scout

French, meaning 'to listen'. The main female character from the classic novel *To Kill a Mockingbird*, by Harper Lee.

Sedona
(alt. Sedna)

Spanish, from the city of the same name. Also the name of a city in Arizona, USA.

Selah
(alt. Sela)

Hebrew, meaning 'cliff'. Also a phrase used in the Hebrew Bible meaning 'stop and listen'.

Selby

English, meaning 'manor village'.

Selena
(alt. Salena, Salima, Salina, Selene, Selina)

Greek, meaning 'moon goddess'. Famous Selenas include singers Selena Gomez and Selena Quintanilla-Perez (known simply as Selena) and actor Selena Royle.

Selma

German, meaning 'Godly helmet'. Versatile actor Selma Blair has starred in a range of film genres as well as Hollywood hits.

Seneca

Native American, meaning 'from the Seneca tribe'. Also the name of a prominent ancient Roman philosopher, Seneca the Younger.

Sephora

Hebrew, meaning 'bird'. In Greek, the name also means 'beauty'.

September

Latin, meaning 'seventh month'.

Seraphina
(alt. Serafina, Seraphia, Seraphine)

Hebrew, meaning 'ardent'. St Serafina was an Italian woman whose illness and suffering contributed to her strong faith.

Serena
(alt. Sarina, Sereana)

Latin, meaning 'tranquil'. Serena Williams dominated women's tennis for long periods.

Serenity

Latin, meaning 'serene'. Also a sci-fi film.

Shania
(alt. Shaina, Shana, Shaniya)

Hebrew, meaning 'beautiful'. Shania Twain is the Canadian country/pop singer-songwriter whose real first name is Eilleen.

Shanice

American, meaning 'from Africa'. Singer Shanice is known for songs including 'I Love Your Smile'.

Shaniqua
(alt. Shanika)

English, adapted from the Swahili word Shanika, meaning 'God is gracious'. More commonly used in the USA.

Shanna

English, meaning 'old'. There is a comic book character called Shanna the She-Devil. Shanna is a name shared by a number of famous Americans, including Shanna Zolman, the female professional basketball player.

Shannon
(alt. Shannan, Shanon)

Irish Gaelic, meaning 'old and ancient'. The name is believed to be a reference to Sionna, who was a goddess in ancient Irish mythology.

Shantal
(alt. Shantel, Shantell)

French, meaning 'stone'. Often used as a spelling alternative to Chantal.

Shanti
(alt. Shantih)

Hindi, meaning 'peaceful'. Also mentioned in T.S. Eliot's poem The Waste Land.

Sharlene

German, meaning 'man'. Often used as a spelling alternative to Charlene.

Sharon
(alt. Sharen, Sharona, Sharron, Sharyn)

Hebrew, meaning 'a plain'. Famous Sharons include swimmer Sharon Davies, presenter Sharon Osbourne and actor Sharon Stone.

Shasta

American, from the mountain of the same name. Also the name of a Native American tribe.

Shauna
(alt. Shawna)

Irish, meaning 'the Lord is gracious'. More commonly used in the USA.

Shayla
(alt. Shaylie, Shayna, Sheyla)
Irish, meaning 'blind'. Shayla Worley is an American gymnast.

Shea
Irish Gaelic, meaning 'from the fairy fort'. Usually associated with the tree and the nut that goes into creating shea butter.

Sheena
Irish, meaning 'the Lord is gracious'. Singer Sheena Easton rocketed to fame when she featured in an early British reality TV show, *The Big Time*, in the late 1970s.

Sheila
(alt. Shelia)
Irish, meaning 'blind'. Actor Sheila Hancock has had a long and varied career that has taken her from the West End and Broadway, through TV and film to Radio 4 and documentary.

Shelby
(alt. Shelba, Shelbie)
Norse, meaning 'willow'. Can be used as a boys' name and girls' name.

Shelley
(alt. Shelli, Shellie, Shelly)
English, meaning 'meadow on the ledge'. Famous Shelleys include skeleton athlete Shelley Rudman and actor Shelley Winters.

Shenandoah
Native American. In the Iroquoian language it means 'deer'. A river in the state of Virginia, USA.

Sheridan
Irish Gaelic, meaning 'wild man'. Actor Sheridan Smith appeared in *Two Pints of Lager and a Packet of Crisps* and *Gavin and Stacey*.

Sherry
(alt. Sheree, Sheri, Sherie, Sherri, Sherrie)
Shortened form of Cheryl or Sheryl, meaning 'man'. Also an alcoholic drink.

Sheryl
(alt. Sherryl)
German, meaning 'man'. Famous Sheryls include singer Sheryl Crow, presenter Sheryl Gascoigne and Sheryl Sandberg, a high-profile businesswoman, currently the Chief Operating Officer at Facebook.

Shiloh
Hebrew, meaning 'his gift'. From the biblical place of the same name, made popular by Angelina Jolie and Brad Pitt's daughter.

Shirley
(alt. Shirlee)
English, meaning 'bright meadow'. Famous Shirleys include singer Dame Shirley Bassey, actor Shirley MacLaine and child star Shirley Temple.

Shivani
Sanskrit, meaning 'wife of Shiva'.

Shola
Arabic, meaning 'energetic'. More commonly a boys' name.

Shona

Irish Gaelic, meaning 'God is gracious'. Also associated with the Shona people of southern Africa.

Shoshana
(alt. Shoshanna)

Hebrew, meaning 'lily'. Made popular by the character of Shoshanna Shapiro in *Girls*.

Shura

Russian, meaning 'man's defender'. In Arabic it also means 'consultation'.

Sian
(alt. Sianna)

Welsh, meaning 'the Lord is gracious'. Famous Sians include presenters Sian Lloyd and Sian Williams, and actor Sian Phillips.

Sibyl
(alt. Sybil)

Greek, meaning 'seer and oracle'. Sibyl was a prophetess in ancient Greek mythology.

Sidney
(alt. Sydney)

English, meaning 'wide meadow'. Used as a boys' name more commonly but also a girls' name.

Sidonie
(alt. Sidonia, Sidony)

Latin, meaning 'from Sidonia'. Also the name of a French-German princess of the fifteenth century.

Sienna
(alt. Siena)

Latin, from the city of the same name. Also the name of a type of yellowy-red earth pigment. Sienna Miller is an English model, BAFTA-nominated actor and fashion designer.

Sierra

Spanish, meaning 'saw'.

Siffhi

Hindi, meaning 'spiritual powers'.

Signa
(alt. Signe)

Scandinavian, meaning 'victory'. Also the name of a town in the province of Florence, Italy.

Sigrid

Nordic, meaning 'fair victory'. Sigrid the Haughty was said to have been the wife of Eric the Victorious in ancient Norse mythology.

Siksika

First Nation, meaning 'silken foot'. The Siksika Nation is a tribe in Canada whose name comes from 'silk' and 'foot'.

Silja

Scandinavian, meaning 'blind'.

Simcha

Hebrew, meaning 'joy'.

Simone
(alt. Simona)

Hebrew, meaning 'to hear'. Female variant of the name Simon, except in Italy, where Simone is the male form of Simon and the female form is Simona. Famous Simones include philosopher Simone de Beauvoir and first female scuba diver, Simone Melchior.

Sinéad

Irish, meaning 'the Lord is gracious'. Used with and without the accent on the 'e'. Famous Sineads include singer Sinéad O'Connor, actor Sinéad Cusack and ice-dancing skater Sinead Kerr.

Siobhan

Irish, meaning 'the Lord is gracious'. Actor Siobhan McKenna is credited with reviving the name in the twentieth century.

Siren
(alt. Sirena)

Greek, meaning 'entangler'. Sirens were beautiful and deadly creatures who lured men to their deaths at sea in ancient Greek mythology.

Siria

Spanish, meaning 'glowing'. Often used as a spelling alternative to Syria.

Skye
(alt. Sky, Skylyn)

Scottish, from the large island of the same name in Scotland.

Skyler
(alt. Skyla, Skylar)

Dutch, meaning 'giving shelter'. The name Skyler has seen a sudden jump in popularity after the success of the drama series *Breaking Bad*, which featured a main character called Skyler White.

Sloane
(alt. Sloan)

Irish Gaelic, meaning 'man of arms'. Usually associated with Sloane Square in London, after which the Sloane Rangers are named.

Socorro

Spanish, meaning 'to aid'.

Sojourner

English, meaning 'temporary stay'. Nineteenth-century civil rights and women's activist Sojourner Truth is known for her phrase 'And ain't I a woman?'

Solana

Spanish, meaning 'sunlight'. The solana is the Spanish word for the side of a mountain or valley where the sun hits.

Solange

French, meaning 'with dignity'. A Christian saint from the ninth century. American singer and actor Solange Knowles is unusual among famous Solanges in that she's not from a French-speaking country.

Soledad

Spanish, meaning 'solitude'.

Soleil

French, meaning 'sun'. Usually associated with performance artists Cirque du Soleil.

Solveig

Scandinavian, meaning 'woman of the house'.

Sona

Arabic, meaning 'golden one'. Sona MacDonald is an actor of film and theatre.

Sonia

(alt. Sonja, Sonya)

Greek, meaning 'wisdom'. Sonia Rykiel is a French fashion designer. Sonia O'Sullivan was a world-class Irish long-distance runner who won medals at World Championships and Olympics.

Sophia

(alt. Sofia, Sofie, Sophie)

Greek, meaning 'wisdom'. Sophia Loren was actually named Sofia. Italy's most famous actor, she won an Oscar, BAFTA and Golden Globes. Other famous Sophias include film director Sofia Coppola and actors Sofia Vergara and Sophia Myles.

Sophronia

Greek, meaning 'sensible'. Usually associated with the character of Sophronia from the epic poem *Jerusalem Delivered*, by Torquato Tasso.

Soraya

Persian, meaning 'princess'. Queen Soraya Tarzi was the wife of King Amanullah of Afghanistan (reigned 1919–1929).

Sorcha

Irish and Scottish Gaelic, meaning 'bright and shining'. Irish actor Sorcha Cusack has appeared in *Coronation Street* and *Casualty*.

Sorrel

English, from the edible herb of the same name.

Stacey

(alt. Stacie, Stacy)

Greek, meaning 'resurrection'. Famous Staceys include actors Stacey Keibler and Stacey Dash and presenter Stacey Dooley.

Star

(alt. Starla, Starr)

English, meaning 'star'.

Stella

Latin, meaning 'star'. Leading fashion designer Stella McCartney is known for her ethics and creativity. She's also a mum of four: Miller, Bailey, Beckett and Reiley.

Stephanie

(alt. Stefanie, Stephani, Stephania, Stephany, Stephenie)

Greek, meaning 'crowned'. Famous Stephanies include actor Stephanie Beacham, tennis pro Stefanie 'Steffi' Graf and author Stephenie Meyer.

Sue
(alt. Susie, Suzy)

Shortened form of Susan, meaning 'lily'. Famous Sues include comedian Sue Perkins and tennis pro turned TV presenter Sue Barker.

Sukey
(alt. Sukey, Sukie)

Shortened form of Susan, meaning 'lily'. Usually associated with the character of Sukey from the nursery rhyme 'Polly Put the Kettle On'.

Summer

English, from the season of the same name. Famous Summers include opera singer Summer Watson and actor Summer Glau.

Sunday

English, meaning 'the first day'.

Sunny
(alt. Sun)

English, meaning 'of a pleasant temperament'.

Suri

Persian, meaning 'red rose'. Suri Cruise is the daughter of Katie Holmes and Tom Cruise.

Surya

Hindi, from the god of the sun.

Susan
(alt. Susann, Suzan, Suzanne; abbrev. Sue, Susie, Suzy)

Hebrew, meaning 'lily'. Famous Susans include actor Susan Sarandon, singer Susan Boyle and suffragette Susan B. Anthony.

Susannah
(alt. Susana, Susanna, Susanne, Suzanna, Suzanne)

Hebrew, meaning 'lily'. Famous Susannahs include artist Susannah Fiennes and actors Susannah York and Susannah Doyle.

Svea

Swedish, meaning 'of the motherland'.

Svetlana

Russian, meaning 'star'. A popular name in Slavic countries, now starting to spread west. Svetlana Stalin was the daughter of Soviet dictator Josef Stalin.

Swanhild

Saxon, meaning 'battle swan'.

Sylvia
(alt. Silvia, Sylvie)

Latin, meaning 'from the forest'. Famous Sylvias include poet Sylvia Plath, suffragette Sylvia Pankhurst and singer Sylvia Robinson.

Girls' names

Tabitha
(alt. Tabatha, Tabetha)
Aramaic, meaning 'gazelle'. A woman raised from the dead by St Peter in the Bible. A very popular name in the USA in the 1970s and 1980s, after Tabitha the child witch TV character.

Tahira
Arabic, meaning 'virginal'.

Tai
Chinese, meaning 'big'.

Taima
(alt. Taina, Tayma)
Native American, meaning 'peal of thunder'. Also the name of an oasis in Saudi Arabia.

Tajsa
Polish, meaning 'princess'.

Talia
(alt. Tali)
Hebrew, meaning 'heaven's dew'. Famous Talias include actors Talia Shire and Talia Balsam.

Taliesin
Welsh, meaning 'shining brow'. Usually associated with the Welsh poet Taliesin.

Talise
(alt. Talyse)
Native American, meaning 'lovely water'.

Talitha
Aramaic, meaning 'young girl'. The name is mentioned in the Bible when Jesus raises a child from the dead.

Tallulah
(alt. Taliyah)
Native American, meaning 'leaping water'. Famous Tallulahs include actors Tallulah Bankhead and Tallulah Riley, and the character of club singer Tallulah in the film *Bugsy Malone*.

Tamara
(alt. Tamera)

Hebrew, meaning 'palm tree'.
Famous Tamaras include socialite
Tamara Ecclestone and actors Tamera
Mowry and Tamara Taylor.

Tamatha
(alt. Tametha)

American, meaning 'dear Tammy'.
Sometimes used as a spelling
alternative to Samantha.

Tamika
(alt. Tameka)

American, meaning 'people'.

Tammy
(alt. Tami, Tammie)

Shortened form of Tamsin, meaning
'twin'. Country singer Tammy
Wynette's best-known song is 'Stand
by Your Man'.

Tamsin

Hebrew, meaning 'twin'. Sometimes
used as a shortened form of
Thomasina.

Tanis

Spanish, meaning 'to make famous'.

Tanya
(alt. Tania, Tanya, Tonya)

Shortened form of Tatiana, meaning
'from the Tatius clan'. Dr Tanya Byron
is a child psychologist, author and TV
presenter on parenting issues.

Tao

Chinese, meaning 'like a peach'. Tao
is also the notion of a route or path in
Chinese cultures.

Tara
(alt. Tahra, Tarah, Tera)

Irish Gaelic, meaning 'rocky hill'.
Famous Taras include socialite Tara
Palmer-Tomkinson and actors Tara
Fitzgerald and Tara Reid.

Tasha
(alt. Taisha, Tarsha)

Shortened form of Natasha, meaning
'birthday'. Famous Tashas include
athlete Tasha Danvers, singer Tasha
Thomas and author and illustrator
Tasha Tudor.

Tatiana
(alt. Tatyana)

Russian, meaning 'from the Tatius
clan'. Famous Tatianas include
actor Tatyana Ali, author Tatiana de
Rosna and the character of Tatiana
Romanova from the James Bond film
From Russia With Love.

Tatum

English, meaning 'light hearted'.
Tatum O'Neal was the youngest
person to win a competitive Oscar,
picking up the award for *Paper
Moon*, in which she starred with her
father, Ryan O'Neal.

Tawny
(alt. Tawanaa, Tawnee, Tawnya)

English, meaning 'golden brown'.
Usually associated with the colour
tawny, as used in the descriptive
name of the tawny owl.

Taya

Greek, meaning 'poor one'. In
several languages the name also
means 'princess' or 'goddess'.

Taylor
(alt. Tayler)

English, meaning 'tailor'. Can be used for boys as well as girls. Famous Taylors include singer Taylor Swift and actor Taylor Schilling.

Tea

Greek, meaning 'goddess'. Actor Tea Leoni is known by her middle name, rather than her first name of Elizabeth.

Teagan
(alt. Teague, Tegan)

Irish Gaelic, meaning 'poet'.

Teal

English, from the bird of the same name. Often associated with the bluish-green colour.

Tecla

Greek, meaning 'fame of God'.

Tehile

Hebrew, meaning 'song of praise'.

Temperance

English, meaning 'virtue'.

Tempest

French, meaning 'storm'. Also the title of a Shakespearean play.

Teresa
(alt. Terese, Tereza, Theresa, Therese; abbrev. Terri, Teri, Terrie, Terry)

Greek, meaning 'harvest'. Famous Teresas include nun Mother Teresa, Prime Minister Theresa May and actor Teresa Graves.

Tessa
(alt. Tess, Tessie)

Shortened form of Teresa, meaning 'harvest'. Tessa Virtue is a Canadian ice dance champion, politician Tessa Jowell has served in the Cabinet and javelin thrower Tessa Sanderson represented Britain at every Olympics from 1976 to 1996.

Thais

Greek, from the mythological ancient Greek concubine of the same name.

Thalia

Greek, meaning 'blooming'. There are half a dozen ancient Greek muses, nymphs and graces who share the name Thalia.

Thandie
(alt. Thana, Thandi)

Arabic, meaning 'thanksgiving'. Thandie Newton is a British film and TV actor.

Names with positive meanings

Allegra – cheerful
Augusta – magnificent
Felicia – lucky
Hilary – cheerful
Lucy – light
Phoebe – radiant
Thalia – flourishing
Yoko – positive

Thea

Greek, meaning 'goddess'. The name Thea can also be a shortened form of Theodora or Dorothea.

Theda

German, meaning 'people'. Theda Bara was one of the silent era's most prolific and popular actors, appearing in over 40 films.

Thelma

Greek, meaning 'will'. Famous Thelmas include the actor Thelma Barlow, singer Thelma Houston and the film *Thelma and Louise*.

Theodora

(alt. Theodosia)

Greek, meaning 'gift of God'. There are dozens of ancient Roman empresses and other figures named Theodora.

Thisbe

Greek, from the mythological heroine of the same name in the ancient Roman poem *Metamorphoses* by Ovid.

Thomasina

(alt. Thomasin, Thomasine, Thomasyn)

Greek, meaning 'twin'. Singer Tammi Terrell, who was known for her Motown duets with singer Marvin Gaye, was born Thomasina Montgomery.

Thora

Scandinavian, meaning 'Thor's struggle'. Famous Thoras include actors Thora Hird and Thora Birch and the figure of Thora Bogarhjort of ancient Norse mythology.

Tia

(alt. Tiana)

Spanish, meaning 'aunt'. Famous Tias include actor Tia Mowry and the goddess Tia from Native American Haida tribal mythology.

Tiara

Latin, meaning 'jewelled headband'.

Tien

Vietnamese, meaning 'fairy child'.

Tierney

Irish Gaelic, meaning 'Lord'.

Tierra

(alt. Tiera)

Spanish, meaning 'land'. Used most commonly in the USA.

Tiffany

(alt. Tiffani, Tiffanie)

Greek, meaning 'God's appearance'. Famous Tiffanys include the singer Tiffany, socialite Tiffany Trump and the book/film/song *Breakfast at Tiffany's*.

Tiggy

(alt. Tigris)

Irish Gaelic, meaning 'tiger'. Tiggy Legge-Bourke (whose birth name is Alexandra) is known for being a royal nanny to Princes William and Harry.

Tilda

Shortened form of Matilda, meaning 'battle-mighty'. Oscar-winning actor Tilda Swinton's full name is Katherine Matilda.

Tilly
(alt. Tillie)

Shortened form of Matilda, meaning 'battle-mighty'. Has seen a rise in popularity in recent years.

Timothea

Greek, meaning 'honouring God'.

Tina
(alt. Teena, Tena)

Shortened form of Christina, meaning 'anointed Christian'. Famous Tinas include singer Tina Turner, comedian Tina Fey and actor Tina Louise.

Tirion

Welsh, meaning 'kind and gentle'.

Tirzah

Hebrew, meaning 'pleasantness'. Found in the Bible.

Titania

Greek, meaning 'giant'. Also queen of the fairies in Shakespeare's play *A Midsummer Night's Dream*.

Toby
(alt. Tobi)

Hebrew, meaning 'God is good'. More commonly used as a boys' name.

Tomoko

Japanese, meaning 'intelligent'.

Toni
(alt. Tony)

Latin, meaning 'invaluable'. Also a shortened form of Antoinette. Famous Tonis include author Toni Morrison, singer Toni Braxton and choreographer Toni Basil.

Tonia
(alt. Tonja, Tonya)

Russian, meaning 'praiseworthy'.

Topaz

Latin, meaning 'golden gemstone'.

Tori
(alt. Tora, Toria)

Shortened form of Victoria, meaning 'victory'. Singer Tori Amos was born Myra Ellen Amos.

Tova
(alt. Tovah, Tove)

Hebrew, meaning 'good'.

Tracy
(alt. Tracey, Tracie)

Greek, meaning 'harvest'. Famous Tracys include singer Tracy Chapman, artist Tracey Emin and actor Tracey Ullman.

Treva

Welsh, meaning 'homestead'.

Trilby

English, meaning 'vocal trills'.

Trina
(alt. Trena)

Greek, meaning 'pure'. Also used as a shortened form of Katrina.

Trinity

Latin, meaning 'triad'. Usually associated with the Christian Holy Trinity. Also the impossibly cool lead female character in *The Matrix*.

Trisha

(alt. Tricia)

Shortened form of Patricia, meaning 'noble'. Trisha Goddard is a TV talk show host.

Trista

Latin, meaning 'sad'. More commonly used in the USA.

Trixie

Shortened form of Beatrix, meaning 'blessed' or 'voyager'. Also a name used frequently in children's television and film, such as the characters of Trixie the Triceratops in *Toy Story 3* and Trixie the Troublemaker in *LazyTown*.

Trudie

(alt. Tru, Truye)

Shortened form of Gertrude, meaning 'strength of a spear'. Famous Trudies include actor Trudie Goodwin and producer and actor Trudie Styler.

Tullia

Latin, meaning 'bound for glory'.

Tunder

Hungarian, meaning 'fairy'.

Twyla

(alt. Twila)

American, meaning 'star'.

Tyler

English, meaning 'tile maker'. More commonly used as a boys' name.

Tyra

Scandinavian, meaning 'Thor's struggle'. Supermodel Tyra Banks is known for her extensive modelling career and is presenter of *America's Next Top Model*.

Tzipporah

Hebrew, meaning 'bird'. Used as a spelling alternative to Zipporah.

Girls' names

Udaya
Sanskrit, meaning 'dawn'.

Ula
(alt. Ulla)
Celtic, meaning 'gem of the sea'. Also the name of a Manchu tribe from China.

Ulrika
(alt. Urica)
German, meaning 'power of the wolf'. Swedish Ulrika Jonsson has made her TV career in Britain.

Uma
Sanskrit, meaning 'flax'. Actor Uma Thurman is known for her roles in *Pulp Fiction*, *Gattaca* and the *Kill Bill* series.

Una
Latin, meaning 'one'. Famous Unas include enduring British actor Una Stubbs and Irish singer Una Healy of The Saturdays.

Undine
Latin, meaning 'little wave'. Also the name of a water element in alchemy.

Unice
Greek, meaning 'victorious'. A spelling alternative to Eunice.

Unique
Latin, meaning 'only one'.

Unity
English, meaning 'oneness'.

Uriela
(alt. Uriella)
Hebrew, meaning 'angel of light'. Found particularly in German-speaking communities.

Urja
(alt. Urjitha)
Sanskrit, meaning 'energy'.

Ursula
Latin, meaning 'little female bear'. A character in Disney's film *The Little Mermaid*.

Uta
German, meaning 'prospers in battle'.

Girls' names

Vada
German, meaning 'famous ruler'.

Valdis
(alt. Valdiss, Valdys, Valdyss)
Norse, meaning 'goddess of the dead', based on the mythological goddess of the same name.

Valencia
(alt. Valancy, Valarece; abbrev. Vale)
Latin, meaning 'strong and healthy'. Also one of the largest cities in Spain.

Valentina
(alt. Valentine)
Latin, meaning 'strong and healthy'. Valentina Cortese is an Italian actor. Russian Valentina Tereshkova was the first female astronaut, in 1963.

Valerie
(alt. Valarie, Valery, Valorie, Valeria; abbrev. Valia)
Latin, meaning 'to be healthy and strong'. Also a song, most recently recorded by Mark Ronson and Amy Winehouse. Valia Venitshaya was an actor in the silent film era.

Vandana
Sanskrit, meaning 'worship'. Also the name of a genus of moths.

Vanessa
(alt. Vanesa)
English, from the *Gulliver's Travels* character of the same name. Famous Vanessas include TV presenter Vanessa Feltz and Vanessa-Mae, the Singapore-born British professional violinist, who represented Thailand in downhill skiing at the 2014 Winter Olympics.

Vanetta
(alt. Vanettah, Vaneta, Vanete, Vanity)
Greek, alternative of Vanessa, meaning 'like a butterfly'.

Vanity
Latin, meaning 'self-obsessed'.

Vashti
Persian, meaning 'beauty'. Also the name of a Persian queen in the Hebrew Bible.

Veda

Sanskrit, meaning 'knowledge and wisdom'. The Vedas are an important set of texts from ancient India.

Vega

Arabic, meaning 'falling vulture'. Also the name of a bright star in the night sky.

Velda

German, meaning 'ruler'. Also the name of a common ancestor named in *The Seven Daughters of Eve*.

Vella

American, meaning 'beautiful'. Also the name of a genus of leafy plants.

Velma

English, meaning 'determined protector'. A character in the *Scooby-Doo* series.

Venice
(alt. Venetia, Venita)

Latin, meaning 'city of canals'. From the city of the same name in Italy.

Venus

Latin, from the ancient Roman goddess of sexuality and fertility. Also the name of the planet.

Vera
(alt. Verla, Verlie)

Slavic, meaning 'faith'. Famous Veras include actor Vera Farmiga, singer Vera Lynn and fashion designer Vera Wang.

Verda
(alt. Verdie)

Latin, meaning 'spring-like'.

Verena

Latin, meaning 'true'. St Verena was a third-century Roman saint who healed the sick.

Verity

Latin, meaning 'truth'. Presenter Verity Sharp is a trained musician and presenter of *The Culture Show*.

Verna
(alt. Vernie)

Latin, meaning 'spring green'. Actor Verna Felton was a voice actor for Disney films and productions.

Verona

Latin, shortened form of Veronica. From the city of the same name in Italy.

Veronica
(alt. Verica, Veronique)

Latin, meaning 'true image'. Famous Veronicas include actors Veronica Lake and Veronica Carlson and the protagonist of the *Veronica Mars* series and film.

Veruca

Latin, meaning 'wart'. Usually associated with the character of Veruca Salt from the children's novel *Charlie and the Chocolate Factory*, by Roald Dahl.

Vesta

Latin, from the ancient Roman goddess of the same name, said to be in charge of the hearth, home and family.

Vevina

Scottish, meaning 'pleasant lady'. More commonly used in the USA.

Vicenta

Latin, meaning 'prevailing'. More commonly used in Italian-speaking communities.

Victoria

(abbrev. Vicky, Vicki, Vickie, Vikki, Vix)

Latin, meaning 'victory'. The name became popular during and after the reign of Queen Victoria in the nineteenth century, and has remained pretty steadfastly popular ever since.

Vida

Spanish, meaning 'life'.

Vidya

Sanskrit, meaning 'knowledge'. Often used in the Hindu faith to refer to learning and knowledge.

Vienna

Latin, from the city of the same name in Austria.

Vigdis

Scandinavian, meaning 'war goddess'. Most commonly used in Icelandic communities.

Vina

(alt. Vena)

Spanish, meaning 'vineyard'.

Viola

Latin, meaning 'violet'. Also a musical instrument like a large violin.

Violet

(alt. Violetta)

Latin, meaning 'purple'. Also a small purple flower of the same name.

Virginia

(alt. Virginie; abbrev. Virgie, Ginny)

Latin, meaning 'maiden'. Famous Virginias include author Virginia Woolf and tennis player Virginia Wade.

Visara

Sanskrit, meaning 'celestial'.

Vita

Latin, meaning 'life'. Often used to refer to the life story of a saint, or their biography.

Vittoria

Variation of Victoria, meaning 'victory'. More commonly used in Italian-speaking communities.

Viva

Latin, meaning 'alive'. Actor Viva was one of Andy Warhol's muses during the 1960s.

Viveca

(alt. Vivica)

Scandinavian, meaning 'war fortress'. Actor Vivica A. Fox is known for her roles in Independence Day, Kill Bill and Soul Food.

Vivian

(alt. Vivien, Vivienne)

Latin, meaning 'lively'. Famous Vivians include actor Vivien Leigh and designer Vivienne Westwood.

Vonda

Czech, meaning 'from the tribe of Vandals'. Singer Vonda Shepard was known for her soft-pop songs and appearances on Ally McBeal.

Girls' names

Waleska
Polish, meaning 'beautiful'. Most commonly used in German-speaking communities.

Wallis
English, meaning 'from Wales'. Famous Wallises include Wallis Simpson, the late Duchess of Windsor, singer Wallis Bird and the clothing retailer Wallis.

Walta
Swahili, meaning 'like a shield'. Also feminine version of Walter.

Wanda
(alt. Waneta, Wanita)
Slavic, meaning 'tribe of the vandals'. Princess Wanda was a queen of Poland in the eighth century, and there are various legends about her.

Waneta
(alt. Wanita)
Variation of Wanda, meaning 'tribe of the vandals'. Also the name of an infamous Yanktonai Dakota Native American tribal chief during the eighteenth and nineteenth centuries.

Wava
English, meaning 'way'. More commonly used in the USA.

Waveney
Old English, from the river of the same name.

Waverly
Old English, meaning 'meadow of aspens'. Can be used as a girls' name or, more commonly, a boys' name.

Wendy
English, meaning 'friend'. Famous Wendys include actors Wendy Richard and Wendy Hiller and the character of Wendy Darling in *Peter Pan*.

Wharton
English, meaning 'from the river'.

Whisper

English, meaning 'whisper'.

Whitley

Old English, meaning 'white meadow'.

Whitney

Old English, meaning 'white island'. Singer Whitney Houston was a pop sensation of the 1980s and appeared in the film *The Bodyguard* with Kevin Costner.

Wilda

German, meaning 'willow tree'. More commonly used in Polish-speaking communities.

Wilfreda

English, meaning 'to will peace'. Feminine form of Wilfred.

Wilhelmina

Old German, meaning 'strong-willed warrior'. There are dozens of members of the German royal family who have been named Wilhelmina.

Willa

(alt. Willene, Willia)

German, meaning 'helmet'. American Willa Cather was a Pulitzer Prize-winning author.

Willow

English, from the tree of the same name. Several celebrity babies have been named Willow over the last few years, including Willow Smith (Will Smith's daughter) and Willow Hart (Pink's daughter).

Wilma

(alt. Wilmer)

German, meaning 'protection'. A character from the cartoon *The Flintstones*.

Winifred

(abbrev. Winnie)

Old English, meaning 'holy and blessed'. Famous Winifreds include Winifred Atwell, prison breaker Winifred Herbert, author Winifred Mary Letts and South African activist Winnie Madikizela-Mandela.

Winona

(alt. Wynona)

Sious Indian, meaning 'first-born daughter'. Actor Winona Ryder is named after the town where she was born, Winona in Minnesota, USA.

Winslow

English, meaning 'friend's hill'.

Winter

English, meaning 'winter'.

Wisteria

English, meaning 'flower'.

Wren

Old English, meaning 'tiny bird'. Often associated with the species of small birds found throughout the world.

Wynda

Scottish, meaning 'of the narrow passage'.

Wynne

(alt. Wynn)

Welsh, meaning 'very blessed'.

Girls' names

Xanadu

A city in Mongolia. Xanadu was the summer capital of Kubla Khan's empire and the inspiration of Samuel Taylor Coleridge's poem *Kubla Khan*. Also a 1980 film starring Olivia Newton-John.

Xanthe

Greek, meaning 'blonde'. Also the name of several characters in ancient Greek mythology.

Xanthippe

Greek, meaning 'nagging'. Also the name of an influential figure in ancient Greek mythology.

Xaverie
(alt. Xaviera)

Spanish, meaning 'the new house'. The female equivalent of Xavier.

Xena
(alt. Xenia)

Greek, meaning 'foreigner'. The popularity of this name rose after the success of *Xena: Warrior Princess*.

Ximena

Spanish, meaning 'to hear'. More commonly used in Mexico.

Xiomara

Spanish, meaning 'battle-ready'.

Xiu

Chinese, meaning 'elegant'.

Xochitl

Nahuatl, meaning 'flower'. Queen Xochitl was a legendary queen of the Toltec culture.

Xoey

Variant of Zoe, meaning 'life'. Often used as a spelling variation for Zoe or Zoey.

Xristina

Variation of Christina, meaning 'follower of Christ'. Usually associated with singer Christina Aguilera, who often spells her name Xristina.

Xylia
(alt. Xylina, Xyloma)

Greek, meaning 'from the woods'.

Girls' names

Yadira

Arabic, meaning 'worthy'. More commonly used in Spanish- and Portuguese-speaking communities.

Yael

Hebrew, meaning 'mountain goat'. Also the name of a character in the Bible.

Yaffa

(alt. Yahaira, Yajaira)

Hebrew, meaning 'lovely'.

Yamilet

Arabic, meaning 'beautiful'. More commonly used in Spanish-speaking communities.

Yana

Hebrew, meaning 'the Lord is gracious'. Also the name of a spiritual practice in Buddhism.

Yanha

Arabic, meaning 'dove-like'.

Yanira

Hawaiian, meaning 'pretty'. Also the name of a character in ancient Greek mythology.

Yareli

Latin, meaning 'golden'. More commonly used in Spanish-speaking communities.

Yaretzi

(alt. Yaritza)

Aztec, meaning 'forever beloved'. More commonly used in the USA.

Yasmin

(alt. Yasmeen, Yasmina)

Persian, meaning 'jasmine flower'. Famous Yasmins include actor Yasmin Paige, model Yasmin le Bon and DJ Yasmin.

Yelena

Greek, meaning 'bright and chosen'. Extremely popular name in Russia and Ukraine.

Yeraldina

Spanish, meaning 'ruled with a spear'.

Yesenia

Arabic, meaning 'flower'. The name was invented in the 1970s for a Spanish-language television production.

Yetta

English, from Henrietta, meaning 'ruler of the house'. Also used in Yiddish-speaking communities.

Yeva

Hebrew variant of Eve, meaning 'life'.

Ylva

Old Norse, meaning 'she wolf'. The name originated in Sweden in the thirteenth century.

Yoki
(alt. Yoko)

Native American, meaning 'rain'. In Japanese the name also means 'happiness' and 'life force'.

Yolanda
(alt. Yolonda)

Spanish, meaning 'violet flower'. There have been several monarchs of Europe known as Yolanda.

Yoselin

English, meaning 'lovely'. Can also be used as a spelling alternative to Jocelyn.

Yoshiko

Japanese, meaning 'good child'. Princess Yoshiko was the Empress of Japan during the eighteenth and nineteenth centuries.

Yovela

Hebrew, meaning 'jubilee'.

Ysabel

English, meaning 'God's promise'. Often used as a spelling alternative to Isabel.

Ysanne

Contraction of Isabel and Anne, meaning 'pledged to God' and 'grace'.

Yuki

Japanese, meaning 'lucky'. Also the name of a popular Japanese singer and songwriter.

Yuliana

Latin, meaning 'youthful'. Often used as a spelling alternative to Giuliana.

Yuridia

Russian, meaning 'farmer'. Singer Yuridia is one of the most popular pop stars in Mexico.

Yusia

Arabic, meaning 'success'.

Yvette
(alt. Yvonne)

French, meaning 'yew'. Famous Yvettes include presenter Yvette Fielding, actor Yvette Nicole Brown and politician Yvette Cooper.

Z

Girls' names

Zafira
Arabic, meaning 'successful'.

Zahara
(alt. Zahava, Zahra, Zayah)
Arabic, meaning 'flowering and shining'. The most famous Zahara is the daughter of Angelina Jolie and Brad Pitt.

Zaida
(alt. Zaide)
Arabic, meaning 'prosperous'. Also a familiar term for grandfather in Yiddish.

Zalika
Swahili, meaning 'well born'. More commonly used in Egypt.

Zaltana
Arabic, meaning 'high mountain'.

Zamia
Greek, meaning 'pine cone'. Also the name of a plant.

Zaneta
(alt. Zanceta, Zanetah, Zanett, Zanetta)
Hebrew, meaning 'a gracious present from God'. More commonly used in Polish and Latvian communities.

Zaniyah
Arabic, meaning 'lily'. Most commonly used in the USA, especially over the last five years.

Zara
(alt. Zaria, Zariah, Zora)
Arabic, meaning 'radiance'. Famous Zaras include Queen Elizabeth II's granddaughter Zara Tindall, actor Zara Cully and fashion brand Zara.

Zelda
German, meaning 'dark battle'. Usually associated with the Nintendo video game series *Legend of Zelda* or American novelist Zelda Fitzgerald.

Zelia
(alt. Zella)
Scandinavian, meaning 'sunshine'.

Zelma
German, meaning 'helmet'. Sometimes used as a spelling alternative to Thelma.

Zemira
(alt. Zemirah)
Hebrew, meaning 'joyous melody'. An opera by Francesco Bianchi.

Zena
(alt. Zenia, Zina)
Greek, meaning 'hospitable'. Usually used as a spelling alternative to Xena.

Zenaida
Greek, meaning 'the life of Zeus'. St Zenaida is recognised as one of the first Christian physicians, during the second century.

Zenobia
Latin, meaning 'the life of Zeus'. Queen Zenobia was the leader of the Palmyrene empire in Syria during the third century.

Zephyr
Greek, meaning 'the west wind'.

Zetta
Latin, meaning 'seven'. In modern maths, zetta means 10^{21} (that's number 1 followed by 21 zeros).

Zia
Arabic, meaning 'light and splendour'. Musician Zia McCabe is known for being a founding member of the band the Dandy Warhols.

Zinaida
Greek, meaning 'belonging to Zeus'. More commonly used in Russian-speaking communities.

Zinnia
Latin, meaning 'flower'. Also the name of a flowering perennial plant.

Zipporah
Hebrew, meaning 'bird'. Zipporah was one of the wives of Moses in the Bible.

Zita
(alt. Ziva)
Spanish, meaning 'little girl'. St Zita is an Italian patron saint of maids and domestic servants.

Zoë
(alt. Zoe, Zoi, Zoie, Zoey, Zoeya, Zoila)
Greek, meaning 'life'. Famous Zoes include TV and radio presenter Zoë Ball and actors including Zoë Wanamaker, Zoe Saldana and Zooey Deschanel.

Zoraida
Spanish, meaning 'captivating woman'.

Zorina
Slavic, meaning 'golden'.

Zosia
(alt. Zosima)
Greek, meaning 'wisdom'. Actor Zosia Mamet is known for her roles in *Mad Men*, *Parenthood* and *Girls*.

Zoya
Greek, meaning 'life'. Zoya Kosmodemyanskaya is one of the former Soviet Union's most revered heroines, after fighting for the Russian rebellion during World War II.

Zula
Swahili, meaning 'brilliant'.

Zuleika
Arabic, meaning 'fair and intelligent'. Also the name of Potiphar's wife in the Bible.

Zulma
Arabic, meaning 'peace'.

Zuzana
Hebrew, meaning 'lily'. More commonly used in the Czech and Slovak republics.

Zuzu
Czech, meaning 'flower'. The nickname for one of George Bailey's children in the film *It's A Wonderful Life*.